AT EVERY BREATH, A TEACHING

AT EVERY BREATH, A TEACHING

Stories About the Life and Teachings of SWAMI CHINMAYANANDA

Rudite Emir

Piercy, California • Langhorne, Pennsylvania

Chinmaya Publications
Chinmaya Mission West Publications Division
Main Office
P.O. Box 129
Piercy, CA 95587, USA

Chinmaya Publications
Chinmaya Mission West Publications Division
Distribution Office
560 Bridgetown Pike
Langhorne, PA 19053, USA
Telephone: (215) 396-0390
Fax: (215) 396-9710
Toll Free: 888-CMW-READ (888-269-7323)

Central Chinmaya Mission Trust
Sandeepany Sadhanalaya
Saki Vihar Road
Mumbai, India 400 072

Printed and Bound by Thomson Press (India) Ltd.

Credits
Design and Layout: Amita Shenoi Design
Photographs: Anjali Singh

Library of Congress Catalog Card Number 99-94693

ISBN 1-880687-31-3

CONTENTS

INTRODUCTION

SWAMI CHINMAYANANDA: A LIVING UPANISHAD

Capturing people's experiences with their guru has been a task fraught with paradox. Swami Chinmayananda's devotees and disciples have been both eager to share what they learned at his feet, as well as reluctant even to try. What can be said when the guru's influence on one's life has been total? Mrs. Kamala of Bangalore sums it up with simple eloquence: "He was the architect of my life."

Another devotee, Sheela Sharma of New Delhi, writes: "I have always wondered if an experience could be written. The moment one makes an attempt to write one, it turns into an event. An experience, and especially a spiritual one, leaves one mute. The deeper the experience, the closer it is to the heart — and, invariably, it leaves one more speechless than ever." [1]

Swami Tejomayananda, the man who inherited Swami Chinmayananda's mantle as the head of Chinmaya Mission worldwide, says of his guru:

> I saw him as a perfect *jivanmukta purusa* — a person liberated while living. Many a time I have felt that it is easier to describe *Brahman* [the supreme Reality] than to describe a *jivanmukta*. We find very many verses in our scriptures in praise of such an enlightened soul. One such characteristic that comes to mind is that the enlightened person is one who is free from worrying over the past or being anxious about the future, one who is totally detached and objective in dealing with the present. Pujya Gurudev himself used to speak about such a person as someone like a mirror. A mirror accepts everything, rejects nothing, reflects everything, but keeps nothing! Pujya Gurudev indeed was that *jivanmukta purusa*.[2]

Vilasini Balakrishnan, who served Gurudev as his assistant for many years, says:

> During Swami Chinmayananda's years of service, hundreds of thousands of people delighted in hearing his talks on Vedanta. What people saw and heard when they sat for his discourses was amazing presence, a force of inspiring dynamism, an energy that swept into one's heart and opened it to greater wisdom. But there is one strong quality of Swamiji's that was not so apparent on stage — and that was his deep, penetrating, soul-stirring silence.
>
> Swamiji taught this silence off-stage. It is this teaching that made him a living Upanishad. It is in this silence that the mind gets hushed, and the joy lying within one's being comes forth. Swamiji was always in this silence.[3]

And because of that silent center within, whatever Swamiji said or did became a living Upanishad. This book is an attempt to capture a small portion of that living teaching through short stories about devotees' experiences with their guru.

"Be quiet, alert, and vigilant" was Swamiji's simple guideline for practicing the sublime Upanishadic teachings in daily life. And those around him who managed to practice such alertness and vigilance even in small measure reaped the benefits of that simple practice, because the alert mind found in his presence — his very life — an uninterrupted stream of teachings, teachings as powerful as those that came pouring forth from the lecture platform.

This is a book about those teachings from the very life of the guru — all the things he did and said that imbued every moment of his life, and those who witnessed it, with a radiant glow. As one devotee says, "I could watch Swamiji slip circles of banana into his mouth along with his breakfast *upma* and know that all I needed to know about Self-realization was contained in that lucid, fully conscious, divinely resplendent act."

I began to gather Gurudev's teaching stories in 1992, at which time a small collection of them was published from issue to issue in *CMW News* (Chinmaya Mission West's monthly newsletter). I had told Gurudev about my idea of gathering stories about how he taught at every step, at every breath. After publishing some stories in the newsletter, I said to him that we could in time fashion a book. Gurudev said: "Aah, good idea, but won't it take a long time?"

He knew, of course, that the time would be long, although I myself did not at that point. Only later did I find out that many of his devotees, bursting with stories, were shy about writing them out on paper and sending them to me, so I had to pack my bags and go after them, especially so to India. I've listened to stories for hours, notebook in hand and tape recorder running, with my daughter Laila assisting me, at Sandeepany Sadhanalaya (Gurudev's ashram in Mumbai), in New Delhi at various gatherings of devotees, at his ashrams in Uttarkashi and Sidhabari, in Chennai, Bangalore, and Tiruvannamalai.

As I continued to collect the stories, especially the more public events witnessed by many, it became evident that I was hearing different accounts of some of the same events. Each account, of course, was seen through the teller's own eyes. Variants of the same story emerged. Memories may have faltered. Legend may have begun to grow to patch over spaces in memory. How to tell what really happened? Was I being precise about the historical record? Besides, not every write-up could be verified in its final rendering with the teller of the story, short of planning more trips to India and to other lands and delaying publication of the book for possibly years. Therefore, small inaccuracies may exist, for which I ask your forgiveness.

However, one conclusion shone clearly through all variants, questions, and anxieties about historical accuracy: The *spirit* of what Swami Chinmayananda had said or done or been was, I believe, captured in every story, no matter what the variant. And it is the *spirit* that most keenly touches our hearts and minds with its message of unconditional love and joyous surrender to God.

My heartfelt thanks go to everyone who has contributed to this volume. It is *your* book, *your* story about the glories of *your* guru.

Rudite Emir
Los Altos, California
May 1999

- On the following pages, all running text that appears in *italic* type reflects actual words spoken or written by Swami Chinmayananda. Text in roman type is an approximation of what people remember him saying.
- Swami Chinmayananda is referred to both as "Swamiji" and as "Gurudev," the latter being the honorific that has been most often used since his passing from this plane.
- Sanskrit or Hindi words are briefly defined at first occurrence in the book. For more detailed definitions, please see the Glossary.
- The sources for all stories are listed in the Endnotes at the back of the book.

PROLOGUE

He folded the letter slowly and deliberately and slid it into the waiting envelope. With his back ramrod straight and his head at a slight angle, his fingers gently folded down the flap of the envelope. Turning the envelope over, with a black felt-tip pen he wrote out the name and address in a flowing, lyric script. The sight of those graceful, swirling letters spelling out one's name had for years brought instantaneous joy to countless people around the globe: a letter from the guru!

Many who had the fortune to sit silently at the feet of Swami Chinmayananda as he worked through endless stacks of correspondence knew how much teaching each silent moment held. The moment spoke of total alertness, dedication to the task, love of service to others, release from one's personal sense of agency — and more. Watching him perform even the most mundane of actions was as powerful a teaching as listening to him expound Vedanta from the lecture platform.

Swamiji never stopped teaching. His every movement and action, no matter how simple, became a lesson in conscious living, dynamic loving, and joyous acceptance of the divine law.

His life itself is a scripture, his words are hymns,
his actions are blessings upon the world.
He is the fulfilled, the perfect.
In such an accomplished man, we watch God and His play.

Swami Chinmayananda
(Describing a God-realized soul)

LIFE

Gurudev's devotees were no doubt first drawn to him because of an innate spiritual hunger. However, as the relationship with him became more intimate, many turned to him not only for answers to deep spiritual questions, but also to seek his guidance with the inevitable problems of life. He knew how to deal with them all, generously doling out support and advice, forever reminding us that our own "Motionless Center" is always at peace, despite all troubles on the material plane.

Although himself a renunciate, Swamiji never once left the impression that he was somehow too far removed from the householder's life to understand its endless ups and downs. In fact, as we listened to him in his lectures, we often wondered how it was possible for him to understand so precisely and in such minute detail some of the ins and outs of our daily lives. He loved telling the story of a family going shopping in a department store, each caught up in his or her own particular attachments, the husband being pulled to the rack with the newest ties, the wife to the display of silk saris, the child to the toys. He could spend long minutes depicting such scenes in intimate detail so revealing of our own frailties that we could but squirm in our seats or laugh as we looked in the mirror he was holding up to us in his jovial portrayal.

With a joke always just seconds away from bursting forth from his amazingly creative mind, he would poke fun now at himself, now at others about the big and small questions in our lives: What should be a Vedantin's attitude toward food? What does enjoyment mean for a spiritual student? And so on, endlessly.

THE HOUSEHOLDER'S LIFE

Gurudev had been known to say: "As a householder, make sure you are the one holding the house, and not the one being held *by* the house." He always knew what advice to give when we became too much "held" by the householder's life:

"All These Add Up to Life"

Lakshmi Reddy was teaching in a college, raising children, and being a wife to her husband — among other roles she had to play as a householder and professional. After she had written to Swamiji, he answered:

> *Your letter has just come. Thanks. Your complaints, problems, busy college work, exam schedules, corrections, valuations, endless household chores, two small growing boys and their boisterous mischief, looking after a busy husband, and yourself not well, marriages, ceremonies in your parents' house which must be attended — I can understand the strains and discomforts around you. But, dear Lakshmi, all these add up to Life. You are not an . . . irresponsible working girl, glamorously living and exhausting a dry piece of loveless life! Rise above all these with infinite Love and Om!*[1]

And so he wrote to many of us caught up in our day-to-day duties, joys, fears, and challenges:

> *Such trials and troubles visit all people now and then. Keep the balance within. They too will pass away. The Motionless Center around which all movements take place is you.*[2]

And again:

> *A chosen seeker is generally dragged through such situations that tease him to learn to accept what the Lord gives with a smile. Accept all that comes your way as the Lord's* prasad *[gift].*[3]

To yet another devotee, Gurudev said in a letter:

> *Things happening around us are interpreted by our mind, and we label them and come to experience them as great tragedies or wonderful blessings. . . . The stream of happenings comes and goes, irresistibly around and above you, and that which gives the balance to face them steadily is prayer. Prayer is not to change the pattern*

around you, but to give you protection from it. We do not travel in a boat to stop the waves, but the sides of the boat do protect us from the raw, direct hits of the waves.[4]

Beauty in the Flood

To a United States-based devotee who had poured out in a letter her tale of woe, which featured her pet animal, her husband, and her unpalatable job, Swamiji wrote back:

> *Your kind letter has crawled up here with its entire load of agony, sorrow, misery, confusion, tears, sighs, dejection, despondency, and protest.*
>
> *In spite of them all, the world moves in its own rhythm. To detach from it, to stand apart and watch the entire surging, rolling, curling, stinking sewage of life gushing out and streaming forth all around you with a smile of understanding is to recognize a beauty in the entire flood, even though there is stink insufferable.*
>
> *Turn your attention to Him, the all-purifying Source of all light, which is constantly drying up the sewage and converting it into life-giving manure.*

Once again, Swamiji had prescribed the surefire remedy to one floundering in the school of hard knocks. Today, almost six years later, she is looking at the sewage in a new light, and the stink doesn't bother her as much.[5]

When the World Kicks You

Bharati Sukhatankar was going through a very difficult time in her life, feeling "kicked about." She went to Swamiji's Sidhabari ashram for a spiritual camp, but never said a word to Swamiji about the troubles she was experiencing.

One day as Swamiji was holding *satsang* [devotional gathering], she approached the group.

"Come, come!" Swamiji beckoned to her to sit directly next to him. She did so. He tapped her head lightly and said:

"When the world kicks you, use it as an experience to grow."

That was all that was said, but Bharati immediately felt that all the things that had been knotted up inside her were dissolved. After many months of turmoil, she felt relief and peace.[6]

Gurudev never tried to give the illusion that just because we had turned to the spiritual life, everything would run smoothly, without obstruction, but warned us instead that on the material plane, change and disturbance and sorrow are part of the mix. He compared life's journey to travel over a long-distance road:

> *When you are traveling across the country a long distance, some part of the road may be under repair or in bad condition. At such patches of rough road, drive slowly and move carefully, and once the smooth road comes, step on the gas. Patches of the road will always be slightly bad.*[7]

Family Heartbreaks

A woman devotee had suffered through a number of heartbreaks in trying to start and raise a family. First there was a stillborn child, then a miscarriage. When a child finally did make it into the world, she turned out to have a serious hearing problem. The mother asked Gurudev, "Why have I had all these problems, Swamiji, in bringing children into the world?"

Swamiji replied, "God sends children like that to such homes where He knows they will be lovingly taken care of."

When another mother asked a similar question, this time about a child who had not developed normally, Swamiji answered, "Because God wants you to take care of her."[8]

Gurudev reminded many a householder about the opportunities that the householder's life affords for growth in the spirit. Just because one may spend many hours on everyday duties of the household, one need not stray from the spiritual path. In fact, he said, fulfilling your duties can become your worship:

> *Even as a wife when you serve your family, leave not the fact that you are worshipping Him as wife, mother, sister, etc.*

Look upon your spouse as the embodiment of the Lord Himself, he said:

> *See [your husband] as the Lord's own Presence at home. . . . You will find how your spiritual life deepens with voiceless meaning.*

Make your whole life a song of worship to the Higher:

> *Keep singing the job of Truth in all your actions, in every look of yours, every word you speak, every thought you entertain. Be in the Silent Beauty Center within and act to the rhythm of devotion unto Him who is ever in your heart.*[9]

Many a devotee often struggled to juggle the duties of the home and the yearnings of the soul. Some who were on the threshold of setting up a new household and planning a family became frightened about the potential conflicts with their *sadhana* [spiritual practices]. Gurudev often quoted the following story:

Criminal or Dignitary

In a letter, Gurudev told the story of a father who pointed out to his son a man who was being hustled along the road between four soldiers. The father said:

"Son, that one who is walking between the soldiers is a great criminal, and he is being taken to prison."

After a few yards, the son and father came to the main road and saw a large crowd waiting on the sidewalk. The road had been cleared of traffic. Soon they saw a procession of soldiers on motorcycles, followed by the president of the country riding inside a luxurious limousine, which was protected on all sides by many soldiers.

The boy cried out, "Daddy, there goes the biggest criminal!"

The father hushed the child as he lovingly explained that they were seeing not a criminal but the president. Gurudev elaborated further:

> *Both of them, the criminal and the president, have soldiers around them. A man is a prisoner when he is under the command of the soldiers. But when the soldiers are under* his *command, he is the president or king himself.*
>
> *Similarly, you may have your own house and child. You will become their prisoner if they come to rule over you. But you shall continue to be the sovereign when you control them, not they you.*[10]

Mind on the Lord

Padma Gupta met Swamiji after her husband had passed on. She had been left with three children, 8 to 16 years of age.

After meeting Swamiji, she longed to spend as much time as possible with him. She saw other devotees traveling with him regularly and longed to do likewise.

"Swamiji," she said, "I would like to follow you around wherever you go. I'd like to be with you all the time."

"That too is a *vasana* [innate tendency, the basis of desire]," he said. "Go home and cook for your children. You can cook and still think of the Lord. The hand does the cooking; the mind is on the Lord."[11]

Although, again and again, Gurudev showed us how the home life is the perfect field of work for the *karma yogi* [a person who follows the path of selfless action], he understood that the struggle with one's lower nature is endless: *"It is not easy to live the real righteous life. The lower in us rises up often to argue, even to quote the scriptures to justify the amoral and the immoral — the unrighteous. The heroism of the seeker is in rejecting the whisperings of immediate happiness and to live nobly fulfilling one's larger duties."* He said that we should learn to face the facts about human nature: that we as human beings are bound to err. But, he said, *"with the right understanding of human weakness, we must fight against it — but with charity and kindness."*[12]

No Molding Required

Radhika Krishnakumar had brought her small infant to Swamiji and asked, "How do I teach him to become a good human being?"

"You don't have to mold him or teach him anything," was Swamiji's reply. "You just keep improving as a person, and he'll be fine."[13]

THE WAYS OF THE WORLD

The Lord, said Gurudev, plays a great, divine game, much of which we don't understand and often question.

In a letter to a devotee he said:

The Lord's games, though apparently unintelligent, have in themselves a great logic, and in the long run they fulfill a mighty purpose of raising man to a higher plane of consciousness. War is one of them — but it has a lot of sweat, blood, and tears in it. [The process of evolution] is called religion or spirituality. This cultural process often gets lost in man's overenthusiasm to indulge and to experience the mere material joys of a sensuous world. Whenever a generation becomes thus blind to the eternal values, a war comes to shake and punish us and so to purify us. It is a great occasion of His infinite Love.[14]

Despite all seeming calamities of life, he encouraged us to keep a cheerful mind at all times:

> *Keep smiling, as there is no occasion which is ever tragic to a student of Vedanta. From the higher standpoint, all the activities around us are but the play of our own mind. Realize this truth and be at peace with yourself.*[15]

Devotees often asked Swamiji about impending natural catastrophes, possibly expecting him to provide a glimpse into the future or to soothe a worried mind. In the sixties, in response to one devotee's fears about possible earthquakes in California, he wrote:

> *Don't yield to such a delusory feeling. No place is safe for man! Even if California is to be drowned, you will not be the only suffering one; there are millions of others there. How are you in any way more sacred than all others who are also Lord's creatures? . . . . You need not move away. Forget all about it. Positively think, "Even if such a thing happens, we will try to serve others even during our last moments." The Lord is great. Warn yourself that no place on the face of this precarious world is safe. Everywhere death can reach us. Therefore, running away from any place is not running away from death. Death is inevitable. Seek life — the glorious Source of all life — . . . the infinite and eternal Reality.*[16]

And he goes on to say in yet another letter that everything in this world is subject to change:

> *Nothing in this world is permanent; everything is in a state of change, your health inclusive. Why do you get despaired about it? Make use of the healthy moments to hold on to His feet, realizing full well that such glorious days are few for anyone. One sorrow or the other will always be pestering us so long as we live as an individual in this world of names and forms.*[17]

Everything changes on the material plane, said Gurudev, yet no fear need haunt us:

> *The human race has survived other perils that logically it shouldn't have: The Ice Age and the flood are two that we know of. What then is the present period of moral decay or even atomic war? The world and life will survive.*[18]

So Many Years to Go

Once a group from the senior citizens association in Mumbai visited Sandeepany Sadhanalaya. Gurudev happened to be in the ashram that day and was about to go out. I requested Gurudev to provide darshan for the old people. To my surprise, Gurudev replied, "I shall address them. Assemble them in the hall." Then he turned to those present around him and continued, laughing, "Mani has brought some *vruddhas* [old people]. He thinks that I am young!"

Addressing the group for thirty minutes, Gurudev pepped them up with his characteristic cheer and dynamism, saying, "Never say you are 'so many' years old. Forget the dead past! Think of the future and say 'so many' years to go! What we have is a gift from the Lord; what we do with what we have is our gift to Him."

The whole crowd dispersed in optimism and cheer.[19]

"You Fight!"

K. B. Shroff of Mumbai was grappling with a severe domestic problem, a conflict with an uncle who was harassing the family for money after the father's death. K. B. Shroff was at his wit's end.

One day, he was invited to a ceremony by one of Chinmaya Mission's trustees, which Swamiji also attended. Shroff sat near the center aisle during the function. When Swamiji was finished, he got up and walked down the aisle in his direction. As he passed Shroff, he looked at him and asked, "Shroff, how is your problem?" (Not one word about his problem had been communicated to anyone in Chinmaya Mission, including Swamiji.)

Then Swamiji presented Shroff with his solution: "Shroff, fight!"

Shroff had received the answer he needed. He went to court and won.[20]

Laughter Solution

Many years ago, S. Subramanian of Mumbai was experiencing a difficult family problem and wanted to run away from it all.

Swamiji said to him: "Face the problem! You'll get all the answers you need from Chapter III of the *Gita*."

And Swamiji added: "Whatever comes, take it with laughter. Never be grim." That is one teaching that Subramanian could never forget, and he has applied it successfully in his own life. People at his work often remarked that he was able to laugh no matter what happened. "That's what my teacher has taught me," he said.

Subramanian recalls: "How Gurudev used to laugh! No one could laugh like him." Once when he started laughing in Gurudev's presence, Gurudev said, "Now, you're coming very close to me!"[21]

Pure Excellence

Anil Sachdev was a 16-year-old student in college, studying for his undergraduate degree in chemistry. He was honored for his achievements, among other youngsters in Chinmaya Mission, by being presented with Swamiji's book entitled *Vedanta Through Letters*.

Swamiji wrote the following words in Anil's copy of the book:

> *Never yield the first rank in any field to anyone. Remember, you are Pure Excellence.*

Whenever later in his life Anil met with any difficulty, those words of Swamiji's always came back to support him, becoming "the cornerstone of his inspiration."

For example, at age 27, Anil was placed in charge of one division in a corporation. He felt overawed by his position. Some time after taking charge of the division, the market slumped; also the union began to agitate. Anil was troubled by the many problems, and his mood sank low.

One night, as though by magic, *Vedanta Through Letters* appeared on his table, even though he had not placed it there. He opened it up and saw Swamiji's encouraging words. Once again, they saw him through.[22]

Cool, Clear Analysis

Once, in Baroda, India, as we sat in *satsang*, a man arrived who was selling spiritual books. It was rare for Swamiji to be involved in such a transaction, and we expected him to decline. Instead, to our surprise, he invited the fellow over to his side and began perusing the books as a prospective buyer might.

One by one, he went through the books commenting on their merits or otherwise. He examined the binding, the number of pages, the quality of print, the content, the reference pages, the index — all in a thoroughly professional and discriminating manner. About one book, in particular, he was almost scathing in his comments, noting that the price was indecent with respect to the number of pages of real content as compared to the number of pages dedicated to the index, references, and blank pages: fancy packaging but not much substance.

After a lengthy period of such considerations, Swamiji finally selected two books that he considered valuable for inclusion in his library.

We were mesmerized watching his cool, clear analysis and careful consideration. The man of perfection may not be of the world, but his eyes are open to its ways.[23]

LEARNING TO LIVE IN A NEW WAY

Swamiji was continually teaching us how to handle life's problems, large or small, often throwing in a dash of laughter to ease the solution. Swami Purushottamananda met up with one such smallish problem when confronted with his own body's inability to handle hot chili peppers:

Hot Chilies

I had given up eating chilies, as they didn't agree with me. Now, wherever I went with Gurudev to a *bhiksha* [a meal prepared as an offering to the guru], particularly in southern India, people would offer chilies to Gurudev and me. I was in a fix. If I said no, the hosts might think that I was being fussy. Here was Gurudev eating chilies, but his disciple would not.

I took the problem to Gurudev and said that in His presence I couldn't refuse the hosts or else they would be unhappy. Gurudev listened very attentively, closed his eyes, and said, "Okay, don't worry. Now when you get chilies, take them but don't eat them. Take an extra *pappadam* [a crisp, flat bread] and cover the chilies and continue eating."

During one evening *bhiksha,* I was sitting near Gurudev. He was watching everything that came onto my plate. When the chilies came, I asked for an extra *pappadam*. Gurudev did not take his eyes off me. I took the *pappadam* and covered the chilies. Seeing that, Gurudev burst out laughing. The host had no idea what the joke was.[24]

Enjoyment Without Attachment

Swamiji was serving one of his devotees, Isabel Taylor, placing food on her plate copiously. He often lovingly served others while being himself served. Sometimes he would call an individual up to the table and say, "Open up!" — and in would pop a morsel of food straight from the guru's hands.

However, this time the devotee had already had her fill and said, "No, thank you; I've had enough."

Ignoring her remark, Swamiji piled on some more food.

"No, thank you. You know it's not good to overeat, Swamiji!" protested Isabel.

"There's no harm in enjoying," smiled Swamiji, "just don't get attached to your enjoyment."[25]

Dealing with Others

"Silently hear everyone," he said. *"Accept what is good; reject and forget to remember what is bad. . . . Accept all and take only what you want; reject the rest and live happily."*

When asked what to do in a case when someone is not necessarily bad, just a "pain in the neck" because of his or her incessant jabbering, Swamiji twinkled his eyes and said: "Just draw down the shades in front of your mind and let the others go on as they will."[26]

"Be a Ram Inside"

The year was 1958. When I was given *Brahmopadesam* [initiation into the *Gayatri Mantra*], our Pujya Gurudev blessed me and gave me golden advice:

"Rajaram! Be a Ram inside and a *raja* [king] outside."

The advice is self-explanatory. One should be serene and divine inside, but outside as we face the world we have to "fight" like a king and be courageous. Being a *sadhu* [person dedicated to a search for God] doesn't mean one should shun fighting the evils or odds in life.

When I was only a shy boy, Swamiji explained it to me thus. It was he who made me a "man" today![27]

Sound Judgment

On the way to the Sidhabari ashram, there was fracas on the platform as we were about to board the train for Pathankot.

A pickpocket had been caught in the act, and a policeman was thrashing him with a *lathi* [club]. Swamiji had just descended the stairs to the platform and came upon the tableau. In spite of the throng and the excitement, there was a little circle of space and silence around Swamiji. Standing straight and tall in his orange robes, he glowed in the lamplight.

Swamiji stared at the policeman intently. The policeman continued his frenzied thrashing until he became aware of Swamiji's gaze. He looked at Swamiji and then quickly looked down, confused. He struck again, and again his eyes were drawn to Swamiji's. Suddenly, all the power disappeared from his blows. He made a few more token strikes, threw a chastened look toward Swamiji, and dragged the thief away.

We were all hushed and a little shaken by the event. In the few moments before we boarded the train, one devotee, obviously very agitated, stammered, "He should not have hit the fellow, Swamiji."

Swamiji shot back at us with a piercing gaze, "The fellow was a thief!"

With his look he had chastened the policeman, whose judgment was clouded by anger and hatred, and with his words he had chastened us, whose judgment was clouded by sentimentality.[28]

Another sort of lesson was experienced by Anjali Singh of New Delhi around the turn of the year one year.

Considering Others

Swamiji was to stop at the Delhi airport for several hours to change flights. Anjali Singh had been waiting for two months with a special New Year present for him and planned to meet him at the airport to present the gift to him. But when she reached the airport, realizing that she had left the present at home, she was deeply disappointed and her mind became very agitated. To appease her mind, she decided to go back home to fetch it, as two hours still remained before his take-off. "That was my first mistake," she said later, "to leave Gurudev's presence and the possibility of *satsang* with him in order to appease the mind."

On the way back to the airport, she got stuck in a traffic jam and vowed to herself that if she did not get to the airport in time, she would punish herself for her forgetfulness by not writing letters to Swamiji for one month.

She did, indeed, miss his flight -- by just three minutes. So she wrote Swamiji a short note explaining why she would not be writing to him for one month, but would he please continue writing to her. And Swamiji did continue to write her letters that month, but in his third and last letter he wrote, "Your one month has ended, and my *two* have begun!"

For the next two months Anjali kept writing to Swamiji and asking, "Why this double punishment for me?" But Swamiji did not reply even once. At the end of the two months he wrote to her, "How dare you take a vow, the consequences of which involve another person? Did you not consider that I might have wanted to receive letters from *you*?"

Anjali's own conclusion about the incident was: "Swamiji didn't need letters from anybody, but this was his way of highlighting a point."[29]

After some years of hearing Swamiji's thoughts about birthdays, a number of his devotees gave up celebrating them altogether. He reveals his reasons in a letter he wrote in 1973:

> *I must acknowledge now the birthday greeting card sent by all of you together. My dear girl, it was not my birthday. There are altogether four birthdays in India for me, and I don't protest, because on each birthday some thousands are collected, which is most useful for the Mission's work. But the truth is: I am Unborn, and there is no existence for me apart from your imagination. But who will believe it?*[30]

In another letter he says jokingly:

> *Thanks for your note of 8th May. I had three birthdays this year. I am confused: 21st April, 26th April, and 8th May. Must be I came out in three pieces —* sattva-rajas-tamas *[the three main qualities of the mind: serene purity, passionate activity, and dull inactivity]; or maybe* karma-bhakti-jnana *[the three main paths to liberation: path of action, path of devotion, and path of knowledge]; or maybe past-present-future. Thanks for your greetings!*

Cycles of Life

A house-warming ceremony was taking place at the home of one of Swamiji's oldest disciples in India. Swamiji visited the house on the auspicious occasion to bless the couple.

As Swamiji was about to leave, the owner brought a brand-new guest book and requested Swamiji to record his visit in it. Swamiji wrote:

> *Grandfather dies, father dies, son dies, grandson dies.*

And underneath those words he added his signature in its characteristically graceful Sanskrit letters.

The host, who was anxiously reading the words as they flowed from Swamiji's pen, couldn't hide his disappointment. Swamiji smiled and assured his host that it was not a joke he had left behind in the guest book, but the sequence he had recorded was meant to be the greatest blessing in one's family life. This sequence is natural and the least painful, he explained. The message of the words was meant to be: "May there be no irregularity in this rhythm. If any irregularity comes, it will be tragic, sad, and painful. May you all remember that it is inevitable that all of us must leave. To remember this always is to tune up all of our attitudes and actions in life."[31]

To Marry or Not

Srichand Krishnani had been vacillating about his marriage plans in the face of his family's insistence that he marry. He had wanted to join Swamiji's ashram full-time, feeling an intense pull toward him. It was a turbulent time for Srichand, as his family was exerting tremendous pressure on him to get married, yet he was utterly consumed by his love for his guru. "The moment he came near me, I forgot everything," Srichand says, "so it was difficult to make the decision for doing anything but being with him."

When a family delegation had approached Swamiji to ask for his help in convincing Srichand to move toward a decision for marriage, Swamiji had said to them, "Leave him alone for now, he will get married later."

At one point, Srichand Krishnani had the opportunity to spend twenty days with Gurudev at Uttarkashi, "a golden time," as he recalls today. At that point, he was still trying to decide if he should join the ashram full-time or not.

One day, he was sitting on the Ganges bank when a storm of confusions and agitations overtook his mind. He ran toward the Tapovan Kuti ashram like a madman. He climbed the stairs to Gurudev's room and flung open the door without knocking first. He fell down at Swamiji's feet.

Swamiji looked at him lovingly while Srichand poured out all the confusions in his mind for some fifteen minutes or more. Without a word, Swamiji just listened to the outpouring.

Then Swamiji looked down where Swami Tapovanam, his own guru, had once sat and said, "What you are feeling is a trick of that old man. Go to Bombay and get married. Why are you scared? Even the great rishis were married people. You, too, can get married and spend your time doing missionary work. There is sufficient spirituality in you."

Some years later, Srichand and his fiancee Mohini had gone to the Sandeepany ashram in Mumbai to attend the engagement ceremony of his friend Jairam Jaisinghani. At the Jagadeeshwara temple, as he prostrated at Swamiji's feet, Swamiji caught hold of Srichand's hand and put a ring on his finger, "You are first married to me; then you're married to her."

"That set me thinking," recalls Srichand. "I asked myself, 'Why did he say that?' I understood that Swamiji had undertaken protection of me. Also, maybe he wanted my mind to continue to be on him without any distractions and to be faithful to him."[32]

Despite his early doubts, Srichand Krishnani did get married, with Gurudev's heartfelt blessings. He also continued to work diligently for Chinmaya Mission, organizing, among other things, the first International Chinmaya Spiritual Camp in Michigan in 1984.

Inopportune Death

Pranji Lodhia, a long-time Chinmaya Mission West Board member, had joined a study group in California even before meeting Swamiji. Then, after the first lecture series by Swamiji that he ever attended, a *yajna* held at Stanford University, Pranji invited Swamiji for *bhiksha* at his house.

After the meal, he asked Swamiji, "How do you explain that a very good person dies very tragically — at a very inopportune time?"

Swamiji looked at him thoughtfully and replied with another question, "Inopportune for whom?"[33]

THIS AND THAT

Head and Heart

One day, overwhelmed with the love she felt for her guru, a devotee burst out to him, "Swamiji, you are so good!"

Swamiji shook his head: "No, not good. Intelligent. Without intelligence you don't survive. If you look at life with your heart only, you weep. When you look at life with your head, you laugh."[34]

Telling a Lie

Swamiji had come to the house of S. V. Acharya for the first time. Four of his children were part of a Chinmaya Mission Balavihar [children's class].

A child in the group asked Swamiji: "Why should we not tell a lie?"

Swamiji's answer was: "By telling a lie, you create two personalities, one weakening the other, with no gain whatsoever."[35]

When Swamiji first arrived in the United States to lecture in the mid-sixties, he spent a large part of his time in California, which was just then moving into the psychedelic age. Recreational drug use was prevalent. His audiences often included listeners who were still taking drugs, or else those who had taken drugs in the past. He was uncompromising in his insistence that a serious spiritual student must not participate in any drug-taking. He called LSD "personality breaking." He said in a letter:

> *There cannot be any controversy about the spiritual harm that will come to anyone who is taking drugs. Spiritual practices are to hasten evolution; drugs and such other artificial methods are striving to bring about a revolution in the personality composition. The delicate human mind can easily be destroyed by such rough methods. LSD cannot bring spiritual experience; it can only bring a hallucination. If I could cry and reach the ears of all America, I would cry out from the housetops to everyone, with no trace of doubt in me, that all such attempts are dangerous for the spiritual possibilities in the individual.*[36]

Often Swamiji likened the administering of drugs to trying to hasten the blooming of a rose by prying its petals open with the fingers. The result: a wilted, broken, ugly bloom. He said the mind is a very delicate instrument, more delicate than a flower; forcing it open with the help of drugs can only create an ugly result. To one very devoted follower who in the past had succumbed to the drug habit he said uncompromisingly — to make certain that person never took drugs again: "If you ever take LSD again, I will withdraw my love from you!"

WORK

At his desk most mornings at 4 a.m. or earlier, no matter where he was on the globe, Swamiji, even in the years of his severely declining health, was the best example of his own definition of work:

> *Work is love made visible. To bring into vivid expression your love of others is work; to drag yourself through each day's schedule, morose, unhappy, and miserable, is labor.*

He rose before dawn, sat himself down at his desk, and began to answer, often in longhand, the many letters continuously piling up on the edge of his desk. Whether the letter had arrived from a worker in one of his Chinmaya Mission centers in India, asking for instructions or advice on a new temple project or school; or from a grade-schooler in Texas, pouring forth her adoration; or from an exuberant devotee from Australia who had sent him five pages filled with effusive questions about fine points of scriptural logic, Swamiji answered them all, without exception.

The rest of the day during a typical lecture tour was taken up with morning meditation classes, morning Upanishad classes, *satsangs*, meetings, *bhikshas*, and evening *Bhagavad Gita* classes, which were often followed by cultural programs. Whenever a free minute or two appeared in his demanding schedule, he would again slip away to sit at his desk, picking up, without a moment's hesitation, exactly where he had left off his work before. Whether on the lecture platform or at his desk or in a meeting in his ashram office, his approach to work was always the same: He reveled in the very doing of it. From the glow on his face and the joy in his limbs, you could see that his work was, indeed, love made visible.

Desk *Puja*

Gurudev had just arrived at Shimoga, in the state of Karnataka, where one of his *yajnas* [lecture series] was to be held. He inquired of the organizers, "Is my *puja samagri* ready?" [The Sanskrit word *samagri* means "material used" and refers to the items used by priests in worship, such as a conch, bell, lamp, sacred rice, sandalwood paste, flowers, and other items.]

The devotees were puzzled.

Gurudev quietly explained, "Are my table, writing pad, pen, and table lamp ready? — That is my *puja samagri*!"[1]

THE LORD'S WORK

The key to Gurudev's source of strength came to light during one of his stays at Krishnalaya, his ashram in northern California:

"He Does It All"

One day in 1992, two people approached Swamiji about doing some healing work on him through a method that analyzes and treats the human system at the energetic level. For the analysis, the practitioner needed a few strands of his hair. His immediate response was, "No! I don't want to keep this body around. I've finished my work here."

However, after some more gentle pressure from the inquiring parties, he tugged vigorously at his beard, but no hairs came loose. "Nothing! Not one!" he said. Then he gave an offhand hint as to where some loose hairs may be lying about. The two devotees took this as a go-ahead sign and located a hairbrush with the required strands.

When the practitioner did her analysis, the results were so astounding that she repeated the measurements over and over again to assure that she had done her work correctly. But the unprecedented results remained the same: At the pathological (physical) level, Swamiji's body was showing readings so low as to indicate death of the body. However, when the readings were taken at his energetic level, they were so high that they went off the scale. The practitioner's interpretation was: Swamiji's as-though-dead physical body was being kept alive by some immense source of energy.

When a devotee relayed the analysis to him, she asked: "Swamiji, how do you do it?" His reply was immediate and vigorous, "*I* do absolutely nothing; *He* does it all. This one is a totally useless fellow. It is His work alone!"

To many devotees who heard this story, it became a scientific corroboration of what they had heard said for many years: A master is an instrument in the hands of the Lord. His life is sustained not by his own desires, for they no longer exist, but by the aggregate desires of those around him.[2]

A similar theme was repeated on many occasions:

Narayana's Work

During one of Swamiji's stays at his Sidhabari ashram, a group of devotees remained as near as possible to Swamiji's side at all times, helping as they could with stuffing envelopes for his correspondence and with other small tasks.

They watched him day in and day out staying up as late as midnight and being up again at 4 or 4:30 in the morning, writing letters at his desk.

After a good many days of watching his schedule, they finally confronted him with a question:

"Swamiji, we have watched you working, on the average, 17 hours a day. Don't you ever get tired?"

Swamiji burst forth with one of his characteristic deep-throated laughs:

"If *I* were doing the work, I would have been *exhausted,* not just tired. But," he pointed to the sky, "with Lord Narayana Himself doing the work, why should I get tired?"[3]

My Master's Voice

Some devotees approached Swamiji and said, "How is it that Swamiji is with us in an ordinary way during the day, talking and joking, and then something quite different happens on the lecture platform. What is it that happens in the evening when you lecture, Swamiji?"

His reply: "I myself wonder, and I listen. It is my Master's voice playing through me."[4]

That Swamiji was not the organizer of his own programs came as a frequent reminder to all of us who, at every parting, demanded to know, "Swamiji, when are you coming back to visit us again?"

Sometimes he would say: "When have I ever left you? I'm always with you!" or, "All I dare to do is work on a travel schedule about one year ahead. Planning past that is interfering with the Lord's Plan. He's in charge, not I!" or, "Certainly I will come gain — when He brings me back here!" And in letters to many a devotee he said words similar to these:

> *Chinmaya* yajnas *are all conducted by Him, and we are all but workers in His army. . . . Let us realize our insignificance and learn to surrender unto Him and be the torch-bearers in His mission.*
>
> *The program of work is sent to me by the Proprietor . . . I don't decide things.*

In one of many similar letters, he said, back in 1969:

> *When I will be able to come is a thing over which I have no control, and I don't know. In fact I never plan my work . . . the work discovers me! When the sudden and irresistible urge comes, I will fly — arrangements or no arrangements! Mother Ganga has not told me a thing about my next trip. Let us see.*[5]

His method of working, in a dynamic yet detached way, is amply illustrated in an account of an incident related from one of his early *yajna* tours in California:

Dynamism in Action

When we landed in San Francisco, we received letters that were waiting for Swamiji. In the car, driving to downtown, Swamiji was silently reading them. He was grave, then smiling, then looking sad, then angry. We could only watch, wait, and wonder. We knew what we would get if we dared disturb him at such a moment when he was evidently working at high pressure in a different wavelength!

We arrived at the hotel and checked in. Swamiji, who had until then been silent and prowling like a tiger at bay, suddenly smiled. He had decided something; he was determined. And for him to decide a thing is to act on it.

"Honolulu speaks of financial difficulties," he said, referring to what seemed a change of plans by organizers in that city who had been planning a *yajna* by him. "They are expressing, I think, their embarrassment. But Trinidad is ready to plan a *yajna*, and they have a committee formed with workers and office-bearers from all the different Hindu organizations there. They have sent me two airplane tickets: They are expecting us. So, I'll go from here back to Los Angeles. Let Miss S. organize it. Let's request all fifty or sixty of our new friends there to help her. Let's call her right away."

We were stunned at Swamiji's dynamism of action: how he plans and readily changes his plans to fit the new situations, how he smiles away his disappointments and dashes forth into new fields with confidence. What gives him this authority, this sense of surety, this amount of self-confidence? We could ask him this, but we know his answer: a big laugh and "Narayana, Narayana!"

Miss S. was instructed over the phone. She was stunned, but said, "Yes, Swamiji." That night, Swamiji wrote forty letters addressing many of our new contacts in Los Angeles: "Contact Miss S.; help her organize this study session on the *Gita* in Los Angeles."

The next day, Swamiji wrote elaborate letters of instruction to Miss S. She must have been aghast at this unexpected avalanche coming toward her: Three different envelopes during the same day were posted to her! That is how Swamiji works; and all of us who have worked with him know it only too well![6]

Another clue to his way of working and decision-making appeared in a letter to one of the workers in Chinmaya Mission:

My method of work is such that when an idea strikes me, I immediately write to the person concerned, but how far the idea is contrary to your local situation and interest is not known to me. You all must decide it among yourselves and do the best. There is no time to check the file, study the entire previous correspondence, and then write a letter as though it were going to be a historical record. This is not possible and hence you must use your own discrimination.[7]

One such message about his inability to plan his course of action came to Anjali Singh *after* his *Mahasamadhi* [the dropping of the body by a highly evolved person]. She writes:

"I Don't Decide Things"

A few days after the installation of Gurudev's statue at Sandeepany, Mumbai, I was sitting near it and thinking: "I know that you never left us, since you were not just a body or a mind or an intellect. I also know that, as all-pervading

Consciousness, you are present right here now. Devotion can invoke your attention in this statue or anywhere else. Yet, I feel the need of seeing your living form walking down this pathway from your *kutiya* [residence], walking stick in hand, laughing or cracking a joke, vibrant with dynamism and making everyone around you feel happy to be alive. But now I can see only a motionless statue that can never match your living brilliance . . . ."

Feeling thus a little dejected, I went back to the work of sorting out old photographs for compiling the life history of Gurudev in pictures. Within about five minutes I came across a photograph of a handwritten message of Gurudev's that could not be read, as the photographic print had been printed in reverse from the negative. Therefore I held it against a mirror and read what Gurudev was trying to convey by this unconventional method. It read:

> *"Come back," you say; even though you admit "we know you have never left." The program of work is sent to me by the Proprietor . . . . I don't decide things. Your request is with reverence sent to Him who orders all activities.*
>
> *Live Vedanta and thus let us all reach That Destination where having met we shall never part. Meet me There. Reach There through love, service, and purity.*

This message must have been written in the past in another context, but it appeared on that day to serve a purpose. I believe that whatever Gurudev has written or spoken is meant for all those whose hearts it touches, especially as he used the same words that I was thinking, "I know that you have never left us . . ."

Strange as it was, I still could not figure out why he sent the message in reverse. Was there a message within a message? It was only later that I remembered that Gurudev spoke about the "lateral inversion" in Sidhabari during a *Vivekacudamani* Camp [*Vivekacudamani* is a Vedanta text by Adi Shankara]. He said that to avoid getting distracted from the theme of *Brahman* [the supreme Reality], one should consider the world as an illusion, just as a city in a mirror. "Whenever the mind is drawn toward it, think of its unreal nature. The world is only a reflection of *Brahman*, having no reality apart from it. The reflection in the mirror looks exactly like to object reflected, but there is lateral inversion of the object; that is, the right side looks like the left side. Consciousness is infinite; the world is finite. Consciousness is all bliss; the world is all pain. *Brahman* is perfect; the world is extremely imperfect."

I realized that after giving an assurance to meet Him there at That Destination, Gurudev was reminding us of the need for more reflection to try to understand that the form of Gurudev was not essentially He. The form has gone down into history, whereas He is in eternity. It was born and grew old, but He is changeless; it was, but He is. But for this difference, it was simply pure *Brahman* that we were seeing functioning in Gurudev.[8]

KARMA YOGA

Especially for people of the Western world, and those of the East deeply affected by the production-oriented ways of the West, Gurudev's most ardent advice always was: practice *karma yoga*, the path of selfless action — do the work you have been doing, but learn to do it in a spirit of selflessness, dedicating all of your efforts to God. Then, he said, you will find joy in all you do, as well as inexhaustible energy. In addition, you will purify your mind so that the sacred message of the rishis can take root in it.

God's Work

On one occasion, Robyn Thompson was mailing some of Swamiji's correspondence but did not have the correct-size envelopes. She solved the problem by taking a larger envelope and folding it over at one end.

Swamiji saw what she was doing and said:

"No, that's not how it's to be done."

He then showed her how to do it. He cut the envelope carefully at the open end and fashioned a flap to fold over for closure. This procedure took a lot of time, but Swamiji was determined that the task be done right, not just expediently.

"This is God's work," he said. "It must be beautiful."[9]

Remember for Whom

One time while doing his correspondence, Swamiji was cutting out an article to send to a devotee. It was getting late for his rest time, but Swamiji was taking his time to do it perfectly. I was getting anxious for him to go for his rest quickly so I offered to cut it for him, and he gave it to me. Since he was still sitting there watching me, I tried to do it fast so he could go for his rest. In my hurry, I was not as meticulous as he had been. He took the paper from my hands and started cutting it himself once again.

As he was cutting it, he said very lovingly, "Always remember for Whom we are doing all this work."

Through that one small incident, Gurudev taught me a very important lesson in how to perform all actions in life. Even today, I try to remember that all the work I do is done for Him, the Lord. Gurudev had made it clear to me that every action should be performed with excellence — for the Lord. That is my gift to Him.

What Gurudev taught me in a few short minutes with profound clarity, I could not have learned in a lifetime with all the books at my disposal.[10]

Dedicating One's Work to God

I remember how during one of Gurudev's early *yajnas* in northern California, I was already looking for opportunities to do something, anything, to support the inspired work he was doing. I had transcribed names of lecture attendees onto small index cards and was sorting them alphabetically as he watched in his characteristic way, with a slight tilt of the head and with utmost concentration:

"Yes, at first you chase the work, and later the work chases you. That's what happened to me," he said, and then he added: "Whatever you do, just keep reminding yourself as you do the work, 'I do this for Him, for the Lord alone. For Him, for Him!'"[11]

In a letter to a worker in Chinmaya Mission Swamiji said:

I am glad . . . that many of you actually experienced that dedicated activities are not personal sacrifices, but they really provide a personal indulgence in a joy and inspiration unknown to us generally![12]

Many a Mission worker remembers the directness with which Swamiji could instill discipline and develop the right attitude toward service. Jairam Jaisinghani, for many years manager at Sandeepany Sadhanalaya, recalls:

Serving with Love

I was in charge of serving food to the devotees at the second *Vivekacudamani* Marathon Camp at Sidhbari. The volunteers and the brahmacharis who helped had a tough time with me if they did not abide by the instructions given. Normally, freshly made sweets were in great demand, and we had to curtail the service to one round. I would not allow a second round and was harsh on the volunteers if they tried to break this rule.

When Pujya Swamiji was told about his, his wrath came into the open at a lecture. He said: "If you serve, serve with love, care, and devotion, not with shouts and roughness."

The impact of his words was so great that I lost sleep for two nights. Tears rolled down my cheeks. The thought of giving up *seva* [service] and running away to Mumbai also crossed my mind. Only with his blessings, I continued serving with enthusiasm from the next day onward — but with a difference.

This is how he trained his workers with love, care, and fire.[13]

Who Did It?

During the Palghat *yajna* in 1983, Kalidas had invited Swamiji to his home for *bhiksha*. The local committee objected, because his ancestral home was in an interior village. However, Swamiji wrote him in a letter that he would be at Kalidas' house for *bhiksha*, following the evening talk.

Kalidas had arranged for a chief priest of the Sabarimalai temple to receive Swamiji with *Purna Kumbha* [a ritual for receiving the guru] and to officiate at the *puja* [worship service]. He himself drove to Coimbatore — a distance of about three hours from his home — to bring the priest for the function. He left at 7 a.m., hoping to be back by noon.

En route to the place he was delayed on the road for about four hours by a road blockage, due to a strike. He started trembling: What about the preparations for the evening? He was stuck midway, unable either to turn back home or go on to Coimbatore. He could only sit and repeatedly invoke Gurudev.

When he finally returned to Palghat after his Coimbatore trip, it was after 6 p.m. There was only time to put the priest in a taxicab and direct him to go on to Kalidas' house, while Kalidas himself cleaned and decorated the car and drove straight to Gurudev's *yajnasala* [lecture hall] to bring him home.

When he arrived at his house with Gurudev, he found the house and compound beautifully decorated — like a temple. All the preparations had been meticulously done. Different people from various localities had contributed to the effort of getting the house ready for Swamiji. It was as though a thousand hands had worked! Swamiji was received with *Purna Kumbha,* just as planned.

Swamiji looked around with beaming eyes, "Who arranged all this?"

"You did, Swamiji," Kalidas answered. As a result of this incident, Kalidas realized that *he* was never the doer himself, as Swamiji had so often taught in his lectures.[14]

Gurudev himself was the best example of the true meaning of working in the *karma yoga* spirit, of providing service, *seva,* to the community. G. B. Bhatia of Mumbai recalls that in the early days of his teaching, before Sandeepany Sadhanalaya was built in the outskirts of Mumbai, Gurudev would take devotees on "spiritual picnics" to visit holy persons and places, demonstrating his own spirit of service along the way:

Chief *Sevak*

During a spiritual picnic back in the early days, Gurudev demonstrated how one should conduct oneself as a worker, a *sevak* [one who serves others]. At the outset of the journey, he declared that he was "Chief *Sevak.*" He boarded his bus only after everyone in the entire convoy of buses was in his or her seat.

En route, one of the buses had a breakdown. Gurudev stopped the whole convoy and remained near the bus that was being repaired. Only after the repairs were completed, did he allow the convoy to resume the journey.[15]

And so he taught us, ever by his own example: how to keep others always in the forefront of the mind and initiate actions that support others' needs and wants. Even a short letter about an organizational detail was often accompanied by a small gift — a photograph, a bookmark, a small memento with a quotation by him. "Even now," says G. B. Bhatia, "when one is sending even a small acknowledgment, Gurudev's care comes to mind, and one makes the effort to do as he did."

Rain or Shine

Jnana Yajna plans were being made in Rourkela. Before the time of the *yajna* arrived, Swamiji had written to K. C. Patnaik: "The *yajna* will go on, come what may."

Although it was not the rainy season, arrangements were made to cover the open-air lecture area. And, indeed, it rained heavily the night before the concluding lecture. Even though the people attending the discourse were protected from the rain overhead, water was seeping in from the surrounding area onto the straw mats on the ground where they were sitting. The seating area was obviously wet throughout, but the audience sat quietly on the ground, without stirring, throughout Gurudev's discourse.

Before the last day of the *yajna*, the cover over the grounds collapsed under the weight of the rain, destroying the dais. Immediately, arrangements were made to hold the last talk inside the college auditorium next to the grounds. And so it happened. The last lecture was held inside a closed hall lit with petromax lights, and thus the *yajna* continued uninterrupted.

In a letter following the *yajna*, Swamiji wrote: "I'm so happy that the *yajna* went on — despite all storms!"[16]

A similar dedication to continuing the planned programs, no matter what the obstacles, is reflected in a letter by Gurudev dated January 25, 1958:

> *Here on 23rd a fire broke out and gutted the entire pandal, just 30 minutes before the lectures. Thank God . . . only some 20 people were there at that time. Before the fire brigade could come, every bit was down. So we held the discourses on the opposite road — an island under the tree — under the street lamp. It was marvelous!!*

Some ten years later, in a letter to a devotee in California, he said:

> *The work goes on. When we work selflessly, as an offering unto Him who dwells in all hearts, there is a bursting joy suffusing our entire being. To be under the halo of this joy is to be in spiritual unison with everyone and everything around us.*
>
> *Live the whole day in quiet, peaceful, unexciting cheer of surrender and dedication. Chant silently "Hari Om" in the mind and go about the little chores of work at home. At dusk, sit down with such a prepared mind for a short but irresistibly dynamic meditation, wherein we surrender all our littleness and rise to the Expanse of the Self.*[17]

He never tired of reminding us that our everyday lives were the best laboratories for practicing *karma yoga*. In a letter in which he was responding to a devotee who had just recounted to him the amount of work entailed in the marriage of her daughter, he said:

> *In such days of work, when you are fulfilling your duties toward others around you, you should not worry if you miss your studies and daily practices. After all, make the work a worship unto Him, by whose law and grace you became the mother of your dear daughter. These are our duties toward others around us. All have emerged from Him — and so all are His own forms. He alone is; everything else is the interpretation of the mind-and-intellect equipment only. Let us dedicate even our breathing unto His service . . . by serving others around us. We need not go out of our way searching for work; but when our duties come to our door, let us do them fully, entirely, beautifully.*[18]

A Master's *Seva*

At a *bhiksha* in Boston, a Christian minister asked Gurudev:

"OK, we realize the infinite, supreme Essence. Thereafter, no individuality, and so no universe. So your personal responsibility to serve the world ends. Is this the state of Perfection?"

Swamiji's answer was:

"The intellectual conclusions arrived at about this state and the life thereafter are authentic — but not true. Social responsibilities and the urge to serve one's fellow men, the urgency rising in our mind to wipe the tears from the eyes of the sad, the melancholy, and the suffering is indeed sacred. It brings about an expansion of our heart. A gush of love fountains up from our heart and streams forth to bathe the life around us.

"When such acts of *seva* are undertaken in a spirit of dedication and love, surrender, and worship of the Lord, they hasten to cleanse the mind of its agitations, and such a purified 'heart' (mind-intellect equipment) discovers the poise and dash needed for contemplation. As a result of steady contemplation, the mind gets transcended to the timeless Essence, the God-state, in a direct subjective experience.

"After this realization, the master, saint, or sage returns to play with his old equipment. In the deepest sense of love for all, he cannot but get involved with the world. The *seva* he does now is the fulfillment of his realization. It is the Lord's play through the saint or prophet."[19]

Serious students on the spiritual path often also became dedicated workers in Swamiji's Chinmaya Mission. Time and again, some would find themselves grappling with trying to keep the right balance between inner purity and outer dynamism, even power.

> *There has never been power with purity — anywhere, at any time. If you want to be pure, you must stand alone. If you want to do positive things, achieve something, leave the world a mite better than you found it, then you must choose power and throw some of your purity away. There is no other choice. What would you have must be your own choice. Now, you choose!*[20]

Gurudev himself was the primary role model for all other *sevaks* — those dedicating their lives to serving others: always ready to give of himself, always filled with an enthusiasm that energized everyone around him to action.

> *Enthusiasm is the very fuel in all great men. By inexhaustible ardor for whatever they undertake, they generate an extraordinary drive for action. In spiritual self-improvement, and in serving the nation in its cultural and spiritual aspects, the workers and the missionaries must discover in themselves the secret of invoking the trajectory force of true and flawless enthusiasm.*

GUIDELINES FOR EFFECTIVE WORK

Swamiji was also eminently practical, providing valuable hints to people who approached him with questions, ideas, and problems from their world of work.

Saying No

One time during his lecture tour in California, Swamiji was reviewing some materials used in management consulting that a devotee had brought in as a sample of how executives are being trained to work with less stress and greater detachment.

"Train yourself to say 'no' — with a smile," he advised. "Many of our problems arise from not knowing how to say 'no.'"[21]

Looking from Afar

At her first meeting with him, Barbara Gee had just been introduced to Swamiji as a management consultant. He made a gesture with his hands as though looking at something from far away and said, "Make sure that you look at the situation from afar." Then he said jokingly with a hearty laugh, "And then leave them alone. They'll create more messes on their own, and you'll never run out of work!"[22]

In a letter he said:

Great results are gained not merely because of the volume of work or the amount of excitement in the worker's bosom. The final results and their glory will depend upon a certain equipoise of the worker's mind, constantly dedicated and surrendered to Him whom a spiritual seeker is adoring and worshipping with every activity that he undertakes.[23]

Swamiji urged us to take things slowly when undertaking a new project, to start small and allow the work to gain momentum:

We could do most things best by easing into them slowly. Don't be in a hurry. The best rule is "hasten slowly." Be careful, but steady, in your pursuit.

Witnessing the speed of modern life in general, he said:

The speed of it all disturbs me. The trouble is we are living in a time of "compressed history," yet so few realize it. Changes that used to take fifty years take now five or fewer, and we can't help it because communication has made it that way.[24]

Situations, Problems, Crises

Swamiji was talking to Barbara Gee, giving her guidelines for her management consulting work: "Just tell the managers you work with," he said, "to keep their minds calm. When the mind is calm, problems become manageable."

He went on to elaborate: "Years ago in the United States, say, around the 1920s and 30s, the newspapers talked of 'situations' — social, political, etc. Then, around the 1940s, those situations had turned into 'problems.' By the 50s and 60s, the words 'situation' and 'problem' had disappeared from our vocabulary, and everything had become a 'crisis.' Now, all we read about in the papers is: 'the education crisis,' 'the health crisis,' 'the oil crisis' . . . Everything has become a crisis. Nothing has really changed about the situations in the world, but we have a reduced capacity to deal with them: Our minds today have a decreased ability to cope. What we need to work on is to *develop that capacity of the mind to cope.*

"If you treat a given event as a situation, it is just a situation to be dealt with. Keeping your mind calm, don't let the situation grow into a problem — and then develop further into a crisis!"[25]

Trust in Him

A devoted couple were trying to start a new business and were feeling despondent: They had little money, the stress level was high, and the future looked uncertain. The wife went to see Swamiji privately. He consoled her:

"Don't worry," he said, "as long as your feet are set on the right path and as long as you work at it diligently, there's no need to be afraid. The Lord will take care of you. Trust in Him."

And his words came true: The couple's business worked out just fine.[26]

Simply watching Gurudev run his vast organization gave untold opportunities to learn about management. Those who witnessed him overseeing the many construction projects (as well as the countless spiritual camps) at Sidhabari had many opportunities to watch the consummate manager in action:

Surprise Inspections

When Swami Subodhananda was first assigned to the Sidhabari ashram, Gurudev gave him the following advice: "If you want to administer effectively, be unpredictable!"

The young swami found out the truth of those words on many occasions. "We had to keep everything here in total readiness at all times," he says, "because Swamiji could appear anywhere at anytime — in the kitchen, the bookstore, the office. He liked to drop by for 'surprise inspections.' This habit of his prevented slacking on our part."[27]

Work Overload

One day, an assistant who was helping Swamiji with his daily correspondence was overwhelmed at the amount of work before her and said to him:

"This is so much!"

He said quietly, "See how every day I work and do a little . . . and slowly it all gets done."[28]

Some devotees who also led active professional lives were distraught because the ethical values they had learned to integrate into their lives as part of assimilating Vedanta seemed to be unduly challenged by certain work environments. Swamiji always had wise words to impart:

Working with Crooks

One man told Swamiji, "I have a problem: The man I work with is a crook. But this work is my livelihood! What do I do?"

Swamiji's answer was: "Do your work; do your level best. When it gets very difficult, wink at the Lord. When the time is right, the crook won't be there anymore."

To another man Swamiji said, "In a tough competitive environment, *know* that you are playing by the rules of that environment — and keep it separate from your personal values."

When another man complained that he had to do business with someone who was unethical, Swamiji said, "In the business room, you fight him. When you go outside, love him as a brother."[29]

Viji Sundaram, who served as editor of the Chinmaya Mission Vedanta journal *Tapovan Prasad,* writes about the lesson she received about journalism from her guru. "In the five years I worked for the Mission as editor of *Tapovan Prasad,*" she said while Gurudev was still alive, "I learned a lot about the profession I had chosen just by watching Swamiji slip into the role of writer. He could, and still can, do it effortlessly. No writer's blocks seem to trouble him. I once asked him how he did it, and he said, 'I let the thoughts flow through me,' and added, for my benefit, 'When you compromise your values, you block the flow of your natural creative instincts.'"

Racing Pen

A few days after my arrival in the United States, in August 1981, I received a letter from Swamiji. I keep the note in a small compartment in my purse and read it every now and then, checking the words like a map that tells me where to go and where not to go. I'd like to title the note "What every journalist should know to be successful."

The letter, in part, reads:

> *Let the pen race through channels of thought opened up by your own natural intuition. This gets blocked when we compromise with unhealthy values or when we get involved with purposeless day-to-day happenings.*
>
> *Flow on with the stream. Let go the world.*

Newspaper editors urge their staff writers to "put a tune into your story and let it sing." What they don't tell them, however, is that the tune can be there only when the writer embraces the let-go-the-world philosophy.

Swamiji, I know, has. That's why there's a tune in everything he writes, everything he says, everything he does.[30]

DEALING WITH ORGANIZATIONAL ISSUES

Many of Gurudev's words, both verbal and written, were dedicated to keeping the workers within his own organization, Chinmaya Mission, motivated, focused, and free from infighting. When difficulties arose within Mission work — as they invariably do in any organization, no matter how well-meaning its members — letters would flood his desk. His medicine by return mail was sometimes sweet, sometimes harsh, sometimes bitter-sweet:

> *A very sensitive heart all the time on your own sleeve will easily get bruised with words and looks. Keep the heart where the Lord has kept it: well-protected by the ribs! Don't be sensitive; rise above while dealing with others. Get out of yourself and watch and hear yourself performing, standing in their shoes.*

Gurudev's devoted workers often worried about collecting the funds necessary to carry out one envisioned project or another. The following answer from a letter was a typical response by him:

> *When Narayana (Spirit) is with us, Chinmaya Family will not worry over the non-arrival of Lakshmi (wealth). She cannot ever be away from Narayana!*

When devotees and Chinmaya Mission workers became overwhelmed with the complexity of the problems they faced, they wrote long, what Swamiji called "exhaustive," letters to him describing their challenges. Often, the letter that came back was one-tenth the length of the one that had reached Swamiji. Situations that were described as complex and insurmountable would often receive a simple, one-sentence salve administered by the deft hand of the Master:

> *A chosen seeker is generally dragged through such simple situations, teasing him to learn to accept what the Lord gives with a smile.*

If the writer had gone far overboard with his or her dramatic portrayal of events, he would shrug off the ego-fed drama with a laugh:

> *I read your letter. I laughed at your despairs and detailed descriptions!*

However, there were other times when a short sentence or jovial laugh did not suffice. At those times, his workers received his doses of medicine in their most scalding form. On one such occasion, the dose was administered in a rather public setting, the closing banquet at the end of a spiritual camp:

A Hurricane of Anger

All camp delegates had gathered for the closing meal to be shared with Gurudev. Decked out in their finest saris and suits, they sat quietly at the banquet tables, awaiting a few inspiring words from their guru.

Then Swamiji stood up to talk. But this turned out not to be a time for quiet or jovial words. All attendees were overcome with shock when Gurudev started shouting angry words at the local organizers, denouncing them about their lack of cooperation among themselves. For several years he had patiently listened to the endless stories of infighting. He had chosen this moment to call a halt to it.

He blasted forth with such a show of anger and at such high volume that those listening could feel the floor under their feet vibrating. Even those who had arrived from other parts of the country and had had little to do with the local organizational problems sat in terrified silence until the barrage of words was complete.[31]

The doctor's treatment worked. After receiving this hefty dose of Swamiji's medicine, the organizers in the area moved toward a more cooperative way of working together.

Gurudev reminded us often that the only way to become effective workers, whether in one's chosen profession or while doing service within Chinmaya Mission, is to cultivate dispassion, "passionate dispassion," as he called it, a state of mind in which one becomes "joyously indifferent." He himself was a perfect example of that joyous indifference, as he moved from continent to continent teaching Vedanta. Whatever the difficulties with travel arrangements, yajna preparations, or a myriad of organizational plans, he moved through them all with a laugh and a shrug of his shoulders.

Swamiji had an unbelievable capacity to detach himself from organizational success or failure. A powerful lesson in that respect — that nothing on the dual plane has absolute value — came in the middle of a painful period in the life of Chinmaya Mission West in the United States. Factions had developed in the organization, and the Mission seemed to be rocking on its foundations, yet Swamiji stood firm and calm:

A Vehicle for Work

I went into Swamiji's room, closed the door, and knelt down in front of him with swallowed tears burning my throat.

We talked for some time about the difficulties the Mission was facing, and I finally managed to force the words out past my gathering storm of emotion:

"Swamiji, but your life's work, Chinmaya Mission, is itself in danger of being destroyed!"

"So what?" was his answer. "The Mission was established to serve a purpose. If that purpose has now been served, what's to cry about? If it's His will, the Lord will provide us with another vehicle for work."

Those few sentences uttered by him in the midst of what we, who were closely associated with the work of his organization, perceived as a major crisis, were an exquisite reminder to me about the absolute nature of Vedanta and the purity of the selfless Teacher who lives in detachment from all temporal events. And Swamiji's Mission did, indeed, survive the tests it passed through at that time and grew stronger with each passing year.[32]

When Swamiji decided to appoint someone to a new job within his organization, no matter how important the job, he usually made the appointment without much fanfare at all, as though just giving an offhand instruction in passing. Narain Bhatia, who since 1990 served as Chief Executive of Central Chinmaya Mission Trust (CCMT) in Mumbai, the central governing body for Chinmaya Mission, remembers how he landed in that position:

Half a Biscuit Plus a Big Job

One day in 1990 Narain Bhatia was passing by Sandeepany Sadhanalaya in his car and said to himself, "Let me stop by for a minute. Maybe Swamiji is there." Indeed, he was — but only because his flight had been delayed by one-half hour.

Swamiji was talking to a group of people at the ashram. Narain Bhatia dared not disturb him, but he still felt compelled to prostrate at his feet, so he did. Swamiji put half a biscuit in his hand:

"Narain, you will take over from him [indicating the then current Chief Executive, who was about to retire from the job]!"

N. Bhatia walked with Swamiji to his car.

"Yes, Swamiji, it is possible," he said.

"If it's possible," said Swamiji, "then better ask your wife first."

All permissions were granted and arrangements made — and Narain Bhatia soon began training in his new post at Chinmaya Mission, thanks to a timely visit and a half-an-hour's delay in his guru's flight![33]

Common Sense

In 1961, Gurudev's monthly Vedanta journal *Tyagi* (later renamed to the current *Tapovan Prasad*) was without an editor. One day, while they were riding in a car together, Gurudev asked Dwaraknath Reddy to become its editor.

Dwaraknath's response was disbelieving and cautious: "Swamiji, how can I edit a magazine with scholarly articles when I've been studying Vedanta for a mere one year?"

Swamiji's reply was simple: "You've got common sense, haven't you? Use it!"

So Dwaraknath took on the job of editor for four years, not only editing the journal, but also writing an editorial for it each month. He recalls, "It was the best thing Swamiji did for me — asking me to be editor. It forced me to consolidate my thoughts. By expressing what I had understood, I had made it my own."[34]

The Guru Knows Best

A *yajna* was about to begin in Mumbai. Some members of the Executive Committee who had organized the *yajna* came to meet Swamiji at his residence. After they emerged from his room, they seemed very satisfied and left.

Then Swamiji emerged from his room. While talking with us casually, he remarked that the organizers wanted him to alter a decision regarding the *yajna*. He himself had decided that the morning Upanishad class should be open only to Mission members. He did not want the general public to attend. The organizers felt that this restriction would deprive a majority of people from reaping the benefits of Swamiji's lectures. To be a member one had to pay a nominal donation. The committee also expressed that people would think that the Mission is being greedy and wants to make more money. A lot of people would enroll as members only to attend the morning talk. It's not clear how they convinced him, but Swamiji gave in to their demands. He remarked to us, "OK, if that's what they want."

We were two days into the morning lecture series. Swamiji was explaining a technical Vedantic term, referring to another Vedanta textbook. Many of the listeners were the regular crowd and were familiar with the other text. However, a large number of new listeners were also present, due to the wishes of the organizers. Swamiji must have seen a blank look on their faces.

He paused and said, "Never mind."

Then, with the next breath, he lashed out at the organizers: "This is what happens when the organizers think that they know more than the Swami. I wanted only Mission members to attend these classes not because I need some extra money. The topic is so subtle that it can only be properly understood by those people who have been attending study groups and studying other texts."

The organizers were cringing in their seats. That day after the lecture they came to Swamiji's residence and apologized for their short-sightedness. Swamiji did not scold them again, but quietly forgave them.[35]

When the Time Is Right

In 1971, at Chinmaya Mission's first National *Gita Jnana Yajna* in Mumbai, the next brahmachari course at Sandeepany Sadhanalaya was announced. K. C. Patnaik, too, filled out an application to join the course. He walked up to the counter to submit his application.

"Sorry," the volunteer at the table informed him, "we can't accept your application. You see, the form is to be changed." It was decided that a modified form would be sent to his home address.

However, when he arrived home, he realized that all his home responsibilities were not yet fulfilled: One sister was still not married, and he had other family responsibilities as well, with old parents depending on him. It was not the right time to join the two-and-one-half-year course at Sandeepany Sadhanalaya in Mumbai.

Later, he went to the United States to study, and on his return to India after obtaining his MBA, he met Swamiji during a *yajna* at Bhubaneswar, Orissa, in January 1984.

"Could I be of any use at CCMT [Central Chinmaya Mission Trust]?" he asked Swamiji.

"You've just landed," was Swamiji's reply with a smile. "Let us see!"

He then assumed a senior executive post with many responsibilities and long hours. In time, he quit the lucrative job to become an independent consultant. He was ardently wishing to write to Swamiji to offer his services, but before he managed to do so, Swamiji attained *Mahasamadhi.*

In December 1994, at a *bhiksha,* Swami Tejomayananda, the new head of Chinmaya Mission, asked him: "What are you doing now?"

"I'm free," was Patnaik's reply.

"Why not join CCMT?" asked Swami Tejomayananda and advised him to relocate to Mumbai.

Patnaik remembered his conversation with Gurudev exactly ten years earlier. This was obviously the right time now. He joined CCMT as General Manager of the Books and Publications Division, looking after publication and distribution of Chinmaya books around the world.[36]

Narayana and Lakshmi Together

A *yajna* was being planned in Mumbai. The organizers realized that the day the lecture series was to begin was Lakshmi Puja Day. The organizing committee agreed that they must convince Swamiji not to start the *yajna* on that day, because too many people might stay away.

When they made their proposal to Swamiji, he said, "Where Narayana is, will Lakshmi [his consort] not come?" So the *yajna* was organized, as initially planned, to begin on Lakshmi Puja Day.

Some 5,000 people came to the *yajna*, and not one problem with attendance was seen. At the end of the *yajna*, Swamiji passed out Lakshmi coins to some 1,200 people who filed by him for two-and-a-half hours; to each, he said something personal.[37]

LOVE

"To give love is freedom. To demand love is slavery," said Gurudev. *"The day you take up the policy of giving love instead of demanding it, that day you will have rewritten your entire future destiny."* Swamiji had taken up that policy long ago, and adhered to it ever more intensely as the years went by. Toward the last years of his life, some of his former strictness had mellowed. The disciplinarian had become the loving guide. In fact, he confessed to unreserved, ardent, "shameless" love:

> *I know nothing about others. I only love them ardently, fully, unreservedly. In that love I act shamelessly, freely, easily, openly. Whether they feel benefited, degraded, roughed up, or mishandled, I don't care: I enjoy such contacts . . . and I cherish such a life of pure and free love! Your permission is not asked; your acceptance is not demanded; your approval is not expected. It is my privilege to love, and I look forward to no return. What will you say to such a foolish one?*[1]

Giving Love

"Above all, he taught me to give love," recalls Jamna Batra. He always used to say, "Give love, give love! Don't think about what you'll get in return, but if you keep on giving love, love will come back to you!"

She tried doing just that for many years. One day she wrote to Swamiji: "You say, 'Give love, give love, and you'll get it back' — but, Swamiji, I don't see anything coming back!"

When he saw her next he said, "You're the mother. You *have* to give love! Don't expect anything back; just keep on loving. Whenever the Lord sees it fit, you'll get love back."

"And," says Jamna Batra, "that is, indeed, what has happened."[2]

Pure Love

Experiencing Swamiji's love was unlike the usual love experiences of the world, with its attachments, longings, and expectations. He knew how to love purely, deeply, unconditionally. At times, when his love-filled eyes looked into mine, I couldn't bear the intensity of it; at times, I could. It all depended on how clear my mind was at the moment. When my focus was on my limited being, with all its wants and imperfections, his loving gaze made the imperfections even more obvious, leaving me in keen discomfort. When my mind was resting in a peaceful space below the layers of mundane thought, I could submit myself joyfully to the guru's loving gaze and be in wordless communion with him.[3]

Unselfish Love

I am a poet and composer. Over the years I've long held an affinity for Ganesha. Having read Chinmaya's excellent book on Ganesha, I wrote him and praised his book for its clarity of thought and readability. Chinmaya responded with a long letter, making the following comments on Ganesha:

> *Ganesha is considered an authority in poetry and philosophy. He is wedded to Mother Knowledge, Sarasvati. To invoke His grace is to deepen your poetry and heighten your music. They will grow all by themselves. Don't beg or demand. Just learn to purely love Him as you and I love flowers or the moon. That is called unselfish, pure love.*[4]

Fatherly Love

During Nalin Vissanji's first trip to Uttarkashi in 1958, Swamiji took a group of devotees for a walk around the grounds near the ashram after classes were over. He led the group over a narrow pathway and lovingly pointed out various Ayurvedic trees and plants, one by one, explaining how each was used for medicinal purposes. Many of those plants they knew from their own gardens, but now Swamiji was broadening their understanding of each plant's use. He poured out his concern and love for them in a most gentle and fatherly way, recalls Vissanji 40 years later.[5]

True Love

In Secunderabad, India, a family had invited Swamiji for *bhiksha* at their home and we tagged along, ever insatiable for his *darshan* [beholding of a holy person]. Swamiji was tired after his mid-morning talk. Shortly after having been received by the young wife of the household, the grandmother emerged tearfully and flung herself at Swamiji's feet, crying that she was depressed and unable to remember the Lord. Swamiji held her hands and advised her to chant her *japa* [chanting with the help of prayer beads]. She was inconsolable and hung onto his feet weeping while he drank a glass of water.

Then, the husband of the household came in to pay his respects, fully decked out in army regalia. Swamiji greeted him accordingly and listened attentively while he outlined the importance of his recent promotion.

The grandmother continued to weep at his feet, the husband held forth about his work, and the wife slipped in questions here and there, seeking advice about the children.

Being quite a new devotee, fiercely protective of my guru, and convinced that these folks could not really love Swamiji or they would not be so demanding of him, I wanted to shout at them to be quiet and see that he was tired. Wishing to express my outrage and concern, I caught Swamiji's eye.

To my shock and discomfort, he sent me one of his Shiva looks, its righteous and chastising anger directed squarely at me. "How dare you judge?" the look in his eyes said. "Is your love so meager and selfish that you cannot extend even a little compassion to my devotees in need?"

Suddenly, the fierce look was gone, and he turned away from me, glowing with love, as he stroked the grandmother's head and nodded appreciatively at the officer's achievements.[6]

LOVE IN ACTION

A devotee recalls: "Gurudev's compassionate love for his devotees and his disciples used to flow spontaneously and in an utterly unique way. Sometimes he would employ sarcasm, at times a scolding, yet other times a hug or calculated indifference to transmit a teaching. Everything was an expression of his pure love."

Swamiji's capacity for loving unconditionally drew people of various backgrounds and types to his side, even those who on the surface appeared to be disinterested in serious spiritual pursuit:

Thwarted Expectations

Once, while I was traveling with Swamiji overseas, I witnessed a lady visitor arriving from a nearby country, a modern Indian woman, who, through family connections, had met Swamiji many times over the years. She was very unlike the usual sari-clad ladies who swarmed around him: She wore her hair short and her make-up generously; she was dressed in Western clothing, and her slender hands were topped off with chiseled, crimson fingernails. She obviously loved being in Swamiji's company, chatting easily about life and her work as a beautician, with no reference to the things of the spirit as far as our ears could hear. He, too, relished the easy interplay between old friends, no doubt relieved for once of the slavish attentions that his many devotees bestowed upon him day after day.

I watched the unusual scene and realized that what drew this earthy woman to Swamiji was the same thing that drew so many of his outwardly devout, sari-clad and mala-draped followers — his capacity to be a genuine, generous, deeply loving human being.

Yet, I felt that the watchful eyes of some of his more traditional devotees, myself included, had a little trouble with the seemingly worldly woman who was taking up the guru's time with idle-sounding talk. One, a particularly devout follower, who exceeded many others in her capacity to rise before dawn and serve his every need with never a sign of fatigue, had just that day gone into town to purchase a special oil for massaging his legs. She, I'm sure, along with many of us, longed to have the opportunity to express her love for the guru by massaging the gaunt limbs that had become emaciated by age and rendered without feeling by diabetes.

The devotee had just entered Swamiji's sitting room with the oil bottle in hand and a shyly expectant look on her face. She was clad, as always, in an immaculately draped sari, her hair pulled back in an elegant bun. She was the picture of classical beauty and grace, a brilliant gem among us regular stones gathered from the side of the road. The beautician was still at Swamiji's side.

I watched the devotee with interest and tense expectation. Knowing what she must feel, I too felt an inward tremble: Will he let her massage his legs, or will he shoo her away, throwing out some curt comment about no need for such nonsense? One never knew.

Then, before any word was uttered, I suddenly sensed what Swamiji was about to do, going in the face of all of our expectations:

"Here, let me have the oil," he said. "We'll have the expert [the beautician who had just been talking to him] massage my legs. She knows how to do it best. She's a professional."

So the dedicated devotee was left to watch as her precious offering was applied to her guru's legs with the crimson-fingered hands of the "worldly" guest. I knew, once again, that our guru had found a grand opportunity to teach us all a whole array of lessons: about drawing conclusions from outward appearances, about expectations, about the judging mind, about surrendering all desires at the altar of the Higher. I had watched him too often in too many situations not to be certain that, once again, he used a simple situation at hand to teach several of us a lesson.[7]

No "Unfit" Devotees

Over the years, we witnessed many instances when Swamiji granted particular attention to someone the rest of us might have declared "unfit" in some way — too unkempt, too boisterous, too demanding of Swamiji's attention.

I remember one time in northern California, a large group of us had gathered for *satsang* with Swamiji and were in the midst of lively questions and answers when a stranger walked through the door, unkempt, dressed in dirty jeans and a jacket, and with an open beer can in his hand. We gave each other uncomfortable glances, wondering what we should do to prevent such a disgraceful entry of the ill-fitting guest. The young man was already beginning to sit down at the back of the room when Swamiji called forth in the delightful way he had of welcoming a new visitor to a *satsang*: A loud, singsong "Hi-iiiii!" and "Come on in!" boomed across the length of the room. This time, though, his greeting didn't stop at that; he insisted that the beer-drinking stranger come closer to the front and sit next to him so he could hear everything that was being said at the *satsang*. The difference between the capacity of Swamiji's loving heart next to our doubting ones became instantly obvious.

Another time I remember a new listener approaching Swamiji after a lecture. The man exuded an air of something extremely fake, even sinister, and once again I felt myself becoming extremely protective of Swamiji, wanting to shield him from the onslaught of this man's obvious insincerity. Then I looked at Swamiji's face. He was standing very close to the man now, beaming down at him with luminous love and tenderness shining from his face, every part of his being focused on answering the question that had been posed to him.[8]

Swamiji's teaching and loving were so intertwined that most of the time one couldn't tell the one from the other. Anjali Singh was traveling with Swamiji in Europe in 1989 and attending to his everyday needs when she had an interesting experience with a lost shawl.

The Lost Shawl

On the eve of departure from St. Gallen, Switzerland, while packing Swamiji's bags on the eve of his departure, Anjali forgot her shawl in Swamiji's room. At the Zurich airport, after all formalities were over and Swamiji and Anjali were waiting in the lounge for the plane departure to be announced, Swamiji asked her, "Where is your shawl?"

"Here," Anjali said, pointing to a second shawl of hers, having completely forgotten about the existence of the first. She took the shawl off her shoulders and placed it on Swamiji's knees, thinking his legs must be cold and that's why his unexpected inquiry.

They flew from Zurich to Madrid, where they changed planes for Las Palmas. On the flight to the Canary Islands, he again asked Anjali, "Where is your shawl?" She quickly put her second shawl once again on his legs and tucked it properly under his feet, thinking, "The blood circulation in his feet must be really low today! It's so warm here, and yet his feet are freezing." On arrival at Las Palmas, they had to drive one hour to his residence. The weather was extremely warm.

Only later, while unpacking his suitcase at the house did Anjali notice two similar shawls lying on Swamiji's bed. One of them was Anjali's, the one she had lost! Swamiji had all along been carrying it on his shoulders, along with his own, despite the heat, for one-and-a-half days — through Switzerland, mainland Spain, and across the sea to the Canary Islands.[9]

Now luminous, now gentle, now seemingly harsh, Swamiji's love sometimes left bruised egos in its wake; other times, melted away ego-created obstructions; and many a time saved his devotees from fear and despair.

R. Krishnamoorthy recounts an incident that demonstrates the depths of Gurudev's love and compassion. The occasion was the installation of the *Sivalingam* [a symbol of Shiva] at Chinmaya Mandir at Thamaraipakkam, Chennai (Madras):

An Embodiment of Love

A large local crowd from the surrounding villages had reached Thamaraipakkam for the installation ceremonies, despite the fact that we had not taken any effort to widely publicize the event in the local area. In addition to hundreds of devotees who assembled for the installation, over a thousand villagers from nearby villages had arrived at the site. They were stopped at the gate by security personnel while the *puja* was being conducted.

After the installation was completed, Pujya Gurudev walked down the temporary road we had laid on the grounds, up to the entrance gate. As we walked with him, the crowd at the gate surged forward to fall at his feet. I was next to Gurudev, along with some Yuva Kendra [youth organization of Chinmaya Mission] personnel, and I tried my best to stop the crowd from falling at the feet of Gurudev, so that he could get into his car parked near the gate.

With his walking cane, Gurudev motioned at me to let the people prostrate. Then a middle-aged woman, with a baby in her arms who was barely ten days old, placed the baby at the feet of Gurudev and, with tears in her eyes, said that she suspects that the baby will die due to high fever and inadequate medicines. Gurudev lifted the child, stroked its head, and told the woman, "Don't worry. Lord Sarveshvara will look after him."

Then he abruptly asked me and the Yuva Kendra personnel to stop the crowd from milling toward him and beckoned me to the side of the road. He struck his cane in the ground and said, "In six months from now, I want a free dispensary at this place. Get it done! I want every child from the surrounding villages to be looked after by our doctors."

He could read the hesitancy in my face. Barely a few minutes before, I had explained that we were falling short of funds to complete the construction of the Dhyana Mandir. Gurudev said, "I know, as usual you are worried where to get the funds. They will come. Take the *sankalpa* [declaration of purpose or powerful thought that manifests itself in the material world]."

That very evening, we met a friend, Mrs. Saraswati Anant, who wanted to talk to Gurudev. We arranged for a meeting the day after, just before lunch. The lady, being old and unwell, had to be taken in a wheelchair to Gurudev by my wife. At the end of the lady's discussion with Gurudev, he said:

"Mrs. Anant will donate Rs. 300,000 for the free medicare center at Thamaraipakkam. It will be named after her husband: 'Anant's Free Medicare Centre.'"

I felt as though I had been struck by lightning. Here I was, not knowing where to get the next thirty thousand rupees, yet, within two days, the decision taken by Pujya Gurudev had taken firm shape. His instructions were: "See that priority is given to the treatment of the children from the surrounding villages."

That was the genesis of Anant's Free Medicare Centre at Thamaraipakkam, an embodiment of Gurudev's compassion and love.[10]

Love went both ways, of course, his to us and ours to him, imperfect though ours may have been.

Two-Way Love

I remember so vividly how I sat in *satsang* after a morning lecture in a small meeting room in the early seventies and couldn't take my eyes off Swamiji's face. He looked at me with loving eyes and smiled, "Don't get attached." I gave myself the challenge then to love no less than in that moment, but to try to leave attachment behind.

And there were times when perhaps in some measure I succeeded. Once, while saying good-bye to him at the airport, I happened at one point to be standing some distance from him and gazed across the heads of the other devotees to meet his eyes. I was suddenly overcome by an inexplicable, strange taste of fierce neutrality. Only paradox could explain my state of mind. I was totally identified with him, loving him, yet absolutely devoid of emotion. His long, meaningful look told me that something of special significance had just transpired.[11]

But most often, many of us, men and women alike, were like weeping *gopis* [milkmaids] at Krishna's side, hardly able to contain our bliss.

Mad Love for the Guru

Isabel Taylor tells of a time when she was massaging Swamiji's feet. Usually during such times her mind would become deeply absorbed in the Higher. However, this one time, Swamiji was holding an interesting conversation with a visiting professor from Germany even as the massaging was proceeding. Isabel was interested in the discussion and was carefully following all of Swamiji's comments.

Then, abruptly, Swamiji withdrew his feet.

As she looked up, startled, he said accusingly, "You were listening to what I was saying!"

"True," she replied.

He said, "So what's the point?"

She answered, "The point is union with God within oneself. The point is practicing what Swamiji keeps teaching us."

The following day, at parting time, Swamiji said to Isabel, "I too loved my guru madly. When I forgot that he was, indeed, *He* [he pointed up as he said this], he would give me a kick. And so will I kick you whenever you forget."[12]

HEALING INNER WOUNDS

A successful businessman in the United States, Sarv Singh, had suffered an unfortunate accident that had damaged his heart severely. He was deeply worried about his health and unable to function dynamically in life when he had his first meeting with Swamiji. He tells his story of what happened:

A New Lease on Life

It was the summer of 1985 when Pujya Gurudev Chinmayananda was holding a spiritual camp here. I was suffering from a major health setback, and, at the age of 38, the future looked bleak. Several top cardiologists had given me five years to live. During the Pomona [a college in southern California] camp, I requested and obtained some time to see Gurudev. He could only spare five minutes, as he was preparing for his next lecture. As I entered his room, I collapsed at his feet and said:

"Swamiji, I am going to die. Can you help me? The doctors want me to have a heart transplant."

He looked at me, got up from his chair, and sat down on the floor next to me. Looking at me with his piercing gaze, he said, "You are not going to need anybody's heart. This heart will do."

My wife quickly interjected and informed him that my heart had lost 90 percent of its capacity.

He answered: "Never mind. Use the 10 percent to the maximum."

He gave me my life back. I returned to work, and my business soared year after year. He graced us with his presence every year. He would ask me each time with an inquiring smile on his face, "How is business?"[13]

During many a spiritual camp, we would often see Sarv Singh sitting next to Swamiji's chair while he was resting or watching television, with Swamiji's hand clasped lovingly over his own. The love between the two was unmistakable.

With so many years of serving and meeting others, Swamiji had met many devotees, disciples, and Chinmaya Mission workers who had suffered the loss of a loved one. He always knew how to reach the bereaved heart.

Consolation in Grief

Gurudev was in Mumbai during the last days of Swamini Pavitrananda, whose body succumbed to a brain tumor in 1991. Swamiji was a great source of solace and strength to the family of the ailing swamini. Despite his own failing health, Gurudev, himself moving about only in a wheelchair, visited Pavitranandaji in the hospital in Mumbai in November 1991 and comforted her family with words of deep profundity and compassion. After Swamini Pavitrananda had passed away, Swamiji consoled the family with poetic words of compassion, urging them to see God as the Magnificent Gardener who seeks to bring his favorite blooms from the garden inside His own house:

When I walk into my house and see a beautiful bloom in my garden and I pluck it for my flower vase to be near me all the time, how can anyone blame and curse me?[14]

The same event is retold from another perspective:

Last Loving Rites

Swamini Pavitrananda, ill with terminal cancer, was in an ICU ward at a hospital in Mumbai. Gurudev himself was not well and had just had an electrocardiogram done. After the procedure he asked someone, "Do you know where Pavitra is? Take me there."

Dr. Asha Chakrabarty, who was with him, was worried that the strain of the trip would not be good for him, as he himself was not at all well. But Gurudev insisted that he be taken to the dying swamini's side, so they went.

He sat at Pavitranandaji's bedside for a full 15 minutes in the ICU ward, where officially he was not even allowed, blessing her for her passage into the next life. When he came out he said, "Remove the oxygen tubes." He had already given Pavitraji *sannyasa* [status of a renunciate, or *swamini*] over the phone from Hong Kong and arranged that her orange robes be sent to her from Sidhabari. Later, he also made arrangements for settling the swamini's full hospital bill.[15]

Lifting Grief

A devotee in India had recently lost her husband to illness and was feeling searing grief. She was sitting at Swamiji's feet at a *satsang* in New Delhi when he unexpectedly placed his foot on her stomach and held it there for a while. She said that after that moment the unbearable weight of her grief lifted, and even though she still mourned her husband's loss, the intense pain of her sorrow had dissipated.[16]

Happiness Stirring Again

Shobha Joshi had lost her only son. All the time she was feeling very sad; she had lost all her confidence.

One day, she went to meet Swamiji for the first time at someone's home. She was standing among a group of devotees when Swamiji came out of his room. The minute she saw him, she said to herself, "Here is a person who loves all of humanity." Swamiji walked directly up to her and held both her hands in his.

"You have come, *Amma* [Mother]," said Swamiji." I knew you would come. I'm happy."

And at that moment, she felt for the first time happiness stirring inside her once again.[17]

Gurudev healed many other hurting and frightened hearts with just the right touch and the right word for each person who approached him in need.

Lifting the Spirits

An elderly man who was gravely ill, wheelchair-bound, and very feeble had been brought to Swamiji's *satsang*. Swamiji beckoned the man to pull the wheelchair next to his own, held his hands, stroked his arms gently, and spoke to him lovingly for many long minutes, now and then cracking a joke to lift the man's mood. By the time the visit was over, the man was beaming.[18]

CARING LOVE AND COMPASSION

Gurudev's compassion knew no bounds: It touched the sick, it bathed newcomers with love and acceptance, it bent low to honor the aged, it touched even total strangers.

No *Pranams*

Many times, we witnessed one of the most endearing sights we had the fortune to behold: An elderly, white-haired Indian woman, bent over with age and obviously hurting in every limb, would approach Swamiji and begin the slow, painful movement toward the floor, intent on doing a *pranam* [bowing at the feet of a holy person]. But at the sight of her, Swamiji's eyes would light up with love, and before she could descend even a few inches toward the floor, he was already out of his chair — even in his later years when his own legs were pain-ridden — pulling her up to full standing position and giving her a big hug.[19]

Many devotees experienced a unique relationship with Gurudev, as though they were his special, chosen disciples. Gurudev had the ability to connect with each devotee in a unique way, ministering to the most personal of his followers' needs. To many, he was both Father and Mother and devoted friend, who took care of them, protected them, and anticipated their needs, big and small. Especially when he played host to a new devotee, Swamiji took every opportunity to protect and pamper the new student, instilling in him or her vast new reserves of confidence.

Loving Pampering

During his early years with Gurudev, Srichand Krishnani had made preparations to spend time with his guru in Chittoor and to visit various other places South India. When he arrived in Chittoor, Swamiji asked him, "What are your plans?"

"I want to visit the entire South," answered Srichand.

"Yes, yes," said Swamiji. "I'll make an itinerary for you and give you letters of recommendation."

Srichand washed up from his journey. Someone brought him a towel, with the words, "Swamiji asked that you have a towel."

At *satsang*, Swamiji beckoned to him, "You come sit next to me!" Swamiji proceeded to do many little things to make the new devotee feel utterly comfortable and cared for. He noticed that Srichand was having some stomach problems and made sure the hosts did not give him any spicy food at mealtimes. Swamiji even went for a swim with him in the host's pool, offering to teach backstroke to the young devotee.

"Everyone will feel 'j'!" Swamiji joked — his way of saying that he realized that others who were watching the two may have felt pangs of jealousy about the special attention the guru was bestowing on one person.

Later, Swamiji wrote twenty-five letters of introduction for Srichand's visits around South India and then bade him a loving good-bye with, "And now, you disappear from here!"[20]

"They Are My Guests"

About eight or nine devotees were traveling by train with Swami Chinmayananda from New Delhi to Pathankot and from there to Sidhabari, in Himachal Pradesh, the site of his ashram Sandeepany (Himalayas). They arrived early in the morning at the Pathankot station, where two brahmacharis had come to greet them. They had brought one small car to carry Swamiji, his luggage, and the two brahmacharis.

The brahmacharis greeted the group and then pointed out to Swamiji where his car was waiting. Swamiji looked at the car, then looked at them and at his group of devotees. He asked the brahmacharis how the rest were going to get to Sidhabari, another few hours' drive from Pathankot:

"I think there is a bus coming in a couple of hours," one of the brahmacharis offered.

Those who witnessed the scene had never seen Swamiji so angry. He took his cane and pounded it down on the earth so hard that the ground seemed to shake all around the group.

"If you want to run this place," he said, "then run it! Find transportation for these people. They are my guests."[21]

An Unexpected Birthday Gift

I had gone to India without my husband, who had meritoriously volunteered to stay behind with our three sons while I attended camps in Sidhabari and Bangalore in March 1989. It was late afternoon. All week long, devotees had gathered two or three times a day to offer *Paduka Puja* [worship of the guru's sandals] at the feet of Sri Gurudev. In fact, the entire camp had been one ceremony after another, interspersed between classes and meditation. It was all I had expected of Sidhabari and more.

But today was very special, and it was a secret known only to me.

As I prepared myself for the evening lecture, my roommate came in, smiling and singing sweetly. She turned to me and said, "Would you like to offer *Paduka Puja* to Swamiji tonight after the lecture?" My immediate reaction was one of shock. I quickly replied in the negative, scared to death at the prospect, for I was a Westerner, and felt inadequate when it came to such sacred rituals. In my heart I was always at his feet and worshipped the foundation upon which he stood, but this was different. This was serious! She mumbled on at how there was no one left to sponsor the *puja*, but perhaps someone would come forward later. I felt compelled to explain to her that my husband had not accompanied me to the camp and that I felt sure it was something we should be doing together. However, I couldn't deny the gnawing sensation within, that this was a rare opportunity being presented, and I was refusing it on a technicality! I kept the conversation going partly out of curiosity and partly because deep inside I was hoping for some miraculous sign that I should be doing this.

Just as she was about to leave, she said, "Don't worry about it. Perhaps it wasn't meant to be. Anyway, these things are often performed on an auspicious day for the devotee, a day of some particular significance."

I asked her what she meant by "auspicious day," and she replied that two of the most auspicious days would be one's birthday and wedding anniversary. Her words were ringing in my ears and I heard myself mutter in amazement, "Today is my birthday."

She looked at me very lovingly.

I said, "Can you help me with this? Because I don't know the first thing to do." Soon, all the preparations were joyfully arranged by the hands of many women, who, I am convinced today, were *gopis* in disguise. It wasn't a coincidence that I had in my luggage a new sari with which to drape the chair upon which Gurudev sat, and new towels to tenderly dry the *padukas* [sandals] that represented his lotus feet.

As if this weren't enough, later on, after all was done, Swamiji's secretary came out onto the porch and handed me a small booklet. "Swamiji said to give this to you," he said.

I looked closely at it. It was the latest copy of *Vedanta Vani* [a periodic bulletin published by the Chinmaya center in Bangalore]. He had written my name on the cover and inside was published one of the poems I had sent to him earlier.

We had never spoken; I had never told him it was my birthday; no one knew except my roommate, who had had no contact with him after our conversation. This was a birthday present for me. I remembered that as a child I would remind everyone in the family at least a month in advance that my birthday was coming. Here, halfway around the world, in a place where I was unknown, on a silent spiritual quest of my own, Swamiji revealed to me that there was nothing kept secret from him and that he was concerned with every aspect of my life. Now when my birthday arrives, I have only one reason to reflect upon the significance of that day — to remember his love and carry on the tradition he started for me of performing *Paduka Puja* at his feet.[22]

Gurudev's unequaled compassion is described with stirring poignancy in a story in the devotee's own words:

The Sweetest of Inquiries

One warm summer evening in July of 1982, I attended Gurudev's seminar at the University of Houston. The next morning I was sitting at his feet. With the sweetest voice I had ever heard, he turned to me and asked, "How is your son?"

I was so shocked that I couldn't answer because my son was in a hospital undergoing drug rehabilitation. Swamiji continued with questions about my life and I could answer none of them: I was too overwhelmed with the awareness that I was sitting in the presence of eternal, all-knowing love, that he already knew more about me than I did.

Six months later, I was sitting on his ashram steps in Bombay waiting for the next brahmachari course to begin — the eternal gift to [oneself] and life.

From the moment I met Gurudev, my life has been permeated by his love and grace. One of my most powerful experiences with him began with his first words to me, which, as it turned out, were the same as his last. At the last Houston Camp *bhiksha* in 1992, he called me to him and asked in the same sweet, caring tone as ten years before, "How is your son?"

"Not well, Swamiji," I replied. "My son is dying of AIDS."

He assured me that my son would be all right.

My son died the same day that Gurudev attained *Mahasamadhi*. Today, I remain in awe of this wondrous . . . eternal love that proves itself eon after eon to be just as dependable in the process called death as in the process called life. He is indeed beyond them both.[23]

A Happy Birthday

Dr. Kshama Metre of the Sidhabari Project, which serves the local village communities, had suffered a fracture, a very bad one, and had to be wheeled around in a wheelchair. When Gurudev arrived at Sidhabari to hold a spiritual camp there, she went to have his *darshan*.

Gurudev told her, "Your back is very bad. Don't come again."

Then, the day of her birthday arrived. Her brother had called to greet her, but since she was not in a position to answer phone calls, some other devotee had received the call. Until then no one had known when her birthday was, although she had been staying at Sidhabari for eight years already. This devotee went to Gurudev and told him that it was Kshama's birthday.

Kshama felt tempted to have Gurudev's *darshan*, despite his admonishments not to come, so she arranged to be wheeled once again to be at his side.

When he saw her, he said, "My legs are better than your back. Stay there. I shall come to you!" — and he walked up to her, hugged her, and sang "Happy Birthday" to her.

When Kshama asked him how he knew it was her birthday, Gurudev very seriously remarked, "Morning and evening you sing *'Tvameva mataca pitatvameva'* [from *Guru Stotram*: "You alone are my mother, you alone are my father"] — and you ask how I know it is your birthday!? If I don't know, then who knows?"[24]

A Much-Needed Apple

When I was leaving a camp in Michigan, I prostrated to Gurudev, and he took an apple and gave it to me, saying, "You will need this!"

On the flight to Washington, D.C., I was given a sandwich, but it looked strange. So I inquired of the flight attendant about it and was told that it was beef! I told her that I had ordered a vegetarian meal. Since one was not available, she went to find something I could eat, but turned up nothing.

I was quite hungry. In a flash I remembered Sri Gurudev giving me the apple and saying, "You will need this!"

I took the apple from my bag and started eating it, much to the surprise of the flight attendant.[25]

No Doors Closed on Love

Whenever Neeru Mehta traveled with Swamiji, she would go into his room before he retired to check on his drinking water, offer her *pranams*, say "Hari Om!" — and then leave the room.

Twice, once in Lucknow and once at Sandeepany Sadhanalaya, when Gurudev stood up to close the door, Neeru bowed and stood facing him. He looked and waited. Then said, "Please turn around. I can't close the door in your face."

"This sentiment is expressed by many persons," says Neeru, "but no one I have met in my life, except for Swamiji, puts it into practice: not closing the door in the face of someone you love."[26]

Even total strangers got a taste of Gurudev's compassion:

Compassion for a Stranger

Swamiji was to arrive at Krishnalaya for a spiritual camp. Nalini Browning was at the Krishnalaya site, awaiting news of his arrival in San Francisco by plane, but the news did not arrive as expected. When she called the airport to inquire, she was told by the airline officials that no one by the name Swami Chinmayananda had been on the plane.

She became very nervous and started making calls to devotees in the town that had been his previous stop. The devotees there insisted that they had put Swamiji on the plane successfully. Now everyone was becoming worried. Nalini called other parts of the country to find out where Swamiji might be, but she was not able to locate him anywhere.

Only later did she find out what had happened that day:

Swamiji had successfully checked in at the departing airport, but somehow his name had been incorrectly entered in the computer, so when Nalini called to inquire at the airline counter, they could not find any trace of him. In the airplane, Swamiji had sat next to an elderly lady who seemed very nervous about her arrival in Phoenix, Arizona, which was also Swamiji's stopover before his connection to San Francisco. The lady was anxious because of an apparent heart condition.

"Who will meet you in Phoenix?" asked Swamiji.

"I don't know," she answered.

So when they arrived in Phoenix, Swamiji accompanied the lady to her relatives' home in a taxicab and then returned to take his flight to San Francisco. However, his scheduled flight had already left without him. He was put on another flight, but no one in Chinmaya Mission knew about the change. When he finally did arrive in San Francisco, nobody was at the airport to receive him. He had to call the organizers to arrange for a ride to his residence.[27]

The kitchen where Swamiji's food was prepared was often the scene of both well-timed and mistimed devotion; of loving and inspired food preparation as well as nervousness, jealousies, and panic. One person could be heard saying, "Swamiji never eats eggplant! That's one vegetable he'll *never* eat!" Yet, another would offer the news that in the special way that *he* had prepared the vegetable in question, Swamiji had indeed not only eaten it, but also praised it! Others offered their "inside knowledge" about his love or distaste for other vegetables or fruits, or for a certain way that any of them had to be prepared to be just right for him.

Since serving the guru his food was one of the ways that his devotees, especially women, could express their devotion in a visible, palpable way, food preparation became the focus of very intense emotions. Swamiji knew this, and was obviously quite aware that such intensities often collided head-on. His loving acknowledgment of such devotion was expressed in a multitude of ways:

Too Many Cooks in the Kitchen

Krishna Varma had gone to a *bhiksha* at the house where Swamiji was staying. She joined a number of women in the kitchen who were preparing his food, and she offered to help by cutting the fruit. Then, along came another devotee who took the knife away from her and took over the fruit-cutting.

Krishna started to reach for her purse and was ready to leave the house when she heard Swamiji calling from the other room. (He had not been near the kitchen to witness the events.)

"Krishna, where are you going?" his voice reached her in the hallway. "You stay! I'm the host in this house now, and I decide who is to stay here with me. You stay and eat with me."[28]

Devotion-Filled Pomegranate Seeds

I was new to the Mission, but devotion to Gurudev came on like a flood, and the desire to serve him was intense. With this objective in mind, I entered the kitchen at Sidhabari and looked around to see how I could best serve him. As though it was an answer to my prayers, a lady who was preparing lunch for Gurudev came to me hurriedly with a pomegranate, which she asked me to peel for him. I was thrilled at this opportunity and promptly went to work at it, all the while praying that he should accept my service. Like a child wanting to be noticed and appreciated by the parent, I wanted to serve the fruit to him myself. I also wanted to watch him fondly as he ate the fruit in which I had poured my love-filled heart.

The lady soon appeared and hastily took away the bowl of fruit from me and placed it before Gurudev, who was having lunch, swaying to the *bhajans* [devotional songs] being sung by devotees in the room. I ran and stood behind a group of people to have even just a glimpse of him enjoying the fruit. Just that would have been reward enough for me.

After his main meal, Swamiji picked up a handful of the fruit and immediately, just as an automatic weapon swinging directly on its target, he looked straight at me and beckoned me to come up to him. Since he did not know me personally and could barely see me behind the group of people standing close together, I thought that he was calling someone else — until he pointed directly at me and again beckoned. The devotees standing in front of me quickly parted, making way for me. I walked up to him as if in a dream. He looked at me with, oh, such loving eyes, stretched out his arm, and gave me the first fistful of pomegranate seeds that he had picked up. As I bowed reverentially to receive the blessing, he said, "This is *prasad* for you."

No, I was not dreaming. It brought home to me and to many others who were at that lunch with Gurudev the truth of the mantra *Om antaryamine namah* ["Salutations to the One who controls from within; salutations to the indwelling Self"].[29]

The Cook Is Not Forgotten

A group of us were sitting with Swamiji in the living room of his residence at a spiritual camp, chatting with him quietly in an informal *satsang,* just enjoying his presence.

Swamiji looked at one of the devotees and said, "Go to the kitchen [which happened to be in a separate building from his] and tell the cook that the Swami sends his love."

We sat there, amazed that even this had not escaped his notice: Someone very devoted to him was preparing his food, but unfortunately at some distance from his side, no doubt missing his physical presence while preparing his food. He knew.[30]

New Confidence

Shobha Joshi was a rather meek person when she first spent time with Swamiji. She had gone to the *Vivekacudamani* Camp at the Sidhabari ashram and made a habit of joining Swamiji at *satsang* when he used to sit outside his *kutiya*, with a group of devotees sitting at his feet in a semicircle around him. The first day he said to her:

"Come, you sit near me."

So she sat down near him and continued to do so during subsequent *satsangs* also, but one day the crowd had grown quite large, and she couldn't find a place near him and sat at the back.

Swamiji called out to her: "Now you're lost in the crowd. I told you to sit near me!"

"I'm OK, Swamiji," she said quietly.

Later, Swamiji told her: "You should not bow down to anyone." It had become a habit with her to be submissive, but now, with Gurudev's loving help, she was learning to become more assertive. He continued to pay special attention to her and pamper her until she grew in confidence and assertiveness.[31]

Probably none of us had ever experienced, through other contacts, the measure of understanding and love that Gurudev bestowed upon us. Both small gestures of deep compassion and grandiose demonstrations of his love left us wondering: "Can he really love me this much — me, with all my imperfections?"

Uninterrupted Love

It was during the early years of listening to Swamiji's lectures, when every word of every lecture opened up new revelations and it hurt immeasurably to miss even one lecture in the series. It was also the first time I had ever heard him teach *Vivekacudamani*, and I was deeply engrossed in every word of every verse and commentary. However, because of family obligations I had to miss one *Vivekacudamani* lecture in the series, and told Swamiji in great sadness that I would be missing one.

"Don't worry," he said. "Just come back when you can."

I returned the following day several hours before the evening class and joined him and a few others at his residence. As soon as I had rushed to his side, offered my *pranams*, and sat down at his feet, he said:

"Now in the first verse of yesterday's lecture Shankaracharya said . . ." — and proceeded to give a summary of the entire missed class![32]

Brahmacharini Robyn Thompson, his frequent assistant during his North American tours, recalls:

Everything Is for Others

During a camp at San Jose State University in California, I was alone with Gurudev after completing some work. At one point, he turned toward me and looked intensely into my eyes with that look that pierced, in all love, to the core of one's being. My mind was stilled, and the words he spoke went deep into my consciousness, never to be forgotten:

Everything is for others!

After a few minutes he added:

Never ask for anything![33]

Gaurang and Darshana Nanavaty, head teachers at the Houston, Texas, Chinmaya Mission center, tell of their early days with Swamiji, back in 1975. They had first heard him in Seattle, Washington, then went to Vancouver, his next stop, to listen to him some more:

Bhikshas Out of Love

In Vancouver, people were vying with each other to invite Swamiji to *bhiksha*. In Seattle, when we had had the opportunity to have him at our home for *bhiksha*, we were not inclined to invite him. Now, I felt guilty and told Swamiji how I missed the opportunity.

The following morning, Swamiji was at a host's house having breakfast, and he said he wouldn't be available for lunch that day. Then he said he would have lunch with Darshana and me. Taken aback by this sudden gesture, I told Swamiji that we lived in Seattle, 150 miles away.

His reply came quickly: "Aren't there any restaurants in Vancouver?"

Immediately, I called a local Punjabi restaurant, reserved the seats, and left special instructions for Swamiji's lunch. After inaugurating a Hindu temple in Vancouver, Swamiji joined us and we went for lunch at the restaurant.

As a 29-year-old in America, it was hard for me to reconcile that a great saint would go to a restaurant to please and inspire an individual who hardly knew him. But it was real. Indeed, his presence, love, and affection certainly transformed us. . . .

At the end of the Vancouver visit, Swamiji called a devotee in Seattle and asked him to inform us that he would come to our house for *bhiksha*.

He left Vancouver at 11:30 p.m. and arrived in his hotel in Seattle at 4 a.m. He was leaving for Ohio by air at 7:30 a.m. that morning, yet he came to our house at 5:30 a.m. and had breakfast with us. Anybody else would have spent those two hours catching up on lost sleep.[34]

Thefts Forgiven

Swamiji established Pitamaha Sadan, an old people's home in a village area by the side of the Ganges, at considerable cost. Always striving for perfection, he had several amenities provided for the ashram. Over a span of ten years, thefts occurred there several times. We did what we could. Arrangements for vigilance were strengthened. The thefts, however, continued to occur. During one of his *jnana yajnas*, Swamiji happened to visit the ashram to learn about the progress of work there. While showing him around, we mentioned the thefts. We also mentioned that we lodged a report with the police. To safeguard against such incidents in the future, it was suggested that we fix wire mesh over the windows.

Swamiji asked us not to lodge any report with the police. He also did not encourage the idea of fencing the windows, saying, "The need of the other person was perhaps greater . . . or else he would not have stolen from an ashram."[35]

"Don't Cause Friction"

Pitamaha Sadan . . . has an ancient temple. With the passage of time, the *Sivalingam* there had become damaged, so Swamiji decided to have a new one installed. A very befitting piece was selected from the South. To perform the installation ceremony with proper rituals, a contingent of a dozen *purohits* [priests] was selected to reach the ashram. All accessories for the ceremony were arranged at a cost of more than 100,000 rupees.

As the auspicious day neared, some of the local villagers near the ashram grew agitated. They did not want the new *lingam* installed. They said, "We would like to worship the *lingam* our forefather have always worshipped."

Swamiji had arrived to give final touches to the event. The matter was placed before him. He promptly decided to respect the will of the villagers.

We argued how a handful of them, driven by ignorance, were the only ones agitated. We implored him to change his mind: that having worked so much and spent so much money, we should probably go ahead with the ceremony.

But he was firm and said, "I do not want the ashram to be a cause of any friction among the villagers. This will be injurious to the healthy growth of the ashram." Then he recollected how when the Sidhabari complex was established, villagers around the ashram spread all sorts of rumors. "But," he said, "we always responded with love towards them. Gradually, harmony and love won over their petty prejudices."[36]

Gurudev's loving care touched everyone. "He never failed to give tips to all the wheelchair porters in the airports," recalls Asha Chakrabarty. He would take a note out of his pocket and slip it quietly into the hand of the porter. When he had stayed some days at a home that had servants who had helped take care of the house during his stay there, before leaving for his next stop, he would offer each of them a monetary gift as a thank you. He gave at all levels — spiritual, emotional, intellectual, and material.

MEETING THE GURU

The stories about meeting Swamiji and recognizing in him one's guru are many and various, some dramatic, some simple, some beyond our usual experience of things and events. Many devotees knew within minutes of meeting him that they had found their guru. For many it happened as soon as they began listening to him lecture from the platform, as it did for Sita Juneja of New Delhi: "A few sentences into the lecture I knew he was the one."

An unnamed seeker tells a story that could be called a classic account of how a person's first meeting with the guru can transform his entire life:

A Memorable Event

Meeting with our beloved Gurudev was the first memorable event in my life. . . . Thereafter, every event in my life has been remembered only in association with Gurudev. . . .

It was 1960. I was informed by a lovely, highly qualified, and intelligent lady colleague that I should listen to the talks of a young, elegant, and eloquent swami at Cross Maidan, Bombay. . . . My impressions about swamis and about *sannyasins* [renunciates] were that they were guys who idly live in the world of heavenly dreams. I believed that Hinduism could have a renaissance only through revolutions and not through any passive evolution or resolutions. So my Ma (the said lady whom I now consider as the one who gave me a spiritual birth) took pains to teach us the Complete Works of Swami Vivekananda and told me that this swami to whom she was directing me was the "modern Vivekananda," who was dedicating his life to fulfilling his vision in a practical mission.

Persuasions having failed, one day she invited us to her residence. After office hours, we went together to Church Gate station through Cross Maidan. To my amazement, my ears were captivated by the beautiful chanting of *Gita slokas* [*Bhagavad Gita* verses], and my eyes noticed the flow of cars into an arena covered neatly with blue cloth. I silently followed Ma, who took me in front of a shamiana. Suddenly the chanting stopped. All the people stood up in utter silence. From one side of the stage appeared a youthful, majestic swami who advanced toward the photo of a saint (Tapovan Maharaj) kept behind a lighted lamp. He stood there a few seconds, then turned toward his seat. He was in an orange *jubba* and *dhoti* with a red bright cloth tied on his head like Shirdi Sai Baba. With his thick and ample black beard reaching down to his chest, he appeared to me a vibrant, silent, royal personality. He looked straight and toward both sides, surveying everyone and everything in the field. His glowing and gleaming face, with a kind but mischievous glitter in his eyes, captured everyone's attention in total silence. He sat down comfortably, removed his wristwatch from his right hand, and placed it in front of him. Closing his eyes, he remained silent for some time, and then broke the silence with a reverberating "Om" . . . . My throbbing mind and eager senses became drowned . . . . That was the beginning of the waking of my spirit. . . .

When the *yajna* was over, I was the most disappointed person. I longed to be with him. After many days of rehearsals and mental preparation, I gathered enough courage to trek my way to Powai [the site of Sandeepany Sadhanalaya, his ashram] and waited before his *kutiya*, in line along with some of the ashramites. My mind was full of prayers to all gods and saints about whom I had heard and read, and my knees were beating together when I heard the "tup, tup" of his sandals. We folded our hands, with eyes resting on his kind and smiling face. We were all melting into oneness to fall at his holy feet. Talking to those visitors who were walking along with him, he slowed his stride, responding to our "Hari Om" while one by one we touched his feet. Some kneeled down and touched with their foreheads, and I fell down at his feet, losing all strength to stand or to kneel. My whole body was shivering, and I was perspiring profusely.

As if he was quite aware of my weakness and helplessness, Gurudev kindly bent down, tenderly but firmly caught hold of my shoulders, and lifted me up. Looking at me, he softly spoke to me in Malayalam: "Come, come to the class."

Ever since, I have remained a student at his feet. "Study! Study! Study and serve!" he has implored me. "More than at the ashram, you can serve me in the society. Go and experience. Hereafter your entire life will be blessed by Him."

> *"Make your home a Tapovan and your mind an ashram. Then you will never be away from me"* were the assurances he gave me in 1969 when I was entering into my *grhastha asrama* [life of a householder]. My house, my wife, and both of my children were all blessed by Pujya Gurudev, and all of us even today consider that without him none of us would have had our fulfillment.
>
> *"Opportunities are plenty all around. You should catch them,"* he wrote to us. We fell at his feet, and our Pujya Gurudev lifted us into a life of eloquent silence.[1]

"True disciples have to meet their Master but once," said Swamiji in a letter, *"even if the Master be not very perfect. The disciple's life-pattern changes, and in his own inner maturity, he climbs the Heights within."* Story after story of devotees meeting their guru in the person of Swami Chinmayananda, the same message is repeated: Lives were transformed.

Swamiji began teaching in 1951. Among his early devotees was Shakuntla Bindra of New Delhi, who met him in 1953. She recalls:

The Touched Heart

> I used to listen to the *Gita* as taught by the great saint Swami Ranganathanandaji of Ramakrishna Mission in 1945 in Karachi. The discourses were wonderful, but I could not grasp the depth and subject due to my lack of knowledge. After the partition, I also used to listen to him at his mission in Delhi.
>
> Then one fine day my grandfather came to my house and told me that a great *mahatma* [holy person or master] from Uttarkashi was delivering discourses in English on the Upanishads. "Go and listen to him," he said.
>
> So the next day I entered the *yajna* hall, which was very, very near to my house. Swamiji was speaking about the sacred syllable *Om* (A-U-M) as described in the *Mandukya Karika*. The way he explained *upasana* [worship] on *Om* touched my heart deeply. From that day onward to this day I have followed this method of worship and all other things that he explained to us.[2]

For others, too, the first meeting with the guru happened to take place unexpectedly close to the very doorstep of their home. As Swamiji himself would often joke, "Back in the old days, the disciple measured long distances to get to his guru in a faraway Himalayan retreat. Now, the guru goes halfway across the world to go to the disciple!"

Synchronous Timing

Since my teen years, I was an ardent reader of the *Gita* and the Upanishads, had tried my hand at meditation and had listened to some fine teachers of Vedanta, but I had not met *my* teacher. Yet, my antennas were always up, ready to pick up any signal of his whereabouts. In 1966, I happened to be living in an apartment house in San Francisco where I befriended a number of young people from India. Among them was a charming young woman who just happened to be, as I found out later, from the Reddy family, who sponsored Gurudev's very first talks in Poona, India, in 1951. She, along with her friends, just happened to mention to me that a very modern, progressive swami was in town (although spiritual topics had not usually been a part of our discussions). And it just so happened that he was giving a lecture series at a hotel, the Bellevue, just two or three blocks from my home, almost at my doorstep.

The lecture hall was hot, I felt a little sleepy, yet my mind was transfixed by the ardor and wisdom of the teacher before me. That one tentative, not-yet-personal meeting with Gurudev set my whole life on a new course and, in time, wove his love, wisdom, and inspiration through every strand of my every day and hour.[3]

As Though Planned

While working in Hong Kong, Somesh Shah came across Swamiji and his teachings. "I realized I wanted to know more. Before leaving on a business trip," says Somesh Shah, "I wrote Gurudev a letter without including where I was from, telling him I wanted to know more about our sacred texts. I mailed the letter and went on my trip. When I returned a few days later, I found information about a Chinmaya Mission study group that would be forming soon and that the Mission was sending an *acharya* [teacher] to facilitate it. Reading further, I found that it was going to be held in the building next door to where I lived!"[4]

Kshama Metre is a medical doctor who gave up a lucrative medical practice in New Delhi to move to Himachal Pradesh and serve the villagers there. Inspired by Gurudev, she became Project Director, Chinmaya Rural Primary Health Care and Training Centre. Her meeting with her guru changed the course of her life:

The Answer to All Questions

A doctor friend and his wife told Dr. Kshama Metre that they were going to see a saint and asked her to come along. She said she could not because they talked of him as if he were the Lord Himself, and she could not accept that. She told them, "It's not right of me to come with you. I don't have the right respect." But they persuaded her.

Once they arrived at the house where Swamiji was staying, Dr. Metre waited downstairs, although Swamiji was upstairs, in *satsang*. Then she thought, "I've come this far; I should go see him." So she hesitatingly climbed up the staircase, but the door to the *satsang* room was shut, with many *chappals* [sandals] gathered outside it. Finally, she opened the door. The minute the door was open, she saw Swamiji resplendent against the window — in orange clothes against the sunset framed in the window. The moment she saw him, "divinity was communicated to me," she says. She walked to him as though drawn.

"I can't say how it happened," she says, "but I knew I wanted to know him, that I did not want to leave him."

She went and sat at his feet. He asked for her name.

Then he said, "You are a doctor. Are you attached?"

"No." She thought he meant if she was married or attached to a hospital. She did not know what significance attachment has in the Vedantic way of life.

"Good," said Gurudev.

Dr. Metre recalls: "I knew that something had happened to me inside. I knew I had met the person I had been looking for all my life."

Later her friends told her about a camp in Sidhabari and asked her to go also, so she did. "At that camp in January 1985, I heard Gurudev recite the *Gita* for the first time in my life. It was like an avalanche. I said to myself, 'Oh, God, it all fits like a jigsaw puzzle! The answer to all of my questions is here!'"

Gurudev asked her to take a walk alone, sit under a tree, and think. She did a lot of walking. By the third day, she was certain that she was not going to leave him. "How could I leave him? Akhilam Amma [now Swamini Nishtananda, the doctor who began the outreach work at Sidhabari] knew I was a pediatrician, so she said she would tell Swamiji that I was interested in a job on the Project, in which a young doctor was required, someone who could do the running around in the villages."

On the last day when her name was called out at the convocation, Gurudev put the *tilaka* [a mark made on the forehead with sandalwood paste] on her forehead and asked her whether she wanted to stay at Sidhabari. Her whole body was answering "Yes," but no words came.

Early the next morning while he was getting into his car to leave, he asked, "Where is the pediatrician *amma*?" He spotted Dr. Metre in the crowd and said, "You can come!"

She knew she was blessed. It took her a few months to pack up and go to Sidhabari, where she has been serving the village community since 1985.[5]

Of course, all those synchronous circumstances were, in fact, no coincidence, because when a disciple meets her guru, a miracle takes place, as the following story of Anjali Singh's first meeting with Swamiji attests:

Love at First Sight

When a student meets his teacher, it is always a miracle. "In fact, it is love at first sight!" said Swami Chinmayanandaji once. My first meeting with Swamiji was on a monsoon evening in July 1961 in New Delhi while sitting on a dozen pairs of shoes, the only seating space available in a hall packed to capacity. What must have transpired in that meeting and how it was communicated I do not know. This I know: that whatever was awakened then never went back to sleep again. It is not that any extraordinary experience happened. Just sitting there listening to him speaking on the "Age of Perception" and how man advanced from that to the "Age of Observation" and thereafter to the "Age of Contemplation" — just listening to that felt as if the first three ages had already been traversed in one hour right there in the lecture hall and that Swamiji had brought us all to the Age of Contemplation by simply relating the history of the stages of man's climb to perfection.

The moment had arrived, a moment that comes just once in one's lifetime, when the miracle happens, and fate or the Grace of God brings a student face to face with her spiritual teacher. This is the sacred moment when the ever-present, invisible essence of Godhood comes out from within one's innermost Self and appears before one in the form of the guru, to lead her along the path that has been set by the Creator Himself.

In those days, *yajnas* used to last twenty-one days. "Shoot!" Swamiji would say after the morning class and shake his crossed-over leg vigorously while waiting for people to ask questions. I liked firing missiles from the audience line, which he would proceed to blow into smithereens each time. After two weeks of "warfare," I formally surrendered and went to see him at his place of residence.

"Where do you manufacture them?" he asked, referring to the ammunition I had been sending out in the form of questions.

I had to smile and say, "My uncle said you liked explosives!" I went to meet him three times after that.

Two days before Swamiji was to leave, I asked him if I might go with him to Allahabad. I did not want to let him out of my sight.

"You had better ask your mummy," he said.

"She has never denied me anything in my life," I replied.

"Please ask your mummy," he reiterated.

"May I *please* have your train ticket so that when she agrees, I might still have time to get my seat next to yours?" I persisted.

Mrs. Bindra and Mrs. Puri raised their eyebrows and looked at Swamiji, warning him not to get taken in by an eighteen-year-old whose dependability had not been established.

"All right. Let her have the ticket. She will bring it back," he said. They hesitated, and it was only after he asked them a second time that they reluctantly obliged. A year later, it was Mrs. Bindra who was to encourage me to visit Swamiji at her home where he was staying and to insist I remain for meals.

At home I met with great opposition. A royal battle followed. My mother appreciated my intention but would not accede to my request. My father was abroad. It was unheard of to be traveling with a swami, especially one whom you had only just met. She decided to go with me and explain her reasons to Swamiji herself. I knew Swamiji did not need any explanations, but I hoped he would be able to convince her.

We both went to his residence the next morning and found him seated on a bed draped with white sheets and decorated with marigolds. Visitors continued to prostrate at the feet of Swamiji, while others sang *bhajans*. Everything seemed so radiant and vibrant. I remember the atmosphere in the room very clearly. It was *Guru Purnima* day [day dedicated to the worship of the guru], my very first.

I did not know then that he was my guru, but I had been brought to him again on that day ostensibly to return his train ticket. I had brought an offering, thereby unconsciously fulfilling the obligations of a relationship that would come to unfold itself in the future but whose beginning had been obscured behind the layers of many pasts.

Swamiji noticed me in the doorway, and his eyes twinkled when he saw my mother accompanying me. He began calling from afar:

"I told you so!" A letdown. It did not seem he was going to help me.

My mummy was already holding his ticket in her hand, but she also had a twinkle in her eye when she handed it back to him and said,

"Swamiji, you *know* I can't let her go with you!"

Then they both laughed as if sharing a secret and he said to her, "I told her 'Ask your mummy!'" disclaiming all responsibility.

He then asked my mother what I was doing, and she told him I had developed a fad for spirituality and had given up the first year of college midway in order to study Vedanta. I had spent one-and-a-half months in Uttarkashi and from there had gone on foot to Jamnotri and Gangotri. He seemed not at all impressed.

"How will you master this great subjective science of the Self, which is very difficult, if you are not able to cope with the objective science, which is so much easier?" I suddenly realized my mistake in having given up my studies for the past seven months.

He turned to my mother and almost shouted, "Go and put her back into college!"

Later, mummy said that I had gotten her a scolding from the swami on her very first meeting. As for me, I went on to study for five years — Swamiji's first gift of grace to me on that sacred occasion of *Guru Purnima*. Ever since then, he continuously poured his gifts upon me, untiringly and patiently, from his limitless treasure house.

"Guru is the radio through which the Lord contacts his student," he used to tell us. "When a student meets his teacher, it is always a miracle. He is immediately attracted to him and his words ring a bell. Another speaker may speak better, but only his teacher will attract him. . . . In case you get the rare privilege of meeting such a master and you happen to understand a little of what he says, then progress *has* to happen. It is unfailing. It is very productive. In case you are benefited, do not forget that the teacher was brought to you by Ishvara [the Lord] Himself — and remember, there is no difference between God and guru, the corporeal entity before you. Therefore, be on the lookout when you meet a master. Search, seek, and fulfill!"[6]

"Swamiji's Here"

My introduction to Gurudev (is timeless, actually) was through a devotee who mailed him my college English paper on reincarnation. I couldn't understand why she sent it, for I had no idea who he was, but that was why I really couldn't care less. I remember completing the paper with a lack of the crystal clarity that I wanted. Still many questions remained, for this was my first venture into reincarnation and Hinduism as a philosophy.

What impressed me most was the reply he sent to me through that devotee. His first words invoked in me a great respect for him. He wrote, "I do admire your unhesitating heroism in trying to attempt a paper before fully preparing for the subject." The heroism part sounded good, but I realized he was laughing at me. After an entire study, I still knew absolutely nothing, but the best part was that he was so right and he had no qualms about telling me so! I had to laugh at myself, too. Many months passed and the letter was brushed aside, the comments forgotten. Then came the day.

My first camp and my first meeting with Gurudev was in Guelph, Canada. I had no idea what to expect and was quite annoyed when, as soon as we arrived, there were noisy whispers and hustling steps sounding about: "Swamiji's here! Swamiji's here!" I kept thinking, "Swamiji's here — so what?" For the first time, I witnessed a line of devotees running to the master's feet to prostrate. And I still thought, "Swamiji's here — so what?" Needless to say, I was there only out of obligation. I had brought a good book with me to tide me through the days. Too little did I know.

I loved his talks from the start. Someone asked me, "Did you understand?" After arrogantly commenting on the "funny" accent, I couldn't help but exclaim, "Of course! It's so obvious, so logical!" After the first day, I respected him tremendously. After the second day, I looked forward to seeing and hearing him again. By the third day, I wanted to meet him.

My chance came when I accidentally passed by his room and saw many slippers by the door. I took a peek to see what was happening. There he sat, being injected with medication, cool and calm, casual and jovial, talking with all those who had gathered around him like a swarm of bees. The whole room was smiling, and I stood hesitantly in the doorway, not knowing if this was a "By Invitation Only" affair. He exclaimed in that royal, masterful tone that reverberates through your whole system, "Come in, come in!" I entered and squeezed into a corner.

More talk, but soon he stood up to retire to his room. All the bees were buzzing, lifting themselves up, shifting over so he could pass. He was saying sweet words to everybody, laughing and joking. At that moment, for some reason, all I could think was: "I wish he'd say something to me — something, anything." An undeserving wish, no doubt, especially after my haughty attitude, but I couldn't help wishing. I was at the edge of the room. He had to pass by that corner to go into his chambers. I kept wishing, "Just one word. So many others, why not me?"

He came right toward me, still talking to others, closer, really close — and then turned the corner, completely passing me by. I had been hoping for some miracle, but I now was so hopelessly, utterly, painfully disappointed that I just stood there, and my head automatically slumped.

Within a split second, his soft beard was twelve inches away from my face. His eyes were roaring Krishna mischief and laughter, and he whispered in a musical tone, "Good niiiiight." I blushed fiercely, smiled ear to ear, and embarrassedly bent my head down lower.

No falling; I was "raised" by his sweet, kind love instead.

I always tell people that Gurudev doesn't just hold you by the hand: He grabs you by the collar! And then you are hooked once and for all. Today, I am among the noisy whisperers and devotees with hustling feet — so infinitely grateful for his love and his grace, exclaiming, "Swamiji's here! Swamiji's here!"

He is.[7]

For some, the guru appeared at a point in their lives that was fraught with so much difficulty that Swamiji's entry into their lives was like a life-line thrown to a drowning person:

Life-Line Just in Time

Nalini Browning recalls that while she was in her teens she had a vision one night before falling asleep. She saw a man holding a staff and wearing a loincloth. She felt great love for him and said to herself: "That's what I want!" Only later did she realize that what she had seen in that early vision was the image of a *sadhu* in India.

Years later, she told Swamiji the story. He asked:

"What year was that?"

"The early 1950s," she said.

"That's just when I began teaching," was Swamiji's comment.

However, it was 1965 before she actually met her guru in person. She had just passed through an extremely difficult period of her life and was desperately looking for someone to help her. One day, she had gone to the Metaphysical Bookstore in San Francisco and, while there, heard the owner of the store talking on the phone about a spiritual lecture. After the phone call, Nalini went to the owner and inquired about the lecture. A swami from India was coming for a talk, she said.

Nalini went to the lecture. Swamiji entered the room wearing an orange headscarf tied in the back. As he sat down, he said brusquely, "I'm not going to talk tonight. You can ask me questions."

Nalini felt no particular reaction while the question-and-answer session was proceeding, but when Swamiji got up to leave, she felt that her life depended upon him. She went up to him.

"Yes, what is it?" said Swamiji with an impatient edge to his voice.

Nalini started to tell him, but he was not being very patient.

Nalini felt angry. She started crying.

"Come see me tomorrow at 8 a.m.," said Swamiji.

She went to his residence one hour early, frightened to see him because he had been so brusque with her the night before. At exactly 8 a.m., she knocked on his door. Someone opened his door and told her, "Whatever he tells you to do, do it."

As soon as her eyes caught sight of Swamiji, she saw a different person than the one she remembered from the night before: He looked so beautiful and kind! Nalini told him her life story, and he listened lovingly to every word. She felt as though they were two friends talking, not a student and a swami. She realized she had been looking into his eyes the entire time, imbibing deep peace from them.

When she was ready to leave, Swamiji took her hands in his, held them, and said, "Thank you, thank you" and asked that she write to him. "Don't worry," he said. "Don't be afraid."

That same year, Nalini heard Swamiji several times more, when he spoke at the Cultural Integration Fellowship in San Francisco. This time, she listened very deeply. In fact, it felt as though Swamiji was talking directly to her throughout the lectures.

When he was getting into his car after the last lecture, he rolled down the window, grabbed her hand and said, "What you're afraid of won't happen." True to his words, all her problems melted away soon thereafter.[8]

Some eventual seekers, full of skepticism and reluctance, arrived at their first lecture by Swamiji simply to please an insistent spouse or friend, only to be overwhelmed and convinced once they were in the presence of the master.

Dragged to the Guru

A future devotee and dynamic worker in Chinmaya Mission said that she was "dragged" to her first lecture by an insistent friend. But, once at the lecture, she decided she liked the dynamic swami a lot and even made a point of meeting him after the lecture. She told him how she had recently separated from her husband, was rearing two children, 8 and 10 years of age, and was teaching *hatha yoga* [a spiritual discipline dealing with the culture of the body].

"How can you help anyone when you can't even help yourself?" was his comment on her life's story.

The woman wept profusely, and others tried to comfort her. Swamiji admonished them: "Don't comfort her," he said and told the woman to raise her children to adulthood before separating from her husband.

The new devotee, red-eyed but convinced of her new decision, returned to her home, reconciled with her husband, raised her children to adulthood, then let the marriage finally dissolve — and became an active worker in Chinmaya Mission West.[9]

Some friends, no matter how hard a devotee tried, could never be "dragged" to the guru. Often a spouse was reluctant, at least at first, until Gurudev worked his special magic on them. Yet he insisted that no one can live the life for another:

> *Please stop worrying for others. Each one has to walk his path all alone. Nobody can help another man by bringing to his attention the possibility of spiritual unfoldment.* When *he will take it seriously and* how *far he will maintain his progress,* where *exactly he will stumble and, having stumbled,* how long *he will rot in that state, all these nobody can foretell.*[10]

"Ah, At Last!"

Veronica Hausman, living in Europe at the time, had had another guru for some years, who had recently passed on. Her mother had heard a swami by the name of Swamiji Chinmayananda and was urging Veronica to attend: "You must hear this extremely jolly monk!" she said. But Veronica declined. Her father attended some lectures and also urged her to attend, "You must go, Veronica!" But still, Veronica declined.

After getting married, she moved to the United States. One day she received a letter from someone she didn't even know, relating to her the news that Swami Chinmayananda was about to give talks locally. She was unable to go and missed the first talk. Later, when she had finally come to the decision to check out this teacher who so many people had been urging her to meet, she discovered that she had mislaid the directions to the lecture. She decided to search through the Yellow Pages in her town for all local Indian stores to inquire of them if any lectures by a swami were being advertised there.

By this circuitous route, she finally located the venue for the lectures and attended her first *jnana yajna* talk. After Swamiji finished his talk that evening, Veronica went right up on the stage where he was still sitting after the lecture and said, "I'm here."

Swamiji put his arm around her and said, "Ah, at last!"

During her first few meetings with Swamiji, she still questioned her relationship with him, wondering if it was right, given her previous teacher-taught association, and plying him with various questions. One day she asked him:

"Swamiji, what about the razor's edge?" referring to the scriptural reference to the great subtlety of the spiritual path and the ease with which a seeker can make the wrong judgment and veer from the correct path.

Swamiji's reply was: "For a devotee there is no razor's edge." She understood:

When you follow your heart, the heart cannot mislead you.

"Then what should I do?" she asked.

"Now, *do nothing*. Let the Lord work," Swamiji replied.

With that answer, her heart began to open to Swamiji as her new guru.[11]

Although in this day and age disciples generally no longer need to walk for hours over mountainous terrain to meet their guru in a faraway Himalayan cave, still, for some, the final challenge of reaching the guru's side has been formidable. The disciple's determination and commitment can be sorely tested:

Unbending Determination

Kalidas was only six years old when he met Gurudev at Guruvayur Temple in 1954. He remembers being very attracted to the imposing image of the Swami, with *rudraksa malas* [prayer beads made from *rudraksa* seeds] on his forearms, his thick hair and beard, and his vibrant vitality.

Kalidas grew up and got married. When his wife was expecting their second child, they happened to go to a picnic at Powai Park, which borders Sandeepany Sadhanalaya, Gurudev's ashram in Mumbai. After the picnic, his wife suggested they go to the temple at Sandeepany Sadhanalaya. They arrived there just as *arati* [a worship traditionally performed at sunset] was in progress. Listening to the Sanskrit chanting, Kalidas felt something awakening in him that had been lying dormant. At that point, he didn't even know that the temple was part of Swami Chinmayananda's ashram.

The following Sunday, he took a taxicab to the ashram, attracted by the serenity of the temple and the Sanskrit chanting. But he still didn't know that Gurudev was in charge of the place. On his third visit to the ashram, someone gave him a copy of Gurudev's book *Kindle Life*, with its Scheme of Study at the end, outlining all the books that Gurudev recommended for close scriptural study and the sequence in which they should be read.

"This was the turning point," says Kalidas today. "Then I knew." It was 1977.

An internal churning had begun, with an ever-increasing desire to meet Gurudev, but every time Kalidas went to Sandeepany, Gurudev had just left. This only intensified Kalidas' desire to meet the Swami. Such near-misses continued for about one year. In the meantime, Kalidas had begun to read Gurudev's many books as outlined in the Scheme of Study he had created to guide seekers.

Kalidas used to go on an annual pilgrimage to Lord Ayyappan's Temple at Sabarimalai, a sacred hill in Kerala. In those days, the temple was open only 61 days of the year. In December 1977, Kalidas was once again on a flight to Kerala to visit the temple. Mid-flight, when he took a walk down the cabin, he saw Gurudev seated in the window seat next to an emergency exit door. Kalidas went up to him and did a full-length prostration at Gurudev's feet. As he was rising from the floor, the pilot's voice announced that they were just then flying over Guruvayur Temple.

When Kalidas began to introduce himself, Swamiji said, "I know you" and called him by the abbreviated version of his name, Kali, a name that only his wife and some work colleagues had used previously.

Kalidas served Gurudev until his *Mahasamadhi*. Since Kalidas was employed with an Indian airline, he became, as Gurudev called him, "his traveling agent," helping to arrange his many flights around the globe.[12]

Some devotees tell of seeing Swamiji's poster announcing his talks and finding themselves catapulted into another dimension by a mere look at Gurudev's face staring back at them from the announcement. Others found themselves dreaming of a swami they had not yet met, then running into a perfect stranger the next day at the airport who ends up convincing them to meet Swamiji, who turns out to be the guru in the dream. Such was Isabel Taylor's story of her meeting with Swamiji:

Premonitions and Promptings

For several years I visited Satya Sai Baba, and every time, on about the tenth day of my stay with him, I would have a dream: In that dream there was Sai Baba, glowing with light and divine love. There were thousands of people, but none recognized him, none paid attention to him — except me. In my mind I asked him why. He explained that he was tired of superficial devotees and had decided to change his appearance and withdraw from the world. Before my very eyes I saw him change. Shortly thereafter the dream ended. Every six months or so, when I went to Sai Baba's ashram, this dream would come gain, and each time I wondered exactly what it meant.

Then, in early February of 1990, I was on my way to Auroville. I planned to stop at Bangalore to visit with Baba for a few days as usual. At the Delhi airport, an Indian lady struck up a conversation with me. It turned out that she, too, was on her way to Sai Baba. After a few minutes she said: "Sai Baba is not my guru. My guru is Swami Chinmayananda, and this is how he teaches . . ." — and she proceeded to write out the BMI (Body-Mind-Intellect) chart that Swamiji used in his lectures and explained it to me.

"Would you like to come with me to hear him? Baba is going out of town on Monday, and my flight is at 2 o'clock on that day."

After a brief hesitation, before leaving the airport in Bangalore, I bought a ticket to Coimbatore to join my new friend on her flight.

Three days later we arrived together at Coimbatore and were taken to where Swamiji was staying. Sitting in an armchair, surrounded by a dozen or so people on the floor, was a very majestic man in orange robes. At the entrance to the room, I knelt and touched my forehead to the floor, then lifted my eyes. There, surrounded by a brilliant light, was the face from my dream, the face that Sai Baba's had repeatedly turned into. Recognition came like an explosion.

He said, "You are welcome!"

Then he turned to his hostess, "You have another guest."

I was introduced and sat down in absolute silence.

For two-and-a-half days and nights I sat at his feet, attended his mesmerizing lectures, and felt my heart expand so much I expected an explosion any second. I could hardly sleep at all, and experienced deep bliss. The day he was leaving, just before 4 a.m., I thanked him for those precious two-and-a-half days. He hugged me, looked deeply into my eyes and heart and said:

"You must come with me. That is why you came to India."

I said, "I know . . . but for how long?"

He replied, "Until you leave India."

Of course I did go with him. I sent telegrams canceling Auroville and my planned social and business program and traveled with him for six weeks. I really had no choice. Because of my dream, I knew he was a form of God come to guide me. I watched him dedicate every moment of each day to helping people, listened to him lecturing brilliantly every morning and evening.

> After that initial time with him, I spent every possible moment traveling with him and serving him, for six to nine months each year. . . . There were many amazing moments: some blissful, some traumatic and acutely painful, but always profound lessons. I am full of gratitude for the grace and blessing of having known him in this form. I aspire to the moment when every living being will be equally an obvious manifestation of the Divine for me.[13]

Among the people who had intimations of their meeting with Swamiji before actually meeting him in person was Leela Nambiar, publisher of the monthly Chinmaya Mission journal *Tapovan Prasad*. She tells how when she went to her first *yajna* by Swamiji and saw a picture of Swami Tapovanam, Swamiji's guru, displayed on the dais, she realized that Swami Tapovanam had been visiting her in her dreams for some time before the meeting. Her very first lecture brought an additional realization:

Vivekananda Speaking?

Leela Nambiar was riding in a car down a main thoroughfare in Chennai (Madras) when she saw a big banner announcing a *"Geeta Gnana Yagna"* by a Swami Chinmayananda. She asked her husband to stop the car and entered the lecture hall from the back and sat down quietly. The lecture was close to finished, but she was spellbound. An overwhelming feeling had gripped her: "I'm listening to Swami Vivekananda!"[14]

Swami Swaroopananda went to his first *jnana yajna* after seeing a poster advertising it. However, he says, later he learned that he had had a connection with Swamiji from birth:

A Connection from Birth

The doctor who helped my mother deliver me was a devotee of Gurudev. The *Bala Ramayana* book read in my childhood was a Chinmaya Mission publication. Another book, *What Is Religion?*, had a preface by Gurudev. But all this came to light only after I listened to Gurudev in Hong Kong. At the end of the *yajna*, Gurudev announced the Vedanta course at Sandeepany Sadhanalaya in 1981. I remember telling myself, "Not me!" But when I went to Sidhabari for a camp, my heart became set on becoming a brahmachari.[15]

Some future devotees made it to the first meeting with the guru only by a hair's breadth:

Guru by a Hair's Breadth

A new friend and I had become close, but I never discussed my guru with her. In those early days as a disciple, I kept my spiritual activities very private. My friend seemed to be very sensitive and open, but I was afraid she'd write me off as not quite normal for following a man in a beard and an orange robe from far-away India. For days before the first lecture was to take place, I had been going back and forth in my mind: "Shall I tell her? . . . No, let it be, don't push your ideas on others . . . But then again, why deprive anyone of the opportunity?" This went on until one hour before the lecture, at which point I said to her as casually as I could manage:

"I'm going to a lecture by a man from India tonight. He's very good. Do you think you'd like to come with me?"

That's all I had said, she told me years later. And yet she went — and became a dedicated Vedanta student who even ended up going to one of Chinmaya Mission's two-and-a-half-year Vedanta courses. As Swamiji himself had said, finding one's teacher is always a miracle.[16]

Many followers of Swamiji in North America who are of Hindu birth were introduced to him through their children. Living in a new land in the midst of a highly secular culture, many Hindu families opted to send their children to Chinmaya Mission Balavihar classes to introduce them to their cultural and spiritual heritage. In many such cases, the parents themselves, at least for a while, continued in the role of the caring but neutrally disposed guardians who dropped the children off at class and picked them up afterward. Even though Vedanta classes for adults may have been offered simultaneously, they chose not to attend.

However, in countless cases the same chain of events slowly unfolded: At first the mother or grandmother of the child decided to attend a Vedanta class or go to a lecture when Swamiji was in town. In time, the husband, too, was persuaded to seek out the teacher of Vedanta, as in this case, among many:

Ramayana Unfolded

Srinivas Sukumar's daughter had been attending Balavihar for some time, and the parents were happy with the results. His wife Lakshmi began to attend the Vedanta classes offered at the local center, but the husband stayed back. Then both husband and wife began to watch the *Ramayana* video series that had been sent to them from India, and in that series they heard Swami Chinmayananda's introduction to a *Ramayana* episode. Both husband and wife were astounded: Their whole perception of the *Ramayana* changed. Although they had heard the story countless times before, with Swamiji's explanation they for the first time understood how the beloved epic depicted the struggle of the soul to regain its divine status after being lured away by desire.

Swamiji's commentary opened up their eyes to a whole new way of thinking. Both husband and wife decided to attend their first Chinmaya Spiritual Camp.[17]

Baptism in Vedanta

On *Gurudaksina* day [last day of a lecture series, when the students make an offering to the teacher as thanks for his teaching], I hastily scribbled a note on a thank-you card, expressing my gratitude to Swamiji for "bringing back into our lives some of the poetry that was lost somewhere over the years."

My joy knew no bounds when I received a reply from Coimbatore stating that *"the poetry of existence was never lost — in the serene quiet within, we can recapture the floating tunes of the Lord's Flute in our hearts."*

This was to me like a baptism in Vedanta, and launched me on a quest for floating melodies "eternally new."[18]

A Sign from God

A man had been with other gurus for some time, yet had doubts if they were the right ones for him. One day he went to the temple to pray.

"Give me a sign, Oh, Lord, when the real guru appears. When he does appear, have him give me some flowers. Let that be the sign."

He then heard of Swamiji's lectures and went to listen to him. When at the end of the lecture he went up to greet Swamiji, Swamiji took one of the flower pots that was used to decorate the podium and handed it to him.

With that, all doubts about having found the right teacher dissipated.[19]

Finding the Right Guru

Someone asked Swamiji in *satsang*: "How do you know if you've found the right guru?"

"Because," Swamiji explained, "whatever guru you meet is the right guru for you at that time. Just be sincere, and the Lord will provide the right guru for you."[20]

Why Need a Guru?

"Why do we need a guru?" inquired someone at *satsang*.

Swamiji replied, "Because the guru helps you sort out your confusions. You cannot ask a book those questions."[21]

For many eventual devotees and Chinmaya Mission workers, the first meeting with their guru occurred during their childhood years, for others in infancy, for yet others, while still in their mother's womb, where they were blessed by Swamiji with a tender touch of the hand and a silent prayer. Children who met him in their early years attended his Mission-sponsored Balavihar programs and later his Chinmaya Yuva Kendra (youth) programs. Some went on to study at one of his Sandeepany institutes of Vedanta; some, after graduating, took on the yellow robe to become brahmacharis; and some of those brahmacharis, in time, were given *sannyasa*, renouncing the worldly life to become swamis themselves.

Br. Atma Chaitanya recalls his early meeting with Swamiji when he was only four years old:

A Four-Year-Old Devotee

"Ours was a huge joint family," says Br. Atma Chaitanya. "Although I was very young, when my father brought Gurudev home, I still remember how much I kept staring at his shining face, black beard, red towel around his head . . ." After that initial meeting, the young boy took every opportunity to be near Gurudev. When he grew a little older, he began to read *Tapovan Prasad*, Gurudev's monthly magazine, and began to attend his *yajnas*. When Gurudev's English was a little hard for the young boy to understand, he would note down the difficult words, look them up in the dictionary, and return to the lecture hall the following day.

The outcome of this early devotion was that the young man, at age 18, joined the Sandeepany Sadhanalaya Vedanta course. Since his graduation, he has been teaching Vedanta in various capacities, including as head teacher at Tamil Sandeepany at Siruvani, Coimbatore, and at Malayalam Sandeepany in Ernakulam, India.[22]

For many devotees some time passed before the first interest in the guru turned into a deep need to serve him and to learn from him. As he watched and patiently waited as we ripened, Swamiji was always many steps ahead of us, making arrangements that at times seemed inexplicable — until later, when in retrospect his actions and words began to be understood. Asha Kamdar of Mumbai, who was to become a trusted assistant of Swamiji's for many years, got to know him through her family, but became a full-fledged devotee only after some time. Asha Kamdar remembers the turning point clearly:

He Knew Best

Initially, that is, until 1973, I was an occasional listener, and I always admired and respected him. In January 1973, when we had gone to meet him, he said, "Asha, you are coming with me to Singapore in April."

After this incident, I completely forgot all about it. In the first week of April, when Swamiji was again in Mumbai, he said, "So, you are coming, aren't you? Now only four days are left."

My passport had expired, visas were not ready, and there were multitudes of problems at the factory. But he insisted, and somehow all formalities got managed within the four days, and I flew along with Mrs. Kamala Chanrai (who was to assist him) and Swamiji himself.

At Singapore, we got a call from Mumbai, informing us of Mr. Chanrai's ill health. Mrs. Chanrai had to fly back to Mumbai immediately. The next day Mr. Chanrai passed away. Then I understood the reason why Swamiji had insisted, ever since January, on me accompanying him.

During the Singapore *yajna*, he really looked after me, woke me up when I overslept, always had breakfast with me, and shared a glass of milk. He is fully responsible for turning my admiration into devotion. I flew with him to the

United States in 1981. At that time I wanted to ask him permission to join the Mission. Three times I tried, but failed. On *Guru Purnima* day, he himself asked me, "So, what did you want to ask me?"

And thus I became his devotee and his Mission worker.[23]

Many devotees' accounts send a powerful message that we can never predict how we will meet our guru, or when will be the optimal time for recognizing his true identity. During one early meeting between an eventual devotee and Swamiji *before* he was a swami, it seems that neither the disciple knew who would eventually become her teacher, nor, apparently, did the guru-to-be know what his future role might be:

Pre-*Sannyasa* Meeting

Malti Prasad met Swamiji before he was a swami and she herself was a 14-year-old girl in India. She recalls that he used to pull her braids in those days and happened to give her her very first ball-point pen. Even then he was always full of jokes and pranks.

Later she learned that he had taken *sannyasa*, but didn't meet him again until she was in America, living in Palo Alto, California. One day, she saw an announcement in the Stanford University newspaper about a lecture series by Swami Chinmayananda.

Malti went to hear Swamiji together with her husband, Raj. She had trouble listening to Swamiji's words, because her mind continued to go back to the time she had known him before, thinking and comparing.

After the lecture, she went up to greet Swamiji, but he didn't recognize her. But when it became clear who she was, he exclaimed: "Malti! You're Malti!"

She introduced her husband.

"You have a husband?" was Swamiji's surprised response.

She invited him for tea at their house. In later years, he often stayed at their home or visited there for *bhikshas*. "I always have to be at Malti's house," Swamiji would say.[24]

Malti and her husband, Dr. Rajendra Prasad, both educators, became active members of Chinmaya Mission. In the 1990s, Dr. Prasad spearheaded the development of Chinmaya International School in Coimbatore, India. And it all began when Swamiji had joked with a fourteen-year-old girl in New Delhi and pulled her braids in jest.

Meeting one's guru is, indeed, a miracle. As Gurudev himself said, "Do not forget that the teacher was brought to you by the Lord Himself! *When* the Lord will bring him and *how* He'll bring him, only He knows."

BLESSINGS AND TRANSFORMATIONS

When we were organizing the first lecture series for Swamiji in the United States, the publicity literature invariably contained the words "the teacher who invites the questioning mind to protest against tradition, to scoff at empty ritual, to challenge ancient dogma, and to accept neither scripture nor saint on hearsay." For the Hindu who was brought up in a household of prayer, Vedic chanting, and daily worship that he barely understood, Swamiji's was a liberating message. Many of his students later confessed: Though reared in an atmosphere suffused with Sanskrit prayers, devotional songs, and daily rituals at the altar, they had nevertheless remained ignorant of their meaning. Then there were those who had vaguely heard of the *Gita* and the Upanishads, but had paid them little heed, having become too immersed in the tantalizing promises of Western secularism. But the fortunate ones wound their way to their first lecture by Swamiji, and the experience, with few exceptions, transformed their thinking. Swamiji burst the pods of the ancient scriptural verses and revealed the fruit-bearing seeds within, opening up new meaning for both the religion-weary former ritualist and the mesmerized secularist.

Also for the Christian grown skeptical about seemingly meaningless knee-bending and Sundays filled with empty intonations from the altar, Swamiji's Vedanta — which underscored the *universality* of humankind's quest for God — once again brought a shaft of light to reveal the essence of their former experiences in houses of worship. And similar were the experiences of Muslims and Jews and people of many and varied religious backgrounds who were touched by the lucid, loving logic of Swamiji's Vedanta.

RITUALS AND BLESSINGS

Having liberated the seeker's mind from ritual as he or she had known it — ritual meaningless and void — Swamiji then proceeded to reinvest it with meaning. Slowly and patiently, he began to teach us the *Guru Stotram*, the song in adoration of the guru. Then came the first *Pada Puja*, worship of the guru's feet. Starting with the first *Pada Puja* we participated in, not one such worship ever took place without Swamiji first explaining its significance (with the exception of some *pujas* in small home settings amid long-time devotees). He admonished us never to think of the worship as one of the physical guru, much less his feet, but instead to raise our minds to a place where we could in gratitude pour forth our reverence to the wisdom in which the teacher was rooted. "The feet," he reminded us, "are symbolic of the wisdom on which the guru stands. When you worship the guru's feet, you are not worshipping flesh and bones, but the wisdom that the teacher represents."

Knowing this, as we sat gathered around his feet covered with blossoms offered by the worshippers, surrounded by the sound of Sanskrit chants and the heady aroma of incense, many a devotee's heart burst open from the intensity of love energy that suffused the place of worship. Tears flowed abundantly and faces glistened in joy. Swamiji sat through much of it immersed in meditation, now and then mouthing the words of the sung prayers himself, as though praying to his own guru. Toward the end of the *puja*, when devotees began to file past him to do their prostrations, he would reopen his eyes, greeting each with a look or a word or a gesture specifically intended for the one in front of him, often with a touch of humor and a twinkle in the eye. In Swamiji's rendering of a ritual there was never even a hint of pomposity or artificial holiness, just simple, down-to-earth participation in the sacredness of the moment.

Overpowering Energy

I remember a time at a temple in Michigan when toward the close of the *Pada Puja* in the newly consecrated space, I stopped in front of Gurudev and did my prostrations. As he handed me a small sacrament (*prasad*) from the *puja*, he looked into my eyes and said, "Salaam Aleikum," this in reference to the fact that my husband is a Muslim. I responded, "Aleikum Salaam" — and made room for the next devotee. But as I moved away, my head reeled, and my entire body shook as though hit by a wall of force. The energy filling me was so overpowering that I hid my face in my hands and cried for some ten minutes or more.

After composure came back to me again, I looked around and saw the face of another devotee who obviously had been similarly transported. She was bathed in tears, barely able to cope with the avalanche of emotion that had burst from her.[1]

A Transforming Moment

Swami Chidananda, teacher of Vedanta courses both at Sandeepany Sadhanalaya in Mumbai and Sandeepany San Jose in California, experienced a deeply transforming moment with Gurudev during an informal gathering. Swamiji had just come out of his room to give some time to a group of devotees. They were singing *kirtan* [devotional songs] when Swamiji walked very slowly into the room. "As he came near me," recalls Swami Chidananda, "he held my folded hands for a while, greeted me, and then proceeded to take his chair. That was it. I do not know what went through me, but I sobbed continuously for perhaps twenty minutes."[2]

Empty ritual had been, indeed, abundantly filled — and to overflowing. In fact, Gurudev could imbue the simplest of moments, in *satsang* or seemingly casual conversation, with the transforming power of ritual, with true communion with the Higher. Simply being in his presence was doing *puja*. In fact, it was utterly effortless worship. Being with him subsumed everything else — home, family, career, all worldly connections.

Yet, on many occasions, we felt that the joy we experienced in his presence could not be contained without sharing it with loved ones:

Four *Tilakas*

My first visit to the Sidhabari ashram was an experience beyond compare. I reveled in the beauty of the surroundings, the immensity of Gurudev's love, the sublimity of his teachings. I was continually saying to myself, "I must return here at the earliest opportunity, and I must bring my family with me. They, too, need to experience the sublimity of this wondrous place!" At the closing ceremony, at which each camp delegate filed past Swamiji to accept his blessings and receive a sandalwood dab on the forehead, Swamiji did not stop with the traditional one *tilaka* for me. After placing the first one, he said, "And these are for the husband and children" — and dotted my forehead with three more!

I had not told him of my desire to bring my family there to share my joy.[3]

Though many of us felt repeatedly blessed by his presence in our lives, Swamiji refused to bestow official blessings on people and places. Sometime during the sixties in San Francisco, he had been taken to a new spiritual bookstore in the city and, after a tour of the place, was asked by the owner if he would bless the store before he left. His reply was simple, "I don't bless."

"I Don't Bless"

A devotee was taking leave of Swamiji after a camp at Krishnalaya in northern California, to return to her home many miles away.

"Swamiji," she said as she approached the table where he was having his breakfast, "please bless me in my *sadhana*."

"No. I will not bless you," was Swamiji's firm but loving reply. "You bless yourself. Ask your Higher Mind to bless your lower mind. Remember the verses of *Vivekacudamani* that you've been listening to at the lecture:

> That which has no caste, creed, family, or lineage, which is without name and form, merit and demerit, which is beyond space, time, and sense objects — That *Brahman* Thou Art . . . meditate on this in your mind. (*Vivekacudamani* 254)[4]

Blessings after Death

At a spiritual camp at Krishnalaya in 1992, a group of devotees were sitting in *satsang* with Swamiji, who was seated in front of a row of stately fir trees next to his *kutiya*. A woman, her mind filled with thoughts about Swamiji's delicate health and advancing years (75), asked: "Swamiji, is it true that the guru's blessings to his devotees increase after he has dropped his body?"

Gurudev answered: "If he is a real guru, he will have dropped his body long ago. The physical guru you think you see before you is only the mind's projection. The real guru is always there, ready to bless you."[5]

His blessings, though unspoken, came powerfully and in a myriad of ways:

A Vision of Swami Tapovanam

In 1993, only weeks before Swamiji's passing from this plane, one new seeker who was attending his lectures for the first time made a habit of going to mid-morning *satsang* in Swamiji's *kutiya* at Krishnalaya. Swamiji had not yet arrived, and the chair he would be sitting in was empty. Yet, the man's eyes were riveted on the chair and began to take on a strange look, but he said nothing. Later, over lunch, he told me what had happened:

"I looked at the empty chair," he said, "and suddenly saw a figure in it, a man with a round face and very short white hair."

He continued to describe the figure, when I exclaimed, "You're describing Swamiji's guru, Swami Tapovan!"

The man's eyes filled with tears, and he rushed out of the dining hall. After a few minutes, I followed him. He was standing next to a tree a little distance from the central building, still weeping, soaking up one tissue after another as he pulled tissues out of his pocket dispenser. He had obviously been shaken to the core. I, too, wept — from the sheer joy of knowing that such heart-opening can take place, a loving blessing from a teacher just barely met.[6]

Blessings and benedictions from Swamiji came in many forms. Often just a glance would suffice.

Demons Banished

I had spent some five hours in the car with someone who was going for a few days to the spiritual camp at Krishnalaya, but more out of duty to a family member than out of devotion or spiritual thirst. Much of the driver's conversation revolved around his doubts about spiritual masters. One story after another was related as to how this or that guru had really proven to have feet of clay. By the time I got to Krishnalaya, I was shocked how negative my mind had become. For almost a day, a black cloud swirled about my head.

But then Swamiji's love broke through the dismal barrier I had managed to create around me, and once again I began to dive deep into the inner spaces that had become so familiar in his presence.

While I was brooding, Swamiji had paid little attention to me. The moment I started opening up again, he glanced over at me during *satsang* and winked. His typically "wink" consisted of batting the eyelids of both of his large brown eyes a few times while a smile played lovingly on his lips.

That's all I needed: a few bats of the eyelids, and all was well, not only well, but blissfully so.

> Oh, Master, Oh Friend of those who reverentially surrender to thee,
> thou ocean of mercy, I salute thee.
> Save me, fallen as I am into this sea of change,
> with a direct glance from thy eyes,
> which rain nectarine grace supreme.
> (*Vivekacudamani* 35)[7]

Many experienced this "nectarine grace supreme" of Gurudev's eyes. Just one look — and all was well. Just one look — and in the depths of our being we were reminded of our true nature. At times, the look went so deep that we felt as though he was looking farther into the recesses of our being than we ourselves, in our most intimate moments, had ever looked. It was a look beyond name or form or worldly association of any kind; it was a look beyond time and space. It was a look that transformed.

TRANSFORMATIONS

In Gurudev's presence, any moment that we ourselves allowed to be such, was a transforming one. And then there were special moments in many devotees' lives that spelled a sudden turn in the way they thought about life and the way they saw the world.

Walking into Our Dreams

Swamiji was giving a *yajna* in a large city in the United States. He was staying at the house of a local devotee, along with several out-of-town devotees.

The hostess and two of the out-of-town ladies were sitting together on the floor, sharing their experiences of seeing Swamiji appear as a visitor in their dreams. One of the ladies described the experience thus:

"And we now interrupt this dream for a special message from Swamiji!" She said that he often appeared in her dreams, as though he had come for the simple purpose of delivering a message of love. After delivering it, he departed.

The husband of one of the ladies was standing nearby and overheard the conversation. Looking down at the group of ladies, he remarked:

"You are all very silly. Dreams are just excretions of the mind."

The husband walked away as the three ladies shared smiles of understanding.

The next day the same three ladies were sitting together in much the same way, chatting. The husband came over to the group, but this time his attitude was markedly different. He said quietly:

"I apologize. Swamiji walked into my dream last night."[8]

Transforming Lecture

Bhanumathi Rao had dedicated her life to dance and music. She had spent much of her life abroad, leading a Western-oriented life.

When she returned to Delhi in 1989, some family members told her that they were going to Sidhabari to hear Swami Chinmayananda. She wanted to join them, so she accompanied them on their trip to the ashram. This was her first meeting with Swamiji, as well as her first exposure to the *Bhagavad Gita* and the Upanishads.

After she heard Gurudev's first talk, she said to herself: "What an utter waste of my life it has been!"

When she returned to her room, she said to herself, "I'm staying here; I'm not going back." She recalls now: "Gurudev changed my whole pattern of life with just one talk." A sense of detachment from the worldly life had taken her over all at once.

After she had made her decision to stay at Sidhabari, she went to Gurudev to seek his permission, but he was busy. She was asked to come back the next morning. She returned to his *kutiya* the following morning and waited from 8 a.m. until noon. Finally, he came out of his room. She told him about her resolve.

"What will you do here?" Gurudev asked.

"I don't know," she answered, "but I want to stay here — with your permission."

"You will be given just one tiny room, one chair, one table," said Gurudev, "and there will be no wall-to-wall carpets."

Then he laughed and called the manager: "Give her a room!"

She stayed in Sidhabari for four years.[9]

Not Self-Realization!

A devotee remembers a particularly inspiring lecture at one of Gurudev's *yajnas*: Her mind reached a state of such incomparable peace and bliss that she wondered if this might be the final crossing over to Self-realization itself. That night she had a dream: She was sitting in lecture with Swamiji, and he said to her straight from the lecture platform: "No, what you are experiencing is *not* Self-realization. Your mind has just gone into a deeper peace than it has ever known before."

At the next day's lecture, Swamiji looked down from the lecture platform, straight into the eyes of the devotee who had experienced the dream, and repeated his message from her dream: "No, the state of peace you experienced was *not* Self-realization! Your mind just went into an incomparably peaceful state, that's all!"[10]

Many stories exist about how Swamiji turned around the reluctant seeker. Often, people came to his lectures dragged along by a spouse or a friend, sat in the back with arms folded across the chest, as if to say, "I dare you to convince me!" And many walked away convinced, despite themselves.

Some were downright rebellious.

Reluctant Seekers

At one of Swamiji's *yajnas* in Kerala, a young student rebelliously disturbed the *satsang* when he got up and shouted from the end of the hall: "Wait a minute, Swami! Only those who respect you will obey you. But a person like me, who has no respect for you, will not obey. So of what use are your advice and your instructions?"

Without pausing even for a moment, Swamiji called out cheerfully to the young rebel, "Is that so? Then come up here and I will show you!"

The crowd, though anxious, made way for the youngster so he could walk up to Swamiji's seat. Determined to show disrespect, the young fellow walked forward, head erect, and reached Swamiji. He stood at Swamiji's right side.

"Please, I think we can talk better if you move over to the left," said Swamiji.

The young man walked over to Swamiji's left.

"No, I think it is better for you to stand in front of me for the discussion, as you don't respect me."

So the young man walked over to stand in front of Swamiji.

"Now, could you come back to where you stood in the first place, here on my right?" was Swamiji's next request.

The young man did so.

"Now, sit down," commanded Swamiji. The youngster sat down.

"Please," said Swamiji, "can you now repeat your earlier statement?"

The young fellow was silent, thoughtful. But the crowd could not suppress its laughter any longer.

"You see, young man," said Swamiji, "respect is not necessary to obey what the elders say. All you need is the anxiety to know. You are obeying me. You are gentle and good."

The young man bowed and left in silence.[11]

"The eloquence of our master was indeed his *vibhuti* [special glory] that casts a spell on even the most 'out-turned' soul to make him pause, think, and change," says Chinmaya Mission's own Swami Chidananda. And he goes on to say:

Overwhelmed First-Timers

Someone once remarked, seeing the crowds that sat to listen to this God-chosen orator, "Ah, what a miracle! In this audience I see hands that once held bottles holding *The Holy Geeta (Bhagavad Gita)*!" Many were those who would sit in the back row on their first visit, move forward a little the second time, and then become very regular and punctual in attendance, seeking out the front rows. Overwhelmed with the new, saving insights into life this great speaker brought to them, many would make a prostration on the dusty ground of the *yajnasala* at the end of an evening's discourse.[12]

Everything — the Lord's *Prasad*

For many years, devotees of Swamiji tried to get him a visitor's visa to allow him to hold public talks in Indonesia, but he was denied the visa by the Muslim government because of his connection to Vishwa Hindu Parishad, the conservative Hindu organization. In 1987, Swamiji was allowed an informal visit to Bali, but was not allowed to speak. The devotees tried again in 1989 to obtain an official visa for him, but again did not succeed. After this unsuccessful attempt, Swamiji wrote a letter to an Indonesian devotee eager for his presence there:

"Don't worry. Accept everything as the Lord's *prasad*. Have patience. Whenever He wishes it, it will happen."

In 1990, the devotees tried once again, but Swamiji seemed to be still on the government's black list. Then, the eager devotee who had received Swamiji's consoling letter decided to spend a month with him, in hopes that, in her absence, her husband might be inspired to use his government contacts to bring Swamiji into the country. And, indeed, the husband succeeded in procuring the necessary documents for official public speaking, and Swamiji, though very unwell physically, arrived for his first Indonesia talks in February 1993.

Gurudev was very happy to be there, his "last frontier." Swamiji laughed his joyous laugh: "How can an entire Muslim country be afraid of *one* Hindu swami?"

The husband, formerly a somewhat reluctant devotee, had, through his efforts to bring Swamiji into the country, became deeply involved with Gurudev's work, and continued to work tirelessly to help organize the *yajnas* that followed, even after Swamiji's passing from this plane.[13]

Many devotees experienced an overwhelming impact when they first heard their teacher, Swami Chinmayananda. For some the impact was immediate, for others, more gradual, but similar stories have been repeated often: How throughout the lecture Gurudev seemed to be talking just to them, to their particular life problems, as though the entire lecture were directed specifically at them. Many remember how, especially in the early days of listening to him, they would walk away from a lecture filled with new, life-saving insights, yet found that the ideas they had heard had created a whole new set of questions that burned in their minds. Invariably, at the very next lecture those burning questions would be answered by Swamiji.

Piercing of the Heart

One young American woman experienced a powerfully transforming first meeting with Swamiji. She had been studying with another Vedanta teacher for a while and found the study deeply satisfying, but wanted to learn more, so she decided to attend one of Swamiji's spiritual camps. At the camp lectures, Swamiji talked a lot about *vasanas*, as he so often did. At one point he explained "addiction *vasanas*," that they are the kind you cannot hope to exhaust; you simply have to stop doing what you've been doing — and as he said that he looked at his new listener, an addicted smoker. She felt as though the entire lecture were addressed to her only. Though some of the lectures were very subtle and difficult to follow, she stuck it out. At the end of the last lecture, Swamiji said, almost in a whisper:

"Your own essential Self is divine, whether you like it or not."

With those words, her heart was pierced. After the lecture, she went off alone to the woods and wept.

The transformation had begun, but still the mind resisted some things she wasn't used to, in particular, the habit of devotees paying respect to the guru by bowing at his feet. The camp was drawing to its close, and leave-taking was imminent. Grappling with her doubts about the proper way to take leave of her newfound teacher, she went to a long-time devotee and confessed, "I can't do it, this bowing to another human being."

Her friend said simply, "It's not the man you're bowing to."

She understood in a flash and rushed up a huge flight of stairs to take leave of Swamiji. Having understood, she finally bowed at his feet. When she straightened up, he laughed lovingly and put his arm around her shoulder.[14]

"At Last We Can Talk"

Veronica Hausman could not look at Gurudev without crying, she was so overwhelmed with devotion. At one point, he suggested that she spend some time in Uttarkashi in North India, the place where he had studied with his own teacher, Swami Tapovanam. At this point in time, Veronica was reluctant to go, since Swamiji would be spending some months in the United States just when he was suggesting she take a trip to India. But Swamiji insisted, so she went.

At Uttarkashi she had deep spiritual experiences. When she returned and met Swamiji, he said:

"Hah! At last we can talk. One little trip to India and we can talk. I have been waiting for this. Up until now, all I could do was slip and slide on your tears!"[15]

HIS ATTRIBUTES

Gurudev delighted in playing the game of life — *lila* in Sanskrit. According to the Hindu tradition, God enacts all roles within the divine play of life. The whole Universe is His playground.

The Master's Dance

> The last day [of the spiritual camp at Sidhabari] was the highlight. The convocation was over. It was going to be a full moon night. The ashram was vibrating with excitement . . . [Preparations were underway for the final ceremonies and celebrations. The workers] were the local *pahadi* boys trained under Br. Vinodji. . . . It was their day. They wanted to serve the special *pahadi* meal to all the delegates out in the open. . . . All the 370 delegates sat while the *pahadi* boys served the food and instructed us as to how to eat the seven varieties of delicious *dals* mixed with rice. To top it all, they served us a dessert of sweet saffron rice. We could not help but overeat. . . .
>
> Everybody had overeaten. Gurudev knew. Imagine the next day's morning meditation! Gurudev could not allow us to sleep with such heavy stomachs, so . . . while the *pahadi* boys sang their lively songs with joy, Gurudev went around picking out the delegates one by one.
>
> "Dance! Dance!" — he commanded by his mere look, all the time a mischievous smile playing on his lips. And then, for the joy of all, the Master of Masters danced with us.[1]

As we watched Gurudev in his daily activities, we witnessed him playing many roles, each role perfectly suited to the situation at hand. We saw an awesome display of qualities that, in sum, began to scratch the surface of what might be called a definition of who he was. Yet, a final definition eluded us.

His most remarkable quality was his unconditional love for others. A separate chapter is dedicated to it.

ASTOUNDING MEMORY

Many stories exist about how well Swamiji remembered people and seemingly impossible details about their lives. As an example, when a brahmachari or brahmacharini completed the two-and-a-half-year course at Sandeepany Sadhanalaya in Mumbai, a new name was given to him or her. From that point on, Swamiji would always remember the name — sometimes seeing the person only once a year. A sprinkling of other examples:

Peanut Memories

Around 1951, Swamiji went on a *yatra* [pilgrimage]. One day during a train trip, a gentleman sitting across from Swamiji offered him some boiled peanuts. Later, the man forgot all about the incident. Thirty years later, this same person (now aged 70) was organizing a *yajna* in Bangalore. At the *yajna*, the man kept looking at Swamiji because he thought he might have met him earlier, but could not remember where. Swamiji looked at him and said, "Peanuts!" Thirty years after such a brief encounter, he still remembered![2]

Interrupted Answer

Swamiji had been a guest at the home of Gulu Advani, long-time member of the Chinmaya Mission West Board of Directors, and his host was now taking Swamiji by car to the home of another devotee. Gulu had a doubt and asked Swamiji for clarification. Swamiji had gotten halfway through his answer when they arrived at the second home. Other devotees were already there awaiting the guru's arrival, opening the car door for him and beginning to converse with him.

Thus, with hellos to everyone, there was no time to finish the conversation that had begun in the car. The following year, Swamiji was once again arriving for a local *yajna*, and Gulu went to pick him up at the airport. The minute they had settled into the car, Swamiji said, "As we were discussing last year . . ." and finished his answer to Gulu's question.[3]

Remembering Means Loving

In 1970, Swamiji took a *rudraksa mala* from his own neck after Uncle Mani had given a Vedanta talk and put it on Uncle Mani's: "Wear this always." One year later at an airport meeting, Swamiji touched Uncle Mani's chest and said: "Is it there?"

Uncle Mani says today, "Gurudev had such love for us — and love means that you remember!"[4]

EXCELLENCE, PRECISION, METICULOUSNESS

Hamir Vissanji had many occasions to witness the level of Gurudev's meticulousness, care, and precision. He writes:

Speedy Answers

A few years after my first contact with Gurudev, he handed over to me the complete administration of the Chinmaya Lesson Course [a correspondence course on Vedanta], which was originally meant for foreign students only but was subsequently opened up for Indian students also.

At that time, each and every query of the Lesson Course students was sent to Pujya Gurudev. Wherever he was in the world when he received the queries, he replied to each letter promptly and meticulously, either in his own handwriting or typewritten and signed by him. Each letter was sent off to the student without delay. This was a great attraction for the students, whose numbers went on increasing.[5]

Only the Right Size Is Right

The *yajna* organizers had published a handsome souvenir for the occasion. Swamiji used to send sample souvenir copies to devotees and Chinmaya Mission workers around the world who were most active in his work. He had inquired about envelopes for the souvenir and was being shown a sample.

"No, not right," he said. "The envelope should be the exact size to match the souvenir. Measure the souvenir," he said, "and make an envelope to match it." So it was done.[6]

Printing, Not Printing Business

During the course of his lecture series in Napa, California, sometime in the 1970s, Swamiji instructed Bill Browning to "learn printing." So Bill began to learn printing by apprenticing to established printers, eventually purchasing his own business in Napa called Family Press. He spent ten years running the business, battling with faulty equipment and struggling to keep the business afloat while fuifilling most all of the printing requirements for Chinmaya Mission West.

When he talked about the difficulties with Swamiji many years later, Swamiji said, "I said to you 'learn printing,' not 'learn the printing business.'"[7]

Following Precise Instructions Precisely

At a *yajna* at Jamshedpur, Swamiji asked the organizers to furnish a list of addresses along with blank envelopes for posting the *yajna* souvenirs to committed Mission workers all over the world.

When the envelopes arrived, he looked at them with displeasure. All addresses were already neatly typed on them!

"Why did you do this?" Swamiji asked. "I didn't ask you to type the addresses!" Swamiji had asked for blank envelopes, but he had received addressed ones, all prepared for him by well-meaning devotees. He had wanted to hand-write the addresses on the envelopes himself. He knew very well what it meant to each devotee to receive an envelope from afar with his characteristic graceful swirls adorning the envelope![8]

The Efficiency of Labor

Swamiji was to give a talk to more than 1,000 senior executives at the Public Sector Steel Plant in Rourkela. The executives had been told that Swamiji would reach the hall exactly at the appointed time, 3:30 p.m., and that they should all be there punctually.

Some officers of the Steel Plant arrived at Swamiji's residence around 3 o'clock. Swamiji was writing letters at his desk. He had been previously told that it would take ten minutes to reach the lecture hall. But the officers started to get worried: "The program is to begin at 3:30, and he is still busy writing!"

However, Swamiji was not moving from his room. By 3:15 the officers who had arrived to take him became seriously restless.

At their bidding, K. C. Patnaik went to Swamiji's room, where he was writing at his desk.

"Yes?" Swamiji asked.

"Swamiji, the Steel Plant officers have come to take you . . . ," said Patnaik.

"But the trip is only a ten-minute drive! Why leave now?"

So Patnaik gave the message to the officers: There would be an additional five-minute wait.

At exactly 3:20 p.m. Swamiji walked out of his room and straight to the car — with no formalities.

His talk at the Steel Plant was on "The Efficiency of Labor," inspiring his listeners to be committed, sincere, and honest in order to increase their level of efficiency.[9]

Swamiji paid close attention to every detail, whether it related to constructing a new building or to managing the finances of an already existing ashram. Jairam Jaisinghani, for many years manager of Sandeepany Sadhanalaya in Mumbai, recalls how Swamiji always said, "One rupee saved is a rupee earned." The ashram, which has served as an institute of training in Vedanta for many batches of students, was and still is run on donations from devotees, and all training and expenses are provided to the students free of charge for two and one-half years. Swamiji used to study the expense statements for Sandeepany in detail, inquiring about any figure that he felt was not acceptable, such as expenditures for telephone calls or gasoline. If the expenditure was deemed too high, he gave instructions on reducing it.

Short-Term Economy

Once I had bought two sets of *dhotis* for the brahmacharis, as I had gotten them very economically from Kerala, at one-half the Mumbai prices. Pujya Swamiji immediately said, "This is short-term economy. Double the soap and effort to wash these will have to be invested until they are torn."

At another time, he saw that several rounds of *chappal* purchases had been made within a two-month period. After inquiring about the purchase, he said that if the brahmacharis lose their *chappals* or misuse them, let them walk barefoot until the next lot is due for them.

Pujya Gurudev advised us that the money at the ashram is the sacred money of the devotees and must be spent with utmost care. He was definitely offended if the receipts were not sent out in time or if the donations were not reported to him.[10]

UNCOMPROMISING STRENGTH

For many devotees, service to the guru and his cause became a paramount life's goal. Many supported Gurudev with hours of dedicated service; others subsidized his many social and educational programs with much-needed funding; many others did both. In the process, he never let his own principles and his adherence to Truth be compromised in the process. He was always teacher first and foremost, allowing himself to serve as the vehicle for truths and lessons that flowed effortlessly through him to those who needed to hear them:

Principles Come First

Around 1956, Swami Chinmayananda went to Calcutta for a *yajna* and stayed with a businessman and his family at their house. Basically, they were good people, but they drank and they played cards in the house, even while Gurudev was there. Swamiji knew that they were drinking and doing all those things. He was in one part of the bungalow and they were in another.

About 3,000 people attended this particular *yajna*, and the two main hosts would sit right in the front of the crowd. On the second or third day of the *yajna*, during the course of the talk, Gurudev intoned in his loud, booming voice, "They think that by bringing a swami or *sadhu* to their house they are doing a great thing! On the other side of the house, they will be drinking, playing cards, and whatnot. Foolish fellows!" All the while Gurudev was sternly staring at the hosts. He was scolding them left and right during the talk, right in front of the crowd!

The two hosts, the subject of his scorn, couldn't take it. They got up and left right in the middle of the talk. Gurudev went on with his discourse without a pause.

At the end of the talk, one of the organizers said to Swamiji, "Swamiji, they are very ardent supporters of the Mission, but Swamiji has said to them that . . ." — and they expanded on what they had heard from the podium.

Gurudev replied, "Did I say that?"

"Yes, Swamiji" the organizer responded.

"If it has come out of me, it must be Truth," was his response.

Gurudev continued to stay in the same house throughout the *yajna*. Feeling insulted, the hosts stopped coming to the talks and declined to talk to Swamiji after the incident. Some twenty years later, they became totally changed and came back to meet him.[11]

A Humble *Mahatma*

When we were studying at Sandeepany Sadhanalaya from 1972 to 1974, one day, Swamiji said that another swami was coming to visit our ashram. His name was Swami Gangeshwarananda. He was very old and completely blind. On the previous day, Gurudev had come to supervise the preparations to make sure everything was all right. We arranged all the flowers and other details on the speakers' podium.

Gurudev saw two chairs on the stage and asked, "What is the other chair for?"

We replied, "It is for you, Swamiji."

He said, "For me? On the stage? A great *mahatma* is coming. When he was a swami, I was a nobody! I was nothing at that time. When he comes, I won't sit on the stage."

We felt so bad; we could not even imagine that our Gurudev would be sitting somewhere below.

The next day, when Swami Gangeshwarananda came, everybody went near the entrance. Gurudev ran across the temple steps like a child to receive him. The visiting swami was taken to the temple, and garlands were placed around his neck.

Swami Gangeshwarananda sat on the single chair on the stage. Gurudev, who sat just below him, started massaging the swami's legs. We can never forget that scene. Such a great *mahatma* "came down" (became so humble) when he was in the presence of another *mahatma*. On that day, the eyes of many of the brahmacharis were opened to the glory of Gurudev.[12]

"OK, We Will Walk"

Someone was to pick up Gurudev from the ashram and drive him to Poona, but the car did not arrive as scheduled. Gurudev waited for a while and then said:

"So, the car has not yet come. Okay, we will walk."

He started walking out of the ashram at a brisk pace. The devotees around him almost had to run to keep up with him. "Luckily," recalls Swami Purushottamananda, "after a few moments, the car arrived, and Gurudev was politely requested to take his seat in the car."[13]

Curbside *Yajna*

One early Saturday morning during a *yajna* in Napa, California, Swamiji and his listeners had already gathered by the high school door where his 6 a.m. classes on *Vivekacudamani* had been held all that week. The caretaker had remembered to open the doors of the building every morning except this, a Saturday. But that didn't stop Gurudev. With a smile on his face, he sat down cross-legged on the cold curb of the sidewalk, motioned the rest of us to sit down in front of him, opened the text, and began to teach. And so he continued for the next one-and-a-half hours as the brisk morning grew gradually warmer around us and traffic noises in the distance slowly beckoned the day awake.[14]

Gurudev's disregard for the discomforts of the body was evident from the earliest years of his study and teaching:

Cramped Quarters

Forty years back when I met Swamiji, he always used to carry a *kamandalu* [a vessel carried by a renunciate] and wear *khadaus* [wooden sandals with a knob between the first and second toes]. He used to walk quite fast with them, even on uneven ground, and his hair was always covered with a saffron scarf, which was tied at the back of the head in a knot. He would take only a glass of milk and some seasonal fruits at night.

I had a chance to see his *kutiya* in Gangotri, where he did penance while staying with his guru, Sri Tapovan Maharaj. It was dug near Tapovan Maharaj's cottage. I peeped into the *kutiya* but could not enter it. I wondered how a tall person like Swamiji used to go in and out of that entrance for years. As it was dug below ground level, one had to bend to enter it . . . With the *kutiya's* low roof, one of decent height could neither stand erect nor sleep with legs stretched. The roof was thatched, and it had a matching thatched door to keep the howling cold wind of Gangotri out.

Once I asked Swamiji how he could manage to stretch his limbs in that *kutiya*, and he answered, "Acrobatics are not allowed for *sannyasins*. For sitting and meditating and relaxing the back it was sufficient."[15]

Once, a devotee asked Swamiji why he ate on a silver *thali* [plate]. His answer was, "It is the host who is giving me food on a silver *thali*. If he serves me in my hand, I'll eat from my hand. I have a comfortable bed now, but if it is not there, I'll sleep on the floor."

Gurudev seemed never to lack anything, even on the material plane. Devotees were forever showering him with gifts, which he then readily passed on to new owners, sometimes within seconds, much to the giver's dismay. Well-to-do followers helped support his many social service activities. Yet, despite the abundance that followed him wherever he went, Gurudev showed to us that material possessions or bodily comforts meant little to him:

Making Do with What's Offered

Soon after Gurudev had stayed at someone's home during his *yajna* in a local town, Swami Brahmananda was being hosted by the same people. He was given the room where Gurudev had previously stayed.

After a night in the room, Swami Brahmananda asked the hosts if the bed on which he slept had been the one that Gurudev also had slept in.

The hosts said, "Yes." The swami then told them that the length of the cot was just sufficient for his own height, and wondered how Gurudev, with his tall frame, might have managed to sleep on it.

During Gurudev's next visit, the hosts apologized and asked Gurudev how he had managed to sleep on such a small cot.

"I slept along the diagonal," was Gurudev's reply.[16]

A *Sannyasin's* Life

When Ram Kirpalani first came in contact with Swamiji in the mid-1970s, he was amazed to see how many *bhikshas* Swamiji attended at which his devotees, disciples, and admirers offered him sumptuous meals. "Unaccustomed to this, I used to look at the whole thing with a certain degree of curiosity," says Ram. "I even began to think that a *sannyasin's* life was pretty good."

Around 1979, Ram and his wife went to India. They joined Swamiji in Tirupati, Andhra Pradesh, where he was holding a *jnana yajna,* with lectures every morning and evening. On a particular Sunday, Swamiji's schedule between morning class and noon included an inauguration of a local Chinmaya Mission Center some 25 miles from Tirupati, a lecture at an ancient temple, and a *bhiksha* at the home of a devotee.

"Knowing of the busy morning schedule, the host served an adequate breakfast to Swamiji," says Ram. "We, too, were the beneficiaries, as we were going with Swamiji. Then we headed toward the site of the inauguration, arriving there in about one hour. The hosts assumed that Swamiji had started from Tirupati early and must be famished. They had therefore prepared a rich breakfast. So Swamiji, in spite of his fragile health condition, ate the second breakfast. So did we, although it was difficult."

Within about an hour, they arrived at their next destination, another site for the inauguration festivities. The hosts must again have assumed that Swamiji would be requiring a meal, for they had made arrangements for an elaborate breakfast.

"Each item on the menu was special," recalls Ram, "but by this time even to look at any food was making me sick." As Ram was considering skipping this meal, Swamiji motioned to him to join him at the table. Swamiji was served ample quantities of breakfast delicacies with great devotion, and since Ram shared the same table, he, too, received bountiful helpings of everything.

"Swamiji started eating as though he had not touched food all morning," says Ram. "I made a slow start, as I was afraid I may not be able to keep the food down." After a number of attempts by the hosts to give second and third helpings, Ram stretched his hands over his plate to avoid any additional helpings, feeling quite sick already. Yet Swamiji continued eating.

"Swamiji obviously sensed my predicament," says Ram. "Not quite looking at me, he said softly, "Ram, this is called true *sannyasa*."

Later that day, Swamiji accepted yet another *bhiksha* at noon, followed by a regular lunch at the host's place. Says Ram: "My mind returned to my earlier thoughts about a *sannyasin's* life. Swamiji went through this kind of life day after day, year after year because of the love in his heart for his devotees and disciples. Not only that, but he would compliment them for their exceptional culinary genius. And he had read my mind and taught me by example how much sacrifice a *sannyasin's* life truly contains."[17]

Gurudev also gave many a devotee opportunities to practice forbearance:

"Don't Complain!"

In 1993, some 800 delegates had arrived at Sandeepany (Himalayas) in Sidhabari for a youth convention. Tents had been set up to help accommodate the many participants. The site was extremely crowded. The organizers had not planned for that many people for food and other necessities.

Swamiji said to the group: "So many of you have come! The organizers had not even dreamed that so many of you would be here. Don't complain. You've come to study the *Bhagavad Gita*. Whatever you get, you eat. If you have a place to stay, good. If not, sit under a tree."[18]

Seek the Lord
in the smiles of your friends,
in the glow of angry eyes,
in the storms of passion.
He is everywhere, in everything.

MIRACLES

Reluctant to discuss the superphysical, the miraculous, Swamiji spoke lightly of seemingly miraculous happenings that transpired in his presence. He dismissed any notion that his powers may be special. Yet, he could be enthralled by the utter miracle of a wrist in motion:

The Miracle of the Wrist

Swamiji had just leaned backward against the back of his chair after having finished a number of letters. He was stretching his right hand upward slightly to release the tension when I saw his gaze intently transfixed on the movement of his wrist as he flexed his hand back and forth.

For several long, silent minutes he seemed totally absorbed — light radiating from his face — in the utter miracle of how a series of muscles worked their wonder inside the wrist to move it back and forth through the air.[1]

"No Miracles" Swami

Newcomers had been brought to a *satsang* in New Delhi. Swamiji was saying to them: "I'm not a miracle swami. Don't expect me to work miracles."

"You are trying to be too humble, Swamiji," objected Krishna Varma. "I know your *vibhutis* [glories, powers]."

"Of course," said Swamiji, "I'm nothing less than God for you. It is the faith of the *bhakta* [devotee] that brings the best out of me."[2]

IN BIRTH, SICKNESS, AND DEATH

Events continued to take place that Gurudev's devotees considered as miracles generated by his presence. Often, he touched people's lives especially deeply when birth, sickness, or death entered their lives, leaving inexplicable results in his path. A longtime devotee of his from Chennai, India, Leela Nambiar, recounts this story:

Rescue from Drowning

In 1965, in the month of August, my cousin came to pay me a visit, along with his wife and their two-year-old son. My cousin and I had grown up together as children and had gone to school together. In the intervening years, we had the fortune to meet only occasionally. So I was very happy to see him again, and we talked about matters of common interest. We got so engrossed in our talk that nobody noticed the child's absence from the room.

Suddenly we heard a splash and a scream. I instinctively knew that the child had fallen into the four-foot deep lily pond near the verandah. As we rushed out, we saw a man, a complete stranger, holding the child dripping in his wet clothes. The stranger handed the child over to me. My cousin and I were greatly relieved to see that the child had not come to any harm. The child was howling in fright, and the mother took him inside to quiet him and change his wet clothes.

Now I turned my attention to the man who had saved the child from tragedy. He was standing quietly near the pond. I asked him who he was and the purpose of his visit. He looked at me seriously and said he came from Swami Tapovan Maharaj in Uttarkashi [Swami Chinmayananda's guru]. I was very surprised, but felt a deep sense of gratitude overwhelming me and wanted to reward the kind stranger. I requested him to wait and went inside, took some cash from my purse, and came out within two minutes, but I could not find the stranger anywhere. I called the watchman and inquired of the stranger's whereabouts, but the watchman said that nobody had come to the house for the past one hour and nobody had gone out.

I was dumbfounded. I was now sure that the guru had come to the rescue of his devotees. Tears started flowing from my eyes, as I mentally prostrated to my guru, Swami Chinmayanandaji.

When this story was related to Swami Chinmayananda during his next visit to Chennai, he kept silent and just smiled.[3]

Beloved Son

Ram Batra of Mumbai was, in Swamiji's own words, his "right arm," helping Swamiji with complex organizational issues in Chinmaya Mission centers around the world. Swamiji used to call him his "son."

Ram had been feeling quite well, with no apparent health problems. One day, he was sitting in his office and felt Swamiji's hand on his shoulder and heard the words, "My son, you're not well. Go have a check-up." So, without delay, he did have a check-up, followed by several others. He had apparently had a minor heart attack.

During that time, Swamiji was in another town, sitting among a group of devotees in *satsang*. He got up and said, "One of my devotees is not well" — and left the room to go pray.

Later, during a *yajna* in their town, Swamiji stayed at the Batra house. He was there an entire month, during which time he took wonderful care of Ram. Some 30 to 40 people were present at each meal, yet there was always enough food for everyone. To her surprise, the hostess saw that her food expenses had decreased to one-half of the usual, despite the size of the meals. She asked Swamiji: "How is this possible? So much food, yet the expenses are cut in half!"

He just laughed and said, "Krishna, Krishna!"

When Ram Batra's heart eventually did succumb, Swamiji took the death very hard. "I have never seen him so emotional," recalls Jamna Batra,

Ram Batra's widow. "At the condolence meeting, Swamiji couldn't talk at all."[4]

Quick Energy

During a *yajna* in the United States, a husband and wife were waiting by the elevator where Swamiji would arrive to enter the lecture hall. The wife was very tired, utterly exhausted from an extremely strenuous day at work. As her husband held the elevator door open for Swamiji, she was leaning against the wall next to the elevator, eyes closed. Swamiji passed by her and touched his hand to her cheek. At once, a burst of energy streamed through her and she felt fully revitalized.[5]

Threat of Cancer Removed

A woman devotee had found a lump in one of her breasts and was quite worried. This was already the second occurrence. Although the first biopsy had turned up benign results, she was worried. She had no intention of talking to Swamiji about it, but her friends decided that she should ask him about it and managed to maneuver her into Swamiji's study so she could say some private words to him.

She was near his desk when she shyly told him her story. Swamiji looked at her, but as he was gazing at her, his look turned into a withdrawn sort of gaze that we sometimes had witnessed in his eyes, as though he were tuning into another dimension. He gazed at her in that way for some time and then said:

"It's benign."

The biopsy that was performed soon thereafter proved his words right.[6]

Return Trip

The wife of a dedicated Chinmaya Mission member in Delhi had become seriously ill. She was taken to Mumbai for testing. Gurudev had himself just undergone an operation on his eyes, and she and her husband went to see him.

Gurudev touched her hand. "Why have you come to Bombay?" he asked.

"I'm under observation at the Tata Institute," she said.

Gurudev held her hand for about five minutes and then said to the husband, "Take her back," he said. Then, looking up, he added, "I had to bring her back from there."

The next day, all tests turned out negative. The devotee says she owes her life to Gurudev.[7]

"Go Laughing"

A woman in Delhi had been diagnosed for breast cancer in a number of different tests. Her friend Krishna Varma took her to see Swamiji. When Krishna went into Swamiji's room, he said, "What's the problem?" Krishna told him about her friend and that tests had shown cancer.

Smiling, Swamiji looked at her and said, "All for a friend — right."

Then he went out to the *satsang* room and hugged the ailing woman.

"Are you scared of the operation?" he asked. "Go laughing and come out smiling!"

When the doctors operated on her, they found no trace of cancer.

Swamiji said later during his evening lecture: "The *bhakta* who has never asked for anything — how can Narayana say 'No' to her?"[8]

Miracle Baby

I had just gone through a very difficult life experience. On the surface, my life was once again in order, yet Swamiji sensed a deeper wound that still needed healing. He insisted that during the course of his San Francisco *yajna*, I sit with him, in private, through every meal. Others cooked the meal, yet I was given the sole privilege of serving it to him in the complete privacy of his room, with doors closed. He ate and we talked, as he gently inquired of my well-being and poured his love and confidence into me. The healing calm of his presence deepened by the day.

At one midday meal, he asked: "Why haven't you and your husband started a family yet?"

He had struck a painful spot. I began to tell him about my long failure to conceive, about my deep longing for a child — and tears began to flow as I remembered the long months of fruitless waiting behind me. Swamiji looked at me lovingly and said in exquisite gentleness:

"Don't worry. Just give it a little more time. The Lord will make sure you get a child."

Three months later I was pregnant with my firstborn.[9]

An Easy Delivery

Radhika Krishnakumar was in the last month of her first pregnancy, about which she had not told Gurudev. She had gone to one of his *satsangs* and was sitting somewhere at the back on the floor. He picked her out in the crowd and said, "Any time, huh? Sit up on the chair, here," pointing to a chair nearby.

When he was leaving the *satsang*, he walked up to her. He touched her shoulder with the little finger of his right hand and said some words that she could not decipher. Immediately, she felt some contractions. She asked Swamiji's assistant whether she had heard what Swamiji had said. "A mantra for easy delivery that Swamiji picked up in the Himalayas," was the answer.

Afterwards, Radhika felt no trace of pain and went home. Later that evening, because of the incident after *satsang*, she said to herself, "Something must be happening inside; let me go to my doctor to check up." The minute she saw her doctor, the doctor was appalled, because, she said, Radhika's labor was three-fourths over.

So Radhika went home, packed her bags, and went to the hospital, where the doctor was already waiting. The doctor was expecting complications because Radhika was very underweight, and a Cesarean section was a distinct possibility. However, the delivery turned out to be very fast and easy, unaccompanied by any pain. In Radhika's own words, "It was like laying an egg." (The next delivery, when no mantra from Gurudev accompanied her labor, turned out to be very difficult.)[10]

Fetal Blessing

Asha Chakrabarty had been going through a very difficult time in her life. She was three months pregnant but still not yet showing much. She had not told many people about her pregnancy, including Gurudev. One day, she went to see Gurudev. The first thing he did when he saw her was put his fingers on her belly. At that very moment, she felt the first fetal movements of the unborn child.[11]

Reading About a Stranger's Death

My brother-in-law had just passed away. Never having met Swamiji in person (though I had attended his lectures), I had not told him about my recent loss.

Soon after the death, I was attending Swamiji's Upanishad class. Instead of starting his class in his characteristic way — by diving straight into the text as though he had finished the previous lecture just short moment before — he said:

"Every day we read in the newspaper: 'So and so has passed away . . . An accident took place on such and such a road . . .' — and we pay no attention, or give the news only scant attention. Then someone we know dies, and tears flow because of our attachment. After that, reading even about a stranger's death touches us."[12]

UNEXPECTED EVENTS

"Change the Aircraft!"

Asha Kamdar and others were accompanying Swamiji to Kathmandu. In the morning, they arrived by train in Calcutta, where they needed to make a connecting flight to Kathmandu around 4 o'clock that afternoon. They had made plans to spend the remaining hours at a devotee's house. Then they learned that a technical problem was delaying their connecting flight by one hour. Swamiji was taken to his host's house, where he had a big breakfast.

Before he went into his room to rest, Swamiji said, "I'll come out of my room at 2:30. You can go to the airport with the luggage then, and I'll follow."

At 1 p.m., quite unexpectedly, Swamiji came out of his bedroom. He walked onto the verandah overlooking the garden and sat down there to meet several devotees who had come to see him. Calling for Asha, he gave her some puzzling instructions:

"Call Indian Airlines. Tell them that I have to reach Kathmandu on time. I can't afford to be late. I can't miss the inauguration. Ask them to change the aircraft."

Asha recalls, "You don't question Swamiji, no matter how illogical his instruction may sound to you." She sat down near the phone and thought to herself, "Now what do I do? Whom do I ring up at Indian Airlines? If I tell them that Swamiji Chinmayananda wants the aircraft changed, they'll probably think I've lost my mind."

Just then one of his devotees from Calcutta arrived at the house. Asha explained the situation. He said, "By the way, you better start picking up your luggage and start moving. They have changed the aircraft, and the flight will be leaving on time after all!"

So they packed up everything and left for the airport.

Balan, Swamiji's secretary, because of the hurry to get to the airport on time, had neglected to put on any footwear (besides, he was used to going barefoot in South India). Then it turned out that he had no identification with him, which was a requirement at the airport.

At the ticket counter Asha explained the situation to a staff member: "We have a small problem. This gentleman has no footwear, nor does he have the right identification."

"Don't worry, we'll take care of it."

Somehow all difficulties were resolved, and they managed to get on board the plane on time. They landed successfully in Kathmandu — and on time to inaugurate the *yajna*.[13]

Miracle Photos

Mimi Robins used to attend many Chinmaya spiritual camps laden down with cameras, lenses, and other photographic equipment, taking every opportunity to photograph Swamiji and the camp delegates. In July 1993, a month before his *Mahasamadhi*, the camp delegates at the camp in Virginia were anxiously awaiting the arrival of Swamiji, who was flying in on a red-eye flight from the West Coast. The plane had landed, and the camp organizers had asked the camp delegates to be at Swamiji's cottage to greet him when he arrived. Since Mimi was the official photographer, she wandered up to the cottage early to inspect the light and the lay of the land. Suddenly a car drove up: Swamiji had already arrived!

Instead of the mass of delegates who had been planning to be there, only an intimate group of devotees had gathered at that point. Swamiji greeted each while Mimi aimed her camera to capture each of these precious moments of meeting.

Swamiji walked into the cottage with the camp organizers, and Mimi followed, camera in hand. As she began to mount the flash attachment to the camera to prepare for some indoor photographs, she noticed with a shock that the film speed setting on the camera was very wrong. The resulting photos would be so grossly overexposed as to be useless. She shook her head in dismay, readjusted the camera, and kept on shooting.

She told the people whose pictures she had been taking upon Swamiji's arrival not to expect any photos — unless there was a miracle.

And there was. When the film was processed, each photo had captured the magical moments of meeting, and with unusual intensity.[14]

Blank Tape

Gurudev's talks were being planned at Stanford University, Palo Alto, California. One devotee asked Gurudev for his permission to record the talks on audio tape, but Gurudev did not grant it. The devotee decided to record the talk anyway. He set up all the equipment, checked it carefully, and proceeded to record the talk. However, when he checked the tape at the end of the lecture, he found that it was still blank.[15]

Shivaratri Miracle

It was Shivaratri at Sandeepany Sadhanalaya in Mumbai. Although Gurudev usually retired to his room in the evening, that night he had said: "I'll come out at midnight and go to the temple. Whoever wants to come with me, come, but just remember one thing: Nobody should touch me!"

Those who were there that night recall that when Gurudev came out of his room, he was "shining," as though light were streaming from him. The brahmacharis and devotees who followed in his footsteps in their bare feet to the Jagadeeshwara Temple say that the spots where Gurudev had placed his feet were warm.[16]

"Be Careful What You Wish For!"

Nalini Browning was with Swamiji at the Sidhabari ashram and was helping him with his correspondence with the aid of the portable electric typewriter she had brought with her from the United States. Then one day the battery in the typewriter went dead, and no quick solution was in sight, since Sidhabari is situated in quite a remote spot.

While she was sitting with Swamiji in his *kutiya*, with the incapacitated typewriter at her side, devotees streamed in and out of the room doing their prostrations, some bringing gifts. A devotee came in with a basket of fruit and offered it to Swamiji. In the middle of the basket were — inexplicably — some batteries, just the kind that Nalini required for her electric typewriter.

"Strange," said Nalini, "I was just now thinking that I'll need to get new batteries for my typewriter."

This kind of coincidence had been happening for several weeks to Nalini while she was at Sidhabari. Whenever an image came strongly in her mind, the object would somehow manifest itself. She'd think about wanting to eat a mango, and a mango would appear, unsought. Or she would be thinking about a glass of water, and Swamiji himself would pour her a glass from his own. Just now the batteries had arrived.

Swamiji's reply to her was: "This is Sidhabari. Whatever you wish for comes true. So be careful what you wish for!"[17]

Thwarted Plans

A woman devotee had made a vow to do a pilgrimage to Gangotri. Before making final preparations, she asked Swamiji, "Swamiji, shall I go to Gangotri now?"

"Yes, go," said Swamiji.

So she made all her final preparations, set the date, and called Swamiji to let him know about her plans.

"I'm going, Swamiji," she said.

To her surprise, his answer was, "No, you're not."

She was deeply disappointed. She had made a vow, her guru had even approved her going, and now he had said "No!" Still, obedient to her guru, she stayed behind.

Only later did she find out that the bus she would have gone on had collapsed on the road.[18]

Miraculous events at times reached back into what our minds perceive as the realm of the deceased. Uttarkashi, the place where Gurudev learned the Upanishads from his own master, Swami Tapovanam, is a spot that has engendered many wondrous stories, among them:

"When *Brahman* Rides on Your Mind"

One day, Kalidas received the news that Gurudev was in Delhi on his way to Uttarkashi. He immediately decided to go to Delhi and Uttarkashi as well. When he walked into Gurudev's residence in New Delhi, he requested Gurudev's permission to travel with him to Uttarkashi. Gurudev said, "Just for that I've brought you here."

That day, he accompanied Gurudev as he attended to Chinmaya Mission business. After the business was concluded, Gurudev went on to a *bhiksha*, and Kalidas was left high and dry, not knowing where to go. The local brahmachari took him to his residence and said, "Now, if you wait until tomorrow to go to Uttarkashi, the same thing could happen. . . . There are only two cars going, and both are full."

Duly warned, Kalidas took a bus to Haridwar immediately after lunch, one day before Gurudev was to head out to Uttarkashi. The brahmachari explained to him how to get to Uttarkashi from Haridwar.

Kalidas had taken along Swami Tapovan's account of his Himalayan experiences, *Wanderings in the Himalayas*. On the way, he read the *Wanderings* book and let himself be guided by it. He was reading about Swami Tapovanji's travels from Rishikesh to Uttarkashi, and it seemed as though everything he was reading in the book was appearing outside before his eyes. For instance, as he was reading a passage about black monkeys, the bus slowed down. When he looked out the window, he saw a group of black monkeys by the roadside!

Once in Uttarkashi, Kalidas headed for Ujeli, where the *mahatmas* live. As he was going up the slope, he saw a *mahatma* walking toward him. From the way he was wearing his *dhoti*, Kalidas surmised that the *mahatma* was from the state of Kerala. His face was serene, aglow with the luster of spirituality. Kalidas greeted him and asked, "Where is Tapovan Kuti?" — in his mother tongue, Malayalam, the language spoken in Kerala.

"Just enter that brick-colored gate," the *mahatma* pointed, replying in the same tongue.

When he entered Tapovan Kuti, he found a room with the door open. Inside was a cot covered with a saffron cloth. Placed on it was an oil lamp with a steady flame. He sat down there, and with no conscious volition was drawn into deep meditation. He was shaken out of his trance when the ashram caretakers arrived.

"How did you come in here?" they asked. "You are not supposed to be entering here. This room is kept closed."

"The door was wide open, so I entered," said Kalidas.

Later, when Kalidas went into the *satsang* hall, he saw a picture of someone on the wall. He realized it was the same person he had just met on the slope who had given him directions. He was informed that it was Swami Tapovanji Maharaj.

Next morning, Swami Govindagiri, a disciple of Swami Tapovanam who had served and cared for his needs from the day Tapovanji arrived in the Himalayas until the end, asked Kalidas to go and have *darshan* at the Saumya Kashisha Temple. He instructed Kalidas to carry a vessel of Ganges water and some flowers and perform an *abhisheka* [ritual bathing of an idol] on the *Sivalingam* at the temple.

As Kalidas neared the road, he saw a car approaching. Gurudev was in the front seat waving out to him.

"Hi, Kali! You've already reached!" Gurudev stepped out of the car and hugged him.

Involuntarily, the Ganges water and flowers fell at Gurudev's feet. The *abhisheka* intended for Saumya Kashisha had taken place at Gurudev's feet!

Holding Kalidas tight, his beard tickling Kalidas' cheek, Gurudev started walking up the slope. Kalidas was choked with emotion, silent.

"So, you've seen him!" asked Gurudev.

"Yes, Swamiji."

"That is why I sent you one day earlier," said Gurudev.

"Swamiji, *how* could this happen?" asked Kalidas.

"This happens," said Gurudev, "when *Brahman* rides on your mind."

"In that case," said Kalidas, "after so many years when everyone says that you also have had *Mahasamadhi* and have gone, will I be able to see you like I've seen him?"

"Guaranteed!" said Gurudev. "When *this* happens, I will walk in front of you — kudu, kudu, . . ." — he made a clicking sound signifying how effortlessly he would manifest his presence in the future after he had left his earthly frame.[19]

The Photograph Speaks

The mother of Radhika Krishnakumar's friend had been in perfect health, but one day she felt some discomfort and sat down on her bed, asking that a photo of Gurudev be placed in front of her. She looked at it and died, very peacefully.

Her daughter felt very disturbed, and was anxious about whether her mother's soul was at peace. "I want to see some sign that Gurudev is taking care of her," she said to her friend Radhika.

The next day, while clearing her attic, Radhika found a photograph she had never seen. Who took it? How did it get into her attic? It was a photo of Gurudev in *satsang* with a large group of devotees. The friend's mother and Gurudev were looking at each other, in clear focus. Every other person in the photograph was out of focus. She gave the photograph to her friend, convinced that the sign that her friend had been looking for had, indeed, been given.[20]

In Gurudev's presence, the fulfillment of unspoken wishes was beyond counting. Especially dramatic was the way people's questions about the teaching got answered even when they were never asked out loud. Such reading of unspoken questions was especially obvious to first-time listeners at Gurudev's lectures. We sat and listened; as we listened, questions would arise that began to agitate our minds. Either later in that same lecture or the first thing at the next day's lecture, the very questions tormenting us would be answered in full.

Yet, when we asked him about his seeming ability to read our minds, his answer was, "*Who would want to waste their time raking through the garbage in your minds?*"

When we persisted that he did, indeed, often answer our unasked questions, he would say:

> *Yes, that will happen. That's the way the universe works.*
>
> *When a lesson is to be learned, the appropriate situation arrives. A question is there, then the answer comes. It's not from an effort or some trick on my part; I am an instrument. Sometimes the solution could come from a stranger on the bus. But because I am a swami, everyone thinks I'm using some special power. Because of certain strong desires of some student, the answer spontaneously manifests through me.*[21]

A Few Strides of Good Luck

Back in the 1960s, Rama Chander and his wife were trying to sell some land they owned because they were passing through a very difficult time financially. Although they badly needed the potential income from the sale, all offers came in very low and were unacceptable.

Rama's mother, who was very devoted to Swamiji, offered some of the land as a donation to Chinmaya Mission. When Swamiji came to view the land, they asked him, "Swamiji, how much land do you need?"

He answered by walking the length of breadth of the required piece of land with his long and stately strides.

Soon thereafter, someone offered a very good price for the entire parcel. Rama wrote to Swamiji: "What shall we do?"

He answered: "Go ahead and sell the land. Give a donation to the Mission equivalent to the portion of land we had marked off as your donation."

Rama and his family have no doubts that Swamiji's blessings made the sale of the land possible, thus saving their family from grave hardship.[22]

Stories of miracles and blessings continue to flow from devotees' mouths and pens. Some stories are told, some still kept secretly sequestered in people's hearts. And yet the greatest miracle may be how Swamiji transformed the seeming insignificance of life's events into moments of splendor and wisdom and miraculous being. "See the Lord playing through everyone and everything," he repeated in many ways. "That is the true miracle of life."

*Greatness is not
in what we do,
but it is in
how we do what we do.*

GREATNESS IN SMALL THINGS

"Gurudev's greatness showed in every little thing. In big things everybody can show greatness, but Gurudev showed greatness even in small things," says Swami Tejomayananda.

NONSTOP TEACHING, NONSTOP LOVING

Swami Sreedharananda, the *acharya*-in-charge at Tamil Sandeepany, where the Vedanta course is taught in the Tamil language, tells what prompted him to decide to dedicate his life to full-time Chinmaya Mission work:

Turning Point

Gurudev had called us Chyksters [youth workers in Chinmaya Mission] to Sidhabari to stage a sound-and-light program on the *Ramayana*. One of the shows brought out Gurudev's penchant for details. He remarked to a performer playing Ravana that he should not have gone up the stage with footwear in a particular scene where Ravana was to worship Shiva, as Ravana was a great devotee of Shiva. No one else had noticed the lapse.

Then, while we were working for Hanumanji's *Kumbha Abhisheka* [a ritual bathing of the idol], Gurudev came to inspect the preparations at 9:30 p.m., 11:30 p.m., and again at 1:30 a.m., when he insisted that we all go to sleep. But what really moved me was that he taught the next morning's meditation class — while we missed it.

So Sidhabari was the turning point when I decided that I would work full-time for the Mission.[1]

Many times Gurudev surprised us with his awareness of the practical aspects of existence, be it in the kitchen or on the road, or relating to the householder's everyday trials at home or irritations in the office. Swami Chidananda of Chinmaya Mission recounts this incident:

Wrong Side of the Road

Harish Chinai is a young man living in the United States. While he was in Mumbai on vacation, his family hosted Swamiji during a *yajna*. The young fellow had the privilege of doing many small acts of service to the Master. He drove Swamiji's car to the morning classes also. One morning, as he was driving the vehicle with Gurudev sitting at his left, Gurudev suddenly reached over to the steering wheel and turned it himself, pulling the car to the other side of the road. Harish was shocked. However, in an instant he realized that Swamiji had saved him from an accident. The young man from the States was driving on the right side of the road, forgetting the difference between the United States and India![2]

A Pencil's Worth

One time Swamiji could not find a small pencil some 2.5 inches in length. He made Asha Chakrabarty search his entire luggage to find it.

She finally found it, and he was very happy she did. He then meticulously sharpened it and put it in its place. "He lived an austere life even in the midst of luxury," comments Asha.[3]

Pappadam Healing

It was banquet time at the end of a camp, and Swamiji was sitting in a horseshoe table formation with the camp delegates. As one young camp member, my younger daughter, aged six, was getting up from her seat to go see him, a man happened to step on her foot.

She rushed over to Swamiji with tears in her eyes and indignation in her voice, "Swamiji, he stepped on me!" she screamed for the whole gathering to hear.

Swamiji took a *pappadam* from his plate, leaned very close to her, and whispered in her ear, "Here, eat a piece of this and your pain will disappear immediately!"

She took one bite and became calm within the span of a second.[4]

Playing with One's *Prarabdha*

Bharati Sukhatankar was helping Swamiji pack. Giving her his cufflinks, he said, "There will be four bags there. Look for one small plastic bag inside a larger plastic bag. Put the cufflinks in the small empty bag."

Bharati remembered some cufflinks that Swamiji had had with a beautiful image of orchids pressed into them. She didn't see them in the suitcase.

"Swamiji, whatever happened to the cufflinks with the engraved orchids?"

Swamiji replied, "My dear, you must learn to play with your *prarabdha* [that portion of one's past karmas that is being lived out in one's current life]. I know the art. You don't."

It was Swamiji's *prarabdha* to receive things from others: gold cufflinks, silver-knobbed *chappals*, silver-tipped canes, gold chains — but he just continued to give them away, playing with his *prarabdha* with ease and joy.[5]

All-Seeing Eyes

In the early days of knowing Gurudev, before she started to serve him as assistant, Padmashree of Bangalore was traveling with him on a train journey. Gurudev was handing out *prasad* to everyone when Padma walked from her cabin toward Gurudev's cabin. She was standing behind him when Gurudev reached his hand behind his back with a fruit in it. Padma was not sure if it was meant for her, for she had just then silently walked in, with Gurudev's back turned to her.

But Gurudev continued to hold his hand behind his back and said, "I don't have to turn around to know who is behind me!"[6]

The Nature of Intuition

A *satsang* was in progress at the ashram in Sidhabari, with people sitting around Gurudev after lunch outside his *kutiya.*

A woman devotee asked, "What is intuition, Swamiji?"

Swamiji looked at the sky and was silent.

The woman repeated her question.

"I don't know anything about intuition," said Swamiji.

Again he was silent, looking at the sky.

Then he said: "You see, it is like this: Countless radio stations are transmitting messages all the time. If your radio is not tuned to any station, all you get is incoherent noise. But when you tune in to one of them, you can get clear, pure music or news or some other program. The radio stations are transmitting non-stop. It is a matter of tuning in."

He looked around and again repeated, "But what do I know about intuition?"[7]

Reading Minds

An *upanayana* ceremony [a youth's formal initiation into Vedic study] was being planned for the son of a devotee. Accompanying the family was a psychic from Delhi who could read minds.

After the ceremony, a group of devotees were sitting around Swamiji in the temple. He said, "This pundit can tell the future. If anyone is interested, go and ask Punditji." The pundit was sitting at Swamiji's feet.

Swamiji, laughing, showed his palms to the pundit and said, "Tell my future; read my hand!"

"It is clear," was the pundit's answer. "The whole future of the world is resting in your palms."

Swamiji laughed, "How do you know?"

"Of course, everyone knows that," said the pundit.

Then someone approached the pundit with a question, but the pundit looked at Swamiji, prostrated, and said, "In your presence, sitting so close to you, I can't do it." He asked Swamiji's permission to move to the other side of the temple and started his readings there.

The devotees who had gathered around Swamiji, fascinated by the pundit's powers, asked, "Swamiji, how does he do it?"

"It is one of the lower *siddhis* [powers]," answered Swamiji. "In spiritual evolution, this is only kindergarten play."[8]

A Mistimed Question

At a large *satsang* in Lucknow, a devotee in the group was singing when one woman decided to weave through the entire crowd of people sitting on the floor and settle herself down next to Swamiji. She whispered something in his ear. When the song was finished, Swamiji said:

"Now, *Amma*, repeat your question for all of us to hear."

"Swamiji, I've heard somewhere that Krishna and Subhadra were brother and sister, but from different mothers. Is that true?"

Swamiji was visibly angry and shouted:

"How should I know? I was not the midwife at that time!"

Then he added in a more gentle voice:

"*Amma*, what does it matter whether they had the same mother or not? You are searching for Krishna. Who the mother is or father is should make no difference."[9]

Not a Word About No Salt

Indra Advani had cooked Swamiji's lunch, but had unwittingly left salt out of the *panir* [soft cheese cubes or balls], not having tasted the food before serving it to Swamiji, as is the custom when serving saints. (Tradition demands that the guest be the first to eat the food.)

Swamiji finished the meal without a word about the taste.

Indra asked, "Swamiji, may I give you some more *panir*?"

"Yes," he said, "and add a little salt this time."[10]

Sour Memories Sweetened

A devotee in San Jose, California, had prepared a meal for Gurudev, which he ate without comment. When he was eating the sweets she had prepared for dessert, he handed a morsel to her also. She took one bite: It was sour!

The woman felt sad that her meal for him had not been perfect.

At her last *bhiksha* for Swamiji before he passed from this plane, she again had prepared some sweets for him. He gave her and another devotee a morsel to taste.

"All candies in the world cannot compare with these *laddhus*," he said — sweetening all of her sour memories from the past.[11]

Swami Dheerananda remembers how even a small, seemingly insignificant act turned out for him to be a mind-transforming experience — in the presence of his guru:

The Touch of His Hand

Chinmaya Mission Hyderabad grandly celebrated Sri Gurdev's birthday on May 8, 1993. Sri Gurudev asked me to sit next to him at the *bhiksha*. When the devotees announced they had a cake for Sri Gurudev, he exclaimed, "Cake for me?! Come, bring it here!" Pointing to me, he said: "You cut it!"

When Sri Gurudev says something, there can be no hesitation or second thought. I rushed to the wash basin to wash my hands and received the knife when I returned. Then alone did I notice that, in my haste, the top of my hand had been left unclean. I was already holding the knife and could not easily return to the wash basin for a second washing. I felt so embarrassed.

At that moment, Sri Gurudev placed his gentle but firm hand over mine. The moment I felt his touch, I forgot my embarrassment and even my hand. I felt his power using my hand to cut the cake. He worked *through* me; his hand was cutting the cake *through* my hand. I totally surrendered to him.[12]

Gurudev was continually showered with gifts from his devotees — candy, books, toys, and many other items. Yet he seldom kept a gift for more than a few minutes. Often, within seconds it was already passed on to someone else —

and more likely than not, the chosen recipient was one for whom the gift was exquisitely suited:

A He-Man's Teddy Bear

One time, someone had given Gurudev a toy teddy bear, and he sat in his chair cuddling it. A woman devotee was eyeing the toy longingly, and asked Swamiji if she might be the one to inherit it from him.

"No," was his firm reply.

Then David Jones entered the room, a man who had spent more than twenty years battling the competitive scene of Hollywood film-making, used to giving directives to his film crews on location — a "man's man" in many respects.

"Here, this is for you," said Swamiji, handing the cuddly toy to David.[13]

Pranams to Ganesha

During an evening program at a Chinmaya Spiritual Camp, the Balavihar children put on a play about Ganesha. Arun and Asha Desai's daughter, who was only about four years old at the time, played the part of Ganesha. Her face was covered with a paper plate, which had been fashioned to look like an elephant's head. Since she couldn't see through her mask, someone led her onto the stage and sat her down in a chair. Then a group of children came onto the stage and sang their prayer to Ganesha. After the prayer, all the children left, but the young "Ganesha" remained. Unable to see through her mask, she no doubt was not even aware that she was alone on the stage, nor could she find her way off the stage alone.

Swamiji, who was sitting in the audience, as he always did at every cultural event at his spiritual camps, burst out laughing. Then he went up to the stage and touched the young "Ganesha's" feet and afterwards guided her down the steps.

Turning to the audience, he said: "The child is still innocent. She was fully the character she was playing."[14]

PhDs Are Few

At the end of a *satsang*, Swamiji was getting up to leave when someone asked him, "Swamiji, when Vedanta is so marvelous to the human ear, why are so few people attracted to it?"

Swamiji answered, "PhDs are not for the many."[15]

LITTLE GEMS

Some of Gurudev's teachings, comments, and sayings fit no ordinary categories — a touch of humor here, a bit of wisdom there. It seems that little was said by him that didn't leave a mark on the listener.

Unexpected Duties

Swamiji was holding a class on *Vivekacudamani* at Sandeepany Himalayas in Sidhabari in 1981. The ashram was just then being constructed, and the delegates were staying in temporary huts.

One day Swamiji arrived five minutes late to the lecture, very unusual for him, who was always so extremely precise and prompt. The subject of the lectures was *vasanas*, the inherent tendencies that rule our lives. While explaining the nature of *vasanas*, Swamiji said, "*Vasanas* make you do everything. They are very powerful. When Swami Sivananda was suggesting to me to take *sannyasa*, I went to Badrinath for 40 days to make the big decision whether to take *sannyasa* or not. Ultimately, I decided to take *sannyasa*. For what . . . .?

Swamiji made a dramatic pause.

" . . . to worry about your toilets and bathrooms!" he announced with a big laugh.

He eased the minds of the perplexed listeners: A problem had developed with the bathroom facilities in the makeshift accommodations at the camp. The camp organizers had been discussing the problem with him when time for the class arrived. That had been the reason for his late arrival.[16]

Gurudev never tired of cracking jokes and setting up humorous situations. Whenever the opportunity arose to have some light-hearted fun, he grabbed it:

Fake Swami

People were used to seeing Bill Browning in rather casual clothes. A printer, he had spent more than twenty years doing printing for Chinmaya Mission publications. Many a time he arrived at Gurudev's spiritual camps with freshly printed camp souvenirs in tow, with hints of printer's ink still visible on his hands. For many years he had also been clean-shaven. Then, one time he arrived at a camp held at Humboldt State University in Northern California wearing a suit and sporting a new beard. Even Swamiji at first did not recognize him. When he did, he let out a yell of surprise and delight.

No one else recognized him either. Bill had tea with Swamiji, with people in an adjoining room looking on. Still, no one recognized the Bill they all knew. After tea, Swamiji led Bill into the room where the devotees had assembled for *satsang* and introduced him to the group:

"Here's my swami friend from India," he said.

People came up to Bill and greeted him with folded hands.

After the two had had their fun, Bill's identity was revealed, but Swamiji continued to call him "Swami Pressananda" for the rest of the camp.[17]

Overcoat Memories

During one of his early San Francisco *yajnas*, Gurudev stayed at a motel by the Pacific Ocean called Seal Rock Motel. I often visited him there to join in *satsang* or to help with various tasks. In those days, I used to wear a long black "maxi-coat," with double rows of silver buttons reminiscent of a military uniform. I remember being quite fond of that coat, especially liking to wear it to Chinmaya Mission functions because it reached down to the floor.

Twenty years later, Gurudev was giving *satsang* at Sandeepany San Jose in California. As I walked into the *satsang* room, I folded away the overcoat in which I had arrived.

"Thank God you're not wearing that ugly coat you used to wear to Seal Rock! Remember Seal Rock?" exclaimed Gurudev.

I was aghast that he had remembered such a small detail — and laughed out loud at this loving slap that reached back twenty years![18]

Tea from a Saucer

An old-time devotee, Urmila, was watching Swamiji sipping tea, then saw him pour tea on his saucer and slurp it up.

"Swamiji," exclaimed Urmila, "I thought I'd never see you doing that!"

"Let me tell you a story," said Swamiji. "Queen Victoria was entertaining an Indian prince when the prince poured his tea on the saucer and drank from it. All the British noblemen looked at the Queen aghast, wondering what she would do, because etiquette had just been breached. The Queen, with a regal air, poured tea on her saucer and drank from it!"

Then Swamiji looked meaningfully at Urmila and said: "But she was a queen!"[19]

Swamiji almost never missed an opportunity to tease people who had managed to accumulate a little extra body weight:

Effect Without a Cause

As it often happens when there are well-fed people around Swamiji, the talk turned to food, with two of us stoutly (pun intended) declaring that a third devotee ate much more than we did (which is probably true anyway). At which Swamiji looked gravely at my companion and said, "Oho! So you are the effect without a cause!"[20]

Untrustworthy Tea-Maker

Gurudev was staying at the home of Rajendra and Malti Prasad in Palo Alto, California. One day, Raj was preparing tea for him, with Raj at one side of the kitchen counter, Swamiji at the other.

Swamiji took a sip of his tea and then asked Raj, "Do you take tea?"

"Yes, Swamiji."

"Do you take sugar in your tea?"

"Yes, Swamiji."

"Put another spoonful in your cup," instructed Swamiji.

Raj added a spoonful of sugar and took a sip: The tea was salty! He had mistaken the salt container for a sugar bowl.

"And you wanted me to drink that?" laughed Swamiji.

Later, whenever Raj tried to give Gurudev something, he would protest, "No, no — nothing from him. I don't trust his tea!"[21]

Like an Army General

Swami Gangeshwarananda was 108 years old when Gurudev dedicated a *yajna* in his honor. Swamiji had great respect for this old, blind swami and visited him whenever he could. One time, Swamiji, with his *padukas* on, had just walked across some wooden planks over a canal and arrived at the blind swami's side without informing anyone.

"Chinmayananda, so you've come!" said Swami Gangeshwarananda.

Swamiji was curious how the blind swami had known that it was he who had arrived.

"The way you walk," answered Gangeshwaranandaji. "Only one swami walks like that, and it is Chinmayananda. You walk like an army general!"[22]

GOD AND GOD'S WORSHIP

"Like God," Gurudev said, *"the vision of God, too, is beyond words."* Yet he himself became, in this century, an incomparable master of painting the Goal of all our seeking in words of great sublimity. At times sublime and at times down-to-earth — as the spirit moved or the moment required — Swami Chinmayananda could capture the essence of divinity in the magic of words that transported the listeners' minds to previously unknown heights of understanding. Yet, minutes later, he could be seen stooping down to the height of a child in front of him, scooping her up his arms, pulling on her fingers one by one and joking, "We have to help God grow you b-i-g-g-e-r!"

He never failed to remind us that all of existence is woven through and through with the Divine Presence. During our initial listening at his lectures, many of us were pleasantly surprised about how freely he talked about the Divine Presence everywhere. He urged us not to confine God to the church or the temple or the mosque, but to realize His Presence in all places, in every part of our lives, public and most private, in the midst of seemingly mundane chores and activities, as well as in our most auspicious efforts.

> *"I am with everyone always, but I can express Myself and manifest Myself only when you keep quiet and dynamically silent, invoking Me with your alert expectation" — so says the Lord. "Give Him a chance, please" is the persistent request of all scriptures of the world.*

All Science Fulfilled

When Gopal Sarma first met Swami Chinmayananda in 1953, Swamiji was conducting a 41-day *Upanisad Jnana Yajna* on the *Mundaka Upanisad* in Chennai, India. This was the second *jnana yajna* of his teaching career, the first one having been a 91-day marathon *yajna* on the *Kena Upanisad* and *Katha Upanisad* in Poona, India.

In 1953, Gopal was studying for his Master's degree in Physics and was preparing for his final exam. Since Swamiji was very accessible in those early days, Gopal would spend precious hours with him exclusively, asking him any question that surfaced in his mind.

When Gopal had his first long interview with Swamiji in Spring 1953, he had his textbook on atomic physics with him. When he asked Swamiji how Vedanta is related to the findings of modern subatomic physics, in answer Swamiji wrote the following in the young student's book:

> *The State that enforces the laws of physics from a neutron to the sun is the State of Pure Consciousness, God! Realize this in and through the observed laws of physics. In this is all science fulfilled.*[1]

Only God!

After a lecture one day, a man went to Swamiji's hotel room to speak with him privately and told him about a vision he had had.

Swamiji said, "You understand that God supports everything, but you don't understand that everything *is* God."

"Sometimes I do understand that I am God," the man retorted.

"No! No! Not you! *Only* God!"[2]

When K. Hemalatha Ramachandra Reddy first met Swamiji in 1956, the first question timidly shot in the direction of the guru was about God:

God's Reality

Gurudev was sitting outside his room in an open space with four or five people around him and was talking, joking, and clearing their doubts. We went in and stood nearby. He looked at us and received us with a gleaming smile on his face. He closed his eyes for a moment and asked us to come and sit near him.

I was very nervous and hesitating to move. Swamiji roared like a lion and said, "Don't be timid! You must be bold. Come on! You have come all this way to meet me and clear your doubts. Why the hesitation then?"

My timidness disappeared. Suddenly, I went to him with full devotion and touched his feet with my forehead. Something happened within me; I felt some vibrations. I felt that I was before Sarveshvara in the Himalayas and did not know what was happening around me for a moment until I heard Swamiji's voice: "Hari Om!" . . .

I took courage literally in both hands and asked some questions:

"Swamiji, is there God? Did you see Him? If so, in what form?"

Swamiji answered, "There is God. There is no doubt about it. Yes, I have seen Him, but not in form. God is not a form. God is a state of consciousness. In order for the average man to conceive of the idea, a form is given. Our national flag is not the form of our country. It *represents* our country. Similarly, God in various forms, whether it is the cross or the crescent of Krishna, represents a state of consciousness to be reached."[3]

Calling the Lord

I was sitting by Swamiji's desk while he worked in his room, helping him with small tasks, when he suddenly shouted through the half-open door into the adjoining room, "Krishna! Krishna!" — beckoning a devotee by that name into the room, as he needed to consult with her about some detail. Then he pointed at the hair on his arm, which was standing straight up:

"See? Horripulations! That's how you should call Krishna!" he said. "Not Krishna, Krishna, . . . as we often hear in *satsangs* or on street corners." He imitated a weak, languid voice chanting with tepid enthusiasm. "When you're calling the Lord, you call Him with your whole being, until the hair stands up on your arm!"[4]

What Does *Brahman* Do?

Someone asked Swamiji at *satsang*:

"Does *Brahman* do anything?"

Swamiji's response was more than a simple yes or no:

"We look at the sun and say that the sun is shining. So we put doership on the sun. But what does the sun say? If anything, it says merely, 'I am.' That's all."[5]

God's Will

Swamiji had been talking in *satsang* about the idea of God's will being done on Earth. One listener, as she reflected upon the idea on her own, came to the realization that God's will is always being done anyway, whether we say or think, "Thy will be done" or not.

So next day in *satsang* she explained this new realization to Swamiji and wondered why we even needed to discuss God's will.

He laughed, "Yes, you're right! God's will will be done anyway, whether you agree to it or not, so it makes it much easier on you if you simply admit it and accept it!"[6]

Everyone Is Sri Krishna

It was October 1990 in Bangalore. Gurudev's *yajna* was going on in the heart of the city. It rained unusually heavily that year, and the roads were overrun with water. After the talk when we started our return journey in the car, we could not use the usual route. Gurudev's host decided to drive the car across the grounds to reach the other side. Swamiji did not know this. When he realized that the car was disturbing the dispersing crowd, he strongly objected.

As the car moved through the crowd, he rolled down the window, and with folded hands he said to the people walking by:

"Krishna, Krishna, I am very sorry to disturb you all. Sri Krishna may forgive me!"

He turned to us, the host family and myself, who were seated in the back seat, and said:

"Everyone who was listening was Sri Krishna Himself. He is the One in all. Who else speaks? Who else listens?"

We could not hold back the tears flowing from our eyes.[7]

Swamini Nishtananda (formerly Dr. Akhilam), a physician instrumental in starting the medical clinic for the local people near Sidhabari, Himachal Pradesh, the site of Gurudev's Sandeepany (Him), experienced a powerful lesson about the meaning of worship:

Delayed *Puja*

Swamini Nishtananda had, for some years, reservations about doing a *Pada Puja*, worship of the guru's feet. She thought that whatever worship she does, she should do in private, resisting the public nature of a *Pada Puja*. Thus, for already ten years she had never performed a *Pada Puja* for Gurudev.

Then, during the last year of Swamiji's life, she was sitting in *satsang* with him near his *kutiya* [residence] during a *Vivekacudamani* Camp there. Swamiji said to someone, "Tell the video people that the lecture will be held at 6 p.m., not 6:30. Inform the kitchen people also."

Someone asked, "From tomorrow onward, Swamiji?"

"No. *Now*!" And then he added in Sanskrit, "Any auspicious resolve must be carried out immediately."

The Sanskrit phrase suddenly convinced the Swamini that she must perform *Pada Puja*, to actualize a thought that had been gathering in her mind. She felt as though Swamiji had just given her a specific instruction, for her own personal use. So she went to the organizers, although she realized that little chance existed that an empty *bhiksha* slot was still available [a *Pada Puja* was traditionally combined with a *bhiksha*, an offering of food to the guru]. Fortunately, a vacancy existed for the next day. She realized that what his comment had meant was that if she had not immediately made arrangements for the *bhiksha*, that vacancy would have already been filled.

She told another devotee about her long "abstinence" from *Pada Puja* and her resolve to perform one now. In front of a large gathering, which included Swamiji, this fact was made public by her friend.

"Why did she do a *puja* ten years ago?" asked Swamiji.

Swamini Nishtananda corrected the impression, "Gurudev, I've *never* done one. I am doing a *Pada Puja* for the very first time now!"

"Yes," said Swamiji, "ten years ago she was a most extroverted young girl [she had been 58 then]!"

At the *Pada Puja*, Swamiji was in very deep meditation. "The whole atmosphere was surcharged with high spiritual vibrations," recalls the Swamini. "Everyone present felt the holiness of his presence." As the Swamini was garlanding Swamiji (while both of them had their eyes closed), he reached out and hugged her, a very unusual gesture during a *puja*.

In retrospect, the Swamini recalls: "He knew I was blocking myself from a great experience, that of worshipping his holy feet, because of false notions. He made the thought come up in me that I must perform the *puja*. He made me bow down so that he could bless me. There never would have been another opportunity. He made the 'most extroverted' part of me bend. Such was his great compassion. He gave without reservations, without counting the fitness of the person. Like sunlight and rain, he showered his Grace on all."

Some days later, when Swamiji was already at his next stop, he wrote to the Swamini:

> *In slow and steady steps move ahead in meditation till you and the world are wiped out. That is all worth striving for. If afterwards,* prarabdha *wants to express itself, let it; you are not concerned with it at all.*[8]

An Unexpected Answer

Bill Sheldon was reluctantly leaving a *satsang* with Swamiji because one of the *yajna* organizers needed a ride home. As he was leaving the room, discussions from the *satsang* were still rolling through his thoughts and continued to engross him as he shut the door behind him. In his mind, he asked Swamiji a question that was troubling him, "How do we *know* that the Lord is working in and through our lives? What proof is there?"

He then drove off in a car he had borrowed from another devotee, the trunk filled with books for the *yajna* hall. As he was going down a steep, winding road in the Berkeley hills, his brakes gave out and the car lurched over the embankment, heading toward the house just beyond the small front yard. However, the crash was averted — by a tree. The car literally ended up in the branches of a tree that sat at a lower elevation than the winding road.

The car was totally destroyed, but Bill and his passenger were left without a scratch. The fearsome collision had been cushioned by the branches of the tree. The tree had literally saved him — and Bill knew that his question had been answered.[9]

Heaven

At one of Swamiji's camps, a devotee asked him at *satsang*:

"Swamiji, what does one need to do to invoke an experience of *Brahmaloka* — Heaven?"

Swamiji gave no answer. Pindrop silence followed for some fifteen minutes. One could hear the leaves rustling outside.

Finally Swamiji said, looking at the questioner: "*Buddhu* [you fool], where do you think you've been for the last three weeks?"[10]

Heaven and Hell

A group of fanatical Christians, who had attended a talk of Swamiji's the night before, were determined to express their grievance over something he had said in the previous night's talk:

"Heaven and hell are not two distinct areas in space, but right here with us. They are the two states of our own mind."

They converged upon Swamiji during his evening walk and stood around him. The most rounded, muscular, and hairy one among them shot at Swamiji:

"Where is heaven and hell?"

"Right here in your own mind!" replied Swamiji.

The man came near to Swamiji, trembling with rage, and grabbed at his shirt: "Where . . . ???" He could not complete the sentence.

Swamiji laughed out loud and said, "Here open the doors of hell for you!"

The man stopped. He released his hold and stood amazed.

Another peal of laughter and Swamiji said: "And here open the gates of heaven for you!"[11]

Sin, Hell, and Heaven

"I am a sinner, Swamiji. You alone can save me. Save me, please!" The visitor had come to a *satsang* with Gurudev and had run forward to fall at the feet of the master. Tears streamed down his cheeks. He was clad in an expensive *dhoti* and *kurta*, and diamond rings gleamed from his fingers. He was evidently a well-to-do businessman, but his face was careworn, and his eyes were sunk deep in sorrow and misery.

"I am a sinner, Chinmayananda!" he repeated. "I have committed every kind of sin. Is there no redemption for me? Will I have to go to hell?"

Gurudev bent down graciously and lifted the man up. "Cheer up, Sitaram. Sit down. No one is beyond redemption. I promise: You will not *go* to hell. You don't have to."

Sitaram, reassured, slowly squatted on the floor and looked up at his guru's benign, smiling face.

"You will not *go* to hell, my son," Gurudev repeated, emphasizing the word *go*. "You are already there. You don't have to suffer any more punishment in hell, because your sins are punishing you even now."

Stroking his beard, Gurudev continued, "Sitaram, you have also to understand that man is not punished *for* his sins. Remember this! The whole thing is subjective. God does not have to punish you. The pangs of suffering following a sinful act are enough punishment. Man is punished *by* his sins. That state of suffering, in religious parlance, is called 'hell.' That is why you don't have to *go* to hell. You are already there."

"Then what are hell and heaven, Swamiji? Why do people talk of 'going' to heaven after death?" asked someone else in the room.

Gurudev replied, "Don't you speak of 'going to sleep' after getting to bed? Where do you 'go'? Do you have to take a flight to some other place when going to sleep? This is the limitation of language. The 'going' is not from one place to another, but from one *state* to another. While sleeping, one 'goes' from the state of waking to the state of sleeping, but in the same place. Similarly, heaven and hell are two states: the first, peaceful, serene, and blissful; the other, miserable, sorrowful, and painful. Both states are subjective and are experienced while one is living, not after death. Heaven is not a postmortem reward, nor is hell a postmortem punishment. Both are immediate, here and now!"

Sitaram, eyes closed, had been listening attentively. He now opened his eyes, still eager to get a specific answer to his own specific problem. He asked: "Then what should I *do* now, Swamiji?"

With a teasing smile, Gurudev replied: "Continue doing whatever you have been doing!"

To Sitaram's discomfiture, the entire roomful of people burst out laughing.

Gurudev bent down to pat Sitaram comfortingly: "Don't worry, I shall explain myself. Suppose you are traveling by car to Poona, and you suddenly find that you have missed the fork at Thane and are actually speeding along on the wrong road toward Nasik. What will you do? You are rushing at 70 miles per hour. If, on realizing your mistake, you rashly jam on your brakes, the car will smash into the roadside ditch; you will be destroyed. Hence, the right thing to do is to bring the car gently to a stop, turn it around, and retrace the road. But, note, you are still on the wrong road until you reach the junction with the right road, onto which you turn and drive toward your destination.

"In the same way, all these years you have been following the wrong road in life — acquiring, hoarding, aggrandizing, all 'sins,' as you say. You have been doing these things because those particular *vasanas* have been strong in you. If you change your way of life all of a sudden, your actions will pull you in one direction, and your tendencies will pull you in another. The resulting suppression and repression will probably land you in a lunatic asylum as a mental wreck. The tendencies are powerful. You should therefore continue your normal way of life, but at the same time make efforts to acquire good and noble values in life, which will form new tendencies and ultimately turn all your actions in the right direction. There is no use in just giving up your present way of life without acquiring positive virtues and values. That will merely be hypocrisy. Think!"[12]

In many lectures, Swamiji repeated this same truth: Heaven and hell are states of mind; liberation from these relative states means abidance in the supreme Reality, the One Consciousness that pervades all. *"In truth,"* he said in response to a devotee's question, *"there is no 'evolution of man.'"* Instead, he explained further:

There is only Consciousness — ever remaining luminous, or from time to time dimming Itself in the endless changing "states." Liberation is not a total obliteration of the individuality and its universe, but it is a state of abiding in the Reality, the Self, or pure Consciousness . . . the state, once reached, from which nobody ever returns.

EGO

Our life-long companion, the ego, was always at our throats, much loved by us and forever battered about by Swamiji. The more we resisted giving up our habitual companion, the more he insisted on reminding us of its presence, in ever-unique ways:

> *The flower must die to be the fruit. The dreamer must die to be the waker. One alone can be: ego must die to become the Self.*
>
> *The courage for this inner death — this total transformation, the secret energy for it, the mental preparedness for it — these are supplied by the words of the scriptures, the examples of the great masters.*

Swamiji was a master at making his disciples' egos squirm. Whenever an event presented itself to give him a chance to pounce on our egos, he would take good advantage of it. Very often he also brewed up a set of circumstances that would set us all in a quandary, test our attachments, and work our egos hard.

Roasted Ego

In 1988, when Swamiji was giving a *yajna* in Melbourne, I had the chance to make an afternoon snack for him. All through the week, I had had an unusual desire to cook something for Swamiji. Normally, I wouldn't even dream of replacing one of the tasty, expertly cooked Indian dishes that appeared before him daily with one of my own creations. I had neither the confidence nor the time to do the task justice. Then my chance came one afternoon, and I planned to cook some spinach pastries for him.

I washed the spinach six times to avoid any grit, bought the finest olive oil, the freshest filo pastry and ricotta cheese, and fresh herbs. I sweated over every detail and watched the pastry triangles bake until they were perfectly golden brown.

Swamiji came out from his afternoon nap in the best of spirits. With a mischievous grin on his face, he watched me as I fussed over arranging the little pastries and stirring his tea.

"What's this?" he asked as he peered interestedly at the snacks.

"Spinach triangles, Swamiji. It's a Greek recipe," I replied, heart in my mouth.

He ate one. "Mmmm," he said. He ate another and then another. "Not bad — delicious! You made these?"

By this time, I was quite rosy with pleasure. "Yes, Swamiji."

He looked at me intently, "What's in there?"

"Greek pastry, Swamiji — and ricotta cheese, spinach, and herbs."

"You really made them?" he asked.

By this time, I was getting a little put out by his questioning: "Yes, Swamiji!"

"You made the pastry dough?"

"Oh no, Swamiji, I bought that ready-made."

"Hmm. You made the cheese?"

"No, Swamiji, I bought that cheese."

"The spinach . . . ?"

"I got it at the market, Swamiji."

"So you made them?" He looked at me with that penetrating, loving, teasing gaze that strips away all the illusions and defenses of the ego, which has the habit of appropriating God's creation for its own glory.

"They're very good," he said with a twinkle in his eye.[1]

Spurned Meal

Some other Western devotees and I had worked all afternoon on preparing a *bhiksha* meal for Swamiji at a spiritual camp. I was feeling pretty good about myself because, next to the other Westerners in the group, I knew quite a bit more about Indian cooking, so I was the acclaimed expert. About an hour before the *bhiksha*, some Indian ladies came in to prepare Swamiji's tea, and, with the efficiency of experts, took over the kitchen in a blink of the eye, making unasked-for decisions for our crew and seriously interfering with our schedule for the evening meal. Trying to keep my calm, I proceeded with the final arrangements, along with the rest of the group. However, the tension was high, because preparing the meal had already been a challenge. Add to that the influx of the tea-ladies in an already crowded kitchen, and our nerves were on edge.

Finally it was time to serve the meal. Despite the nervousness, the long hours of work, and the unexpected and unasked-for culinary advice in the middle of our sincere preparations, the meal looked quite good, and we expectantly waited for Swamiji to start eating, hoping for a few words of encouragement. But his usual exuberance seemed to be at a low point that night — that is, until a devotee from a nearby town emerged from the shadows with a covered vessel in hand and said, "Swamiji, I have brought you *aviyal* [a specialty from his home state of Kerala]. May I give you some?"

"Of course!" said Swamiji, all exuberance now.

And he proceeded to praise that one dish lavishly, asking for additional helpings several times. In fact, most of the eating that evening was from that one imported dish only. Not a word was said about the meal we had been laboring over for hours.[2]

But one never knew what his reaction would be. If a certain reaction was expected, it was sure not to come:

Lavish Praise for Humble Beans

When a local devotee was hosting Swamiji at her home, I prepared one simple green bean dish for him to supplement the hostess' efforts and brought it for his lunch. I knew fully well that I could not compete with the hostess' culinary efforts and had no pretensions about the success of my own, but I wanted to contribute something, so I did. My simple bean dish received much lavish praise, while the hostess' generous spread of delicacies were eaten without a comment.[3]

Spurned Tea

I had prepared tea to take up to Swamiji's podium after meditation class. While others took a tea break in a specially designated area, Swamiji remained in the hall and took his tea there before the commencement of the lecture that was to follow.

Many people had already returned to their seats after their own cup of tea, many of them sitting cross-legged on the floor, and I had to weave through the entire throng, stepping carefully between bodies to finally reach him with intact tea cup in hand. I was very self-conscious of the whole procedure and wished with all my heart that I would get to the podium without a spill. When I got there, Swamiji took a sip and waved the tea away, an obvious rejection in front of the entire group. Shame-facedly I wove through the crowd again, back to the kitchen, to prepare a second cup of tea.[4]

Public Rejection

One devotee, during her early years with Gurudev, had made the decision to make arrangements to travel some distance to be with him for several days in another city. She felt overwhelmed with love for him and wanted to take every opportunity to be near him. When a trip was planned for Gurudev to pay his respects to another spiritual teacher in the area, she joined the group who would be accompanying him.

Gurudev looked at her sternly and said, without any further explanation, "You are *not* going!" So she stayed back, while others gathered around him to accompany him on the visit.

She was in despair. She wept hurtful tears for many long hours afterward. But as she wept, she felt her ego washing cleaner, her mind becoming lighter. She then realized what his four simple words had accomplished in lightening the load of her ego.[5]

However, when our thoughts were not attached to the result — the dish, the tea, or whatever else — Swamiji was all openness and poured out exuberant and lavish praise. After many years of watching him deal ego-blows to others and myself, it was quite clear that offerings of food, drink, and other things were accepted or rejected not because of his own want or liking, but as a means for teaching the bearer of the goods about attachment and ego.

Glass of Water

One time, on a rather sultry day, I watched Swamiji being offered a glass of water a number of times by a devotee, who was offering the refreshment with quite a bit of solicitude, but always with the same result: "No, I don't want it." The informal *satsang* continued. Then, only some short minutes later, I was suddenly overwhelmed with an overpowering feeling that Swamiji needed some water. Without giving it any thought or analyzing what this conviction might mean next to his obvious dismissal of water just minutes before, I rushed to the kitchen and brought him a glass of water. "Ahh," he breathed gratefully and took it without hesitation and downed it in a few quick gulps.[6]

Attachment to Serving

Veronica Hausman had assumed the job at one *yajna* of taking care of Swamiji's footstool, slippers, and cane at the end of each lecture. Every night, as soon as the lecture was over, she would unobtrusively position herself next to where Swamiji was sitting, move the footstool out of his path, place his *chappals* in front of his feet, and hand him his cane. In order to do this, she took a seat on the floor very close to the front, near his seat.

One night, another woman had taken her spot. When the time came to help Swamiji with the footstool, she said to herself, "Don't worry. The person who took my seat will take care of things." But her rational mind didn't listen to her own advice, and at the end of the lecture she got up from her seat, positioned herself in front of the other woman, and crawled toward the stage to be in position to move the stool.

Swamiji stood up, and she took the footstool away and handed him his cane and *chappals*. But instead of walking off the stage, he sat back down in his chair and said in a very loud voice for the entire hall to hear: "If I had remained standing, she would have taken away my chair also!"

On several other occasions, at *satsang*s and *bhikshas*, Swamiji repeated the same line in her presence: "If I had remained standing, she would have taken away my chair also" — just to make sure that Veronica got the message that attachment has no place in doing any kind of work, including service to the guru.[7]

Taking Things for Granted

"One never knew whether our experience with Swamiji would be one of the ego being hugged or kicked," says Robyn Thompson, who spent many hours in Swamiji's proximity as one of his assistants during his lecture tours. Since she spent so much time near him, there were repeated occasions to become the subject of his ego-blasting exercises. Whenever she began to take certain aspects of her relationship with Swamiji for granted — that is, when she began to feel that a certain mode in which he responded to her would remain constant — he would abruptly change his ways, or, in her own words, he would "hit the ego in the bull's eye."

During certain periods, Swamiji would be very demonstrative in the attention he gave her. As a result, a certain expectation settled into her thoughts: "Gurudev will respond to me with a smile, hug . . ." As soon as such expectant thoughts began to form in her mind, Swamiji's response would turn out to be just the opposite. "But as soon as I would let go of everything," Robyn says, "such as the tears from a hurt or feelings of rejection, there he would be — smiling, full of love, as though nothing had ever been wrong."[8]

Guru as Mirror

Brahmacharini Robyn Thompson says that it took some years for her to realize the utter truth of the guru's mirror. One day, someone who had been with Swamiji for many years said to her:

"Don't you know that he reflects yourself back to you?"

She now became very alert to how that mirror worked: "I remember occasions when I approached him in a tense, closed mood, and he would respond likewise: His replies would be short and to the point, and my time with him would be cut short as well. In contrast, if I went to him in an open, happy mood, not asking for anything, not expecting any particular result, he would respond with hugs and easy conversation — in other words, the way I myself was feeling."[9]

Gurudev served as our mirror in many ways. If, for instance, a worker in Chinmaya Mission ran into organizational problems and wrote him a letter filled with complaints about another person, he had the habit of sending the complaint straight to the person who was being complained about. When the original writer discovered what had happened, the image in the mirror became frighteningly clear: a face etched with negative lines, a mind lacking in forthrightness. Those who suffered through such humiliation once, thought twice before sending scalding letters to Gurudev.

Sometimes the ego lessons were very subtle. When Gurudev saw that our hearts were closed or our minds suffused with negativities, he turned his usual enthusiasm and lovingness to cold indifference. That hurt as much as an outright mental slap.

Ganges Water for Everyone

Veronica Hausman had gone to Uttarkashi to spend some time at Gurudev's ashram there. Someone in India suggested that she take some Ganges water back with her so that she could wash Gurudev's feet with it upon her return to the United States. So she poured Ganges water into a bottle and carried it with her throughout her journey home — first to Sidhabari, then Delhi, Mumbai, London, and finally to Philadelphia, where she went to meet Gurudev.

When she saw Gurudev, she walked up to him and prostrated. As she got up from her bending position, she got entangled in his robe. She herself felt quite flustered about the incident, but Gurudev went calmly to his room as though nothing unusual had happened. For days thereafter, she waited for just the right moment to bring out her Ganges water and wash his feet, but Gurudev made a point of ignoring her. She said to herself, "I'm doing something wrong."

Then one day Swamiji told a beautiful story, and she felt her heart opening up. That day she said to Swamiji: "I have brought some Ganges water for you." She put some water in his hand.

"Share this with everyone," said Swamiji, and she did.

Hers was a double lesson, Veronica recalls, not only about an opened heart but also that Gurudev wanted his devotees not just to look to him as someone to serve but to look at everyone as the focus of their caring and love.[10]

Who Is Who?

One devotee recalls how she was sitting with Gurudev in his room when a telephone call arrived for him. As he began to talk on the phone, she was overwhelmed with the feeling that he had turned into *her*. He was not just a mirror: He was actually acting her out! On the phone, he had suddenly become the "garrulous monk," carrying on the sort of conversation that she recognized as her very own — many words, much detail. He was mimicking back to her her own mind, her own ways.[11]

The Frightened Ego

It was a few weeks after some intense private *sadhana*. One day, I began to sense an unseen presence hovering right by my shoulder, a foreboding presence of unknown origin. This sort of experience was totally new to me and made me fearful, especially so because my children were small, and I was alone with them at home while my husband was away on an overseas assignment. I didn't know where my strange experiences were leading, and I wasn't sure if this phenomenon might interfere with my motherly duties.

Fortunately, in a few days, the unusual presence disappeared. However, I resolved to ask Gurudev what it all meant when I next saw him.

The annual summer *yajna* arrived, and I had many opportunities to spend much time with Gurudev. I tuned in to his presence very deeply. As often happened near him, all previous doubts disappeared, including my big question about "the presence." Now and then I recalled in some far corner of my mind that I had had a serious question to ask him, but, blissfully content, I was totally disinclined to ask him anything.

Then one day as Swamiji met me in a hallway of the residence he was staying in, he looked at me intensely and said:

"There's nothing to fear. It's all right. There's no harm to you."

For a moment I wasn't sure what he meant.

Then he continued, "All that was going on was your ego getting a little scared that you may want to squash it! It was just trying to give you a fright so you would quit your *sadhana*! Nothing to worry about."

Now I realized that he was referring to my earlier frightening experiences, though I had breathed not a word about the incident to him.[12]

Ultimately, Gurudev said, ego binds us because of attachment:

> *The entire* Bhagavad Gita *is a screaming cry to end ego and egocentric desires and then relate yourself to things, beings, and situations. Then you are free to give love, to show anger, to express tenderness — without getting yourself involved, bound, tied down, gagged by your own emotions.*
>
> *Love, but let not your love twist your arm. Eat food, but let not food eat you. You drive life — let not life drive you. This is detachment. End ego and egocentric desires — and then act.*

SADHANA

"Whatever leads man to God is acceptable," Gurudev said. *"Whatever stands in the way of realizing God should be rejected totally and unceremoniously."* And to be a sincere spiritual seeker, he added, one must *"never ever, ever, ever pay attention to the world."*

Yet he cautioned us:

> *What we are seeking is not a thing or a being. It is not an objective experience; it is a movement, a shift in consciousness. Our own values — and so our attachments to this present plane of consciousness — alone are that which obstructs us from moving into the altered state of consciousness.*

And again:

> *The Infinite can never be gained by the finite. All* sadhanas *are finite, indeed. . . .* Sadhana *only prepares us. It quiets our mind, calms the intellect, purges the* vasanas. *And also, positively, the seeker fills himself with the assertion of the holiness of the Self — its beauty, bliss, beatitude.*

But Swamiji continued to give us encouragement that all the efforts were worth it, for, he said, "Remember, every saint had a past, and every sinner has a future." And then he added with a chuckle, "And if the kind of fellow that I used to be in the past could make it, anyone can!"

Divine Prescription

Asha Chakrabarty, a physician, once said to Swamiji, "We're so busy with our everyday lives. How do we do our *sadhana*?"

"It's not difficult at all," he answered. "Every time you write a prescription, just say, "*Om Namo Narayana*." Then tell me if your patient does not recover!"

Dr. Chakrabarty says today, "Those words of Swamiji's have stayed with me all this time, guiding my work and my *sadhana*."[1]

BEING QUIET, ALERT, VIGILANT

Gurudev never tired of reminding us, in and out of lecture, "Be quiet, alert, and vigilant." But he added with a twinkle in his eye, "Sounds simple. Try it. Most of us can't do it. When our minds are quiet, our physical bodies are asleep. The mind that can achieve a state of quietude while being alert and vigilant is the meditating mind. And the meditating mind is the one that can realize the presence of the Lord."

An important part of being alert is leaving behind all mechanical action, Gurudev reminded us repeatedly. He would say, "Learn to act — don't react." And again, "Know what you do and then do it. If you don't know, don't do it."

If we appropriately heeded his words and were alert in his presence, we picked up invaluable tips about our own *sadhana*.

Some of those teachings were, in fact, about alertness itself.

Alertness and Intensity

Gurudev had been invited to give a talk at a church some distance from Napa in northern California. Some of us who had been attending his regular *yajna* talks in Napa for a week decided to accompany him to the lecture. I was driving a small Volkswagen then and had committed to transporting several passengers to the destination, the exact address of which was unknown to me. Swamiji's driver assured me that if I followed him, I could get to the church easily.

But the trip was far from easy. Swamiji's car went very fast, and my small Volkswagen and rather conservative driving style made it difficult to keep up with him. Yet I had no choice but to speed, as otherwise I would have lost all chance of finding the venue of the lecture, so I dashed over the country roads near Napa at speeds quite unusual for me, turning corners with squealing wheels, my mind pushed to a new limit of intense alertness.

As I walked into the church, my mind was fairly buzzing with the heightened state of alertness that the fast chase had elicited. I sat down and listened to Swamiji's lecture with such an unusual intensity that I felt as though every sense and every part of my mind had been honed to a new precision. As a result, it was an incomparable lecture experience for me. At the end of it, Swamiji gave me a long, knowing look. Then I understood: This kind of alertness is what he wants out of me all the time!

Some hours later I learned from the driver of Swamiji's car that during the "chase" Swamiji had turned the rear-view mirror away from the driver and toward himself, so that he could watch the progress of the hapless devotee-driver behind him![2]

Those who drove Swamiji to and from his talks became quite familiar with his love of speed while traveling in the car. He was always urging his drivers to step on the gas pedal a little more, turning many a sluggish disciple into a picture of alertness.

Narain Bhatia, Chief Executive of Chinmaya Mission, tells this story:

Jet Speed

After his heart bypass surgery in 1980, Gurudev had returned to India and was back to normal routine. A devotee from Thane invited him for a noon *bhiksha*. He was a young man from a middle-class family who neither owned a car, nor had anyone else whom he could request to drive Gurudev to his residence. Then he thought of me and requested me to drive Gurudev to the *bhiksha*.

I didn't want to lose such an opportunity to drive Gurudev, to sit next to him on a fairly long drive from the city to the distant Thane suburb. As luck would have it, a day before the *bhiksha*, the differential gear of my car started emanating constant noise. Conscious that Gurudev would have a constant disturbance throughout the journey, I tried to get it rectified, but it was too late in the day to have the repairs done.

When we started our journey, the noise of the differential gear was immediately apparent to Gurudev. He commented that the car was fitted with a new musical instrument! To curtail embarrassment, I had no choice but to slow down a bit.

After the *bhiksha*, we were returning via the pipeline road to the ashram when Gurudev looked at his watch. It was close to 2:30 p.m. My slow speed was eating into his afternoon rest time. Just then an airplane appeared in the sky as it was descending toward the Mumbai airport. Gurudev said:

"Narain, can you see that airplane hurrying to reach its destination — Bombay?"

"Yes, Swamiji," I replied.

Swamiji continued: "In the morning it went to London, had breakfast, and is now coming back for lunch. But we are yet to reach the ashram!"

The message was clear: that Gurudev wanted "jet speed" in his missionary work.[3]

Swamiji called alertness the price of Self-unfoldment. Over the years, he caught many of us off-guard, as we often did not put his alertness teaching into practice. So he continued to nudge us at every opportunity.

No Slouching Allowed

Swamiji was having lunch in the main dining hall at Sandeepany Sadhanalaya, with students serving him the meal. The serving had just finished, and several of the students were standing behind a table near the wall, which was just a few inches from their backs.

During a slight pause before grace was chanted, one student relaxed a little and leaned back to let the wall support her. At that moment she happened to look at Swamiji: He was gazing straight at her. He threw back his shoulders and straightened his back purposefully. The student received the message and immediately returned to an erect posture away from the wall.

Alertness at all times, in matters large and small, seemed to be the message.[4]

Nothing was ever left unnoticed by Gurudev. He was his own best example of the "alert and vigilant" mind he urged us all to cultivate. Those around him were constantly amazed at what details he picked up and commented on, whether relating to householders' lives, the political scene, the physical surroundings he found himself in, or devotees' actions and behaviors. Those who worked with him on various construction projects at Chinmaya Mission centers around the world attest to the fact that no detail was too small for him, no expertise out of his domain. Whether architectural engineers were sharing with him their plans for a new temple or he was watching workers laying bricks, he always had specific directions to impart, which in retrospect always turned out to have been just the thing that was most needed.

UNEXPECTED TEACHINGS

Desire for Sweets

Isabel Taylor recalls a conversation during an airplane journey she shared with Swamiji that went something like this:

Isabel: "Swamiji, ego is desire, right?"

Swamiji: "Right."

I: "Self-realized beings don't have any desires, right?"

S: "Yes."

I: "Then how come you keep asking for sweets and things that are bad for your body?"

S: "The body always has desires, but it doesn't matter."

I: "Then why do we spend so much time on giving you medicines?"

S: No answer.

Two days later at lunch at a devotee's home, Swamiji suddenly burst out laughing while sitting at the lunch table. Nothing had been said to prompt such a response.

"What's so funny?" those sitting around him inquired.

"The other day Isabel asked me if I had a big ego. She asked how is it possible for a person without a big ego to still desire sweet things."

Immediately, pindrop silence settled over the people gathered around him. Swamiji was the only one making a sound: His laughing continued.

"Of course," he said, "what she doesn't understand is that no body is there to be damaged."

He laughed again.

"Of course, no one is there to ask the question either."

Some time later Isabel said to Swamiji: "But you were giving your answers from a very high Vedantic perspective. That's not enough."

Swamiji replied, "Yes, from the lower point of view, I have a *big* ego!" And he laughed again.[5]

A number of Swamiji's followers heard him tell them in various ways, by word as well as by action, that they needed to be selfish about their spirituality. "If you want it," he said in a variety of ways, "you need to go after it."

One devotee recalls how, when she had listened to her first lecture by Swamiji, she was so convinced that she needed him as a teacher that she made a dash for him as though her life depended on it. Not caring whether she was being impolite or forward, she ran after him in the hall and managed to get his attention. That was the beginning of a long, intense *guru-sisya* [teacher-taught] relationship that spanned many decades.

"To act opposed to your spiritual fervor," he said to someone else, *"is to run in reverse gear at top speed from your destination — the Bliss Absolute."*

When Being Nice Isn't Nice

A long-time devotee of Swamiji's finally had a chance to be his personal assistant for the length of one *yajna*. Part of her job was to travel with him to all the *bhikshas* and to prepare his diabetes syringe for him, so that he could administer his insulin shot before the meal. (Unless a doctor or nurse was around, he performed this procedure himself.)

After one evening's lecture, a devotee was clamoring to squeeze into the back seat of Swamiji's car: She wanted to be near him for those precious 20 to 30 minutes to the site of the *bhiksha*. After much jostling and rearranging, it became obvious that there would not be enough room for both the ardent devotee and the personal assistant.

The assistant said to herself: "Why be so selfish? Every day you have the opportunity to be near him for so many wonderful minutes. Why not take the second car that's being offered and let this lady have the chance to ride with Swamiji?" She got out of the way to allow the ardent devotee into Swamiji's car and slipped into the second car herself.

On the way to the site of the *bhiksha*, the driver realized that his directions to the house were not clear. It was dark, and the area was strange to him. He was obviously lost. He found a public telephone, made some frantic calls, and finally determined the correct route.

When they entered the house, Swamiji's assistant rushed to Swamiji apologetically, explaining what had happened — and expecting that he would be forgiving in view of her sacrifice (giving up her seat for someone else). But Swamiji's face was hard and his voice gruff.

With a turmoil of emotions in her mind, she managed to hand over the syringe to Swamiji just seconds before his meal began. The assistant promised herself never to forget this lesson. She vowed to herself always to remember to give highest priority to one's duty and to live in quiet surrender to the guru's needs. Then no foolish decisions will take place. [6]

Great humorist that he was, Swamiji often doled out meaningful teachings in a humorous wrapping:

Curing the Disease of Life

In a 1954 letter addressed to one of his earliest devotees, Sheila Lal Keswani, Swamiji gave the following remedy for the "disease of life":

How to cure the disease of life? The disease of life is called the perception of plurality. This is caused by a very powerful germ called "ego" — or separative idea. This thrives on the mind and intellect. If you take the following mixture regularly, the cure is sure:

Rx

Sincerity	*11 g*	*Love*	*10 oz*
Regularity	*10 g*	*Meditation*	*9 oz*
Honesty	*8 g*	*Serve all*	*6 ml*
Courage	*9 g*	*Be pure*	*3 ml*
Pursuit	*7 g*		

Shake the bottle (intellect) before use; after use, cork it with a controlled mind.

1. *Never taste scandal-mongering; if you want, drink plenty of* Om *chanting.*

2. *Don't roam about much in animalism and sensuousness.*

3. *Rest in meditations.*

4. *Once a day, take a cup of Upanishad soup.*[7]

Once an eminent doctor came to meet Gurudev at his ashram with a copy of Gurudev's *Holy Geeta* (*Bhagavad Gita*) and asked for his autograph. Gurudev wrote the following message in her copy of the book:

> *Rx. Two stanzas, three times a day, for three months. To be repeated if symptoms persist.*

DEALING WITH THE MIND

When troubled by life's problems or our own minds, we would inevitably request a private interview with Swamiji. In *satsangs* and at lectures, he would often poke fun at our insistence on privacy: "Swamiji, could I please have a *private* interview? I have a very special problem" — and he would mock our pious tones. "Why private?" he asked. "Don't think 'private interview' — all of you have the same problems."

Many times, private tortures were resolved in unique ways — and without the benefit of a private interview:

Torturing Thoughts

One devotee recalls how he was struggling with some negative emotions relative to his guru: The emotions seemed inappropriate and uncalled-for, and he tried to suppress them. One night after Swamiji's local *jnana yajna,* the devotee saw Swamiji in a dream. Nothing much was said, but he had taken a very unusual pose in a reclining chair, leaning back elaborately, with a long, searching look in his eyes. The next day during *satsang,* the devotee sat among the others, still struggling with his inner turmoil, attempting to suppress it in hopes of hiding it from his guru. Then Swamiji leaned back on the couch in the exact pose he had seen in his dream. He shuddered inside: It was obvious that Swamiji knew exactly what was going on in the devotee's mind. Trying to hide the turmoil was futile.[8]

Swamiji helped with a powerful methodology for dealing with unwanted thoughts. He said: "When unwanted thoughts come to torture you, don't try to hold them back. Don't suppress them! Instead, shine a very bright spotlight on them. They will shy away from so much attention and scurry away out of view!"

And also:

> *When any sensuous thoughts, regrets, agitations, loneliness, fear, sorrows, sadness, etc. reach your bosom, disassociate yourself from them — do nonviolent non-cooperation. This is successful only when you "violently" cooperate with Him and His divine qualities.*

Anger Cure

A devotee went to Gurudev and demanded to know how he could get cured of his bouts of bad temper. He sincerely wanted to be rid of them, as he realized how much sorrow they caused him and also for those around him.

"Show me the anger in you, please," requested Swamiji. "There are some varieties that can't be cured. Show me *your* type."

"Right now I can't show it to you, Swamiji. It comes suddenly, makes me do stupid things, and then just as suddenly leaves me," explained the devotee.

"Then it is not your own nature. If it were so, you could show it to me. You were not born with a bad temper; nobody gave it to you; your education didn't train you in it. It is not yours. Please think this over and come to disown it — quickly!"[9]

"We all know Swamiji got angry at times, but anger never controlled him," says Nalin Vissanji. He recounts an episode from the early days of Sandeepany Sadhanalaya in Mumbai:

Anger for a Purpose

During the early years of the Sandeepany Sadhanalaya Vedanta course in Mumbai, when Swamiji himself was not at the site, another speaker gave talks on Sundays, which householder devotees also attended. At one point, Swamiji indicated that these classes should be discontinued, that the students could benefit more from their own individual study following his prescribed Scheme of Study.

A small group of householder devotees, all study groups members, decided to ask Swamiji if he might not change his mind about the Sunday talks. So on a day when Swamiji was giving a class on the *Mandukya Karika* to a small group of serious students, the householder devotees joined the class so that they could talk to Swamiji afterwards about the Sunday talks. Since the *Mandukya Karika* is an advanced text, membership in that class had been restricted.

At 7:30 a.m., they were all gathered for the *Mandukya* class. Four or five householders were sitting at the back of the class. As Swamiji entered the room, he shouted at the top of his voice, "I don't want anyone in class but those assigned to it!" As Nalin Vissanji recalls, "There was no question of our staying in the room, so we left," but one lady persisted in staying and arguing the point with Swamiji, who was now showing even more anger.

Finally, after the lady, too, left the room, Swamiji switched to a totally normal voice as he spoke with the students in the class. All signs of anger were gone within seconds.[10]

Keeping Anger in the Pocket

Once when he was traveling with Gurudev, Swami Shantananda recalls that a devotee had changed Gurudev's flight plans without telling him. Just as Swamiji was getting ready to board the plane, he was informed that he now had to board another.

Swamiji got very angry. Enraged, he told the man that he had to follow directions, and that if anything ever changed, Swamiji was to be told. The man was quivering in the face of Gurudev's fury. Just then, a couple came up to Swamiji and prostrated before him. Apparently, they were unaware as to what dialogue Swamiji was just then engaged in. Gurudev's mood changed immediately. He welcomed them with open arms, blessing them with a big smile and much love.

"This is what Gurudev taught us: to keep anger in the pocket, take it out when necessary, and then put it away," says Swami Shantananda.[11]

Gurudev warned us not to become too involved with the vagaries of the mind while we struggled to create some semblance of control over it. While working with devotees in the United States in the sixties and seventies, he soon became aware of the popularity of various techniques such as encounter groups. He warned his study group leaders not to allow group discussions to deteriorate into "mind-raking sessions," seeking to make us aware that encounter group techniques, wrongly applied, could backfire.

Encounter Groups

Referring to the indisciplined use of some encounter group techniques, Gurudev wrote in a letter to a study group leader:

> *The mutual exploration of the mind is a dangerous game. It is scavenging work. It is dangerous. Beware! . . . The cleaning of your own mind itself is sufficient work. Don't try to clean all "commodes." If you must, then wear a mask and a pair of thick gloves. Teachers do it often. They have the defense equipment plenty.*
>
> . . .
>
> *If you keep on analyzing yourself, your despair will increase — and your thoughts will unnerve you. Please stop it. Rise above them.* Viveka *and* vairagya, *right knowledge and dispassion, are the wings for the bird of life in you to reach the roof-gardens of liberation.*[12]

"Soar beyond the mind," Gurudev continued to implore us. Don't try to make a dark room bright by shoveling out darkness with a shovel, he said. Instead, simply bring in the light. Similarly, don't try to vanquish *Maya* [illusion, ignorance of Reality] by battling the mind one thought at a time, as though you were shoveling darkness out of the room one shovelful at a time. Simply open up to the Divinity within you: Let the Light in.

Making the Mind Strong

Someone asked Swamiji toward the end of a spiritual camp, "Swamiji, why in your presence is meditation so easy, but then when we are no longer near you, our ability to be still and dive deep fades away?"

"Because," said Swamiji, "when you're in my presence, I hold you with my mind, and my mind is much stronger than yours right now."

To make the mind strong, he said, you need to integrate the personality. You cannot have one thought pushing you in one direction and another thought yanking you back in another. "When you say one thing and do another, you dissipate energy," he said. "When you say one thing and then do it, you build inner strength."[13]

Drinking *Vasana*

At a *satsang* at a Chinmaya Spiritual Camp, a person said to Swamiji: "I have a problem. I'm an alcoholic. I come to these camps and enjoy them very much. I understand what you're saying, but when I get home, I start drinking again. While I'm here, I have no problem — only when I return home again. What do I do, Swamiji?"

Swamiji answered, "Drinking is only a *vasana*, the same as an anger *vasana* or an overeating *vasana*. If you decide that you are tired of this *vasana* and you want to get rid of it, all you have to do is decide: 'I don't want it anymore.' Then, with full awareness, watch how the *vasana* functions, and you will get rid of it. Try this:

"Before the *vasana* pulls you to enter the drinking booth [pub], say to yourself, 'I have a drinking *vasana*, and I'm ashamed of it. I want to get rid of it.' But if the *vasana* is still too strong, you cross the street, open the door, sit down on the bar stool, and meet your drinking companions. With every step, whatever you do — opening the door, walking up to the counter, sitting down on the stool, greeting your friends — you do in full awareness. As you order the first drink, say to yourself, 'This is the drinking *vasana* doing this.' Then you swallow the burning liquid consciously, with full awareness that this is the drinking *vasana* at work. After that, you may not remember anything else, but next morning as you wake up with a splitting headache, you remember again, 'This is the drinking *vasana* that's done this to me.' And you suffer the hangover in full consciousness that the drinking *vasana* caused it.

"You go through this exercise again and again, because if the *vasana* is strong; it will not leave you easily. But one day you will find that you may cross the street, enter the bar, meet your friends, and walk out without buying a drink. Then, sometime later, you cross the street, walk through the door, look at the whole bar scene in full consciousness — knowing now that you have a choice to get sucked in or walk away, never to enter the drinking booth again. It is *your* choice. If you go through these experiences with full awareness, one day you will be free."[14]

New Toys Every Day

The aging parents of my husband had been admitted to the hospital with serious ailments. Being greatly attached to them, my husband felt very disturbed, and the demon of personal loss loomed large.

Just then Pujya Gurudev visited New Delhi. Since we could not manage time off to meet him, as we were kept busy with home and hospital duties, we thought it a good idea to attend the Chinmaya Vidyalaya annual function, where Gurudev was to address the students.

There he was, a grand, majestic figure of spiritual strength and moral courage. He told us of a little boy who went to nursery school and cried when his mother left him there. The teacher, to calm the little one, quickly gave him brightly colored toys to play with, and he was soon fascinated. When it was time to go home, the teacher started collecting the toys from the children. The boy, pained at his loss of his new-found joy, clung to the toys and cried out loud. He would not let go. Finally, he gave in to the teacher's entreaties and loosened his grip. When he came to school the next day, he got different toys, new ones, different from the previous day but more enchanting.

Thus, each day the teacher took away the old toys and gave him new ones that were better than the previous ones. Soon the child learned not to cling to what he had but to laugh when it was taken away and look forward with assurance to new toys waiting in the wings for him.

The suffocating burden of attachment fell away from us instantly, and we realized the glory of God's love for us.[15]

Mind in a Rut

Swamiji was standing outside the *yajna* hall, taking a look around. He said, "*Tat Tvam Asi* [That Thou Art]."

"Yes, I know," said a devotee near him.

"Yes, but you know with the intellect only."

She went home and thought about what he had said. At a *satsang* later that day she said, "Swamiji, remember what you said earlier today about knowing '*Tat Tvam Asi*' with the intellect only?"

"Y-e-e-e-s?" he stretched out the syllable long, as he often did with certain words, and raised his eyebrows questioningly.

"I have been practicing the witness for some time now. But how do I transcend the intellect? Please tell me."

"No," he said. "You come to class and let Adi Shankaracharya tell you."

She didn't look very pleased. He went on to say:

"The mind is like a child. You say to your child, 'Don't jump on the bed,' but the moment you leave the room, the child jumps to his heart's content. Any *sadhana* you undertake you have to keep changing now and again, because the mind goes into a rut."

She concluded that the mind must have gone into a rut with her witness practice and adjusted her *sadhana* accordingly.[16]

Reading the scriptures and listening to the teacher, many of us began to feel with excruciating clarity the disparity between the Ideal portrayed in the holy texts and our own current state of mind. How to reach it? How to know what's right and what's wrong at any given moment in one's life?

Knowing What's Right

Questions about right and wrong were burning fiercely in my mind during one of Gurudev's first *yajnas* in San Francisco. I had sat down on the carpet next to his chair and asked him, "Swamiji, how do I make the right choice each moment of my life? How do I always make the correct judgment as to what is right and what is wrong?"

Swamiji proceeded to tell me an analogy, one that became indelibly etched in my mind to help guide my actions — and has been much used in many a study group discussion since then. It went something like this:

"You know how a master painter teaches his apprentice how to mix colors? The master himself is an expert in the subtle use of color; his rich browns and greens and oranges are incomparable. But he doesn't just squeeze the brown out of the tube and dab it onto the canvas, no! He takes a bit of brown with his brush and dabs it onto his palette. He then takes a bit of black and mixes it with the brown; then some red, maybe also a dab of green or blue or yellow," Swamiji demonstrated with an imaginary palette and brush. "The master keeps mixing various colors in various proportions until he's achieved just the right shade. Only then does he apply the paint to the canvas.

"His apprentice first watches, making mental notes while observing the master at work. He then picks up his own tubes of paint and begins to experiment with the mixing of colors, following the master's example. Some of his experiments are total failures, some fair, others *almost* successful. In time, and with practice, he *develops a feel* for what is just right.

"In the same way, the spiritual student first watches the master or masters at work — either through reading the scriptures or by listening to spiritual teachers or by watching a teacher in daily life. He observes how the teacher handles difficulties, how he relates to people of various temperaments, and so on. These observations become the student's guidelines for right action. Then he starts applying those guidelines to his own life, experimenting with their application to everyday problems and challenges. Sometimes he succeeds, sometimes he doesn't — but, with practice, he develops a *feel* for what is the exact right thing to do at any one moment. You have to give it time."[17]

Ever-present *Vasanas*

Michael Mayzel of Toronto was driving Swamiji from meditation class in the morning and was waiting with Swamiji in the car until it was time to enter the lecture hall for the morning's lecture. They saw a man sitting on the curb with an open Upanishad in front of him, one hand holding a cup of coffee, the other, a lit cigarette. Swamiji gave a running commentary on what must have been going on in the reader's mind: "Ram, Ram" . . . "Coffee, coffee" . . . "Ram, Ram" . . . "Cigarette, cigarette" . . . "Ram, Ram" . . .

Then a beautiful young woman came within view. Swamiji's comment, with a loud gust of laughter, was:

"Oh, oh . . .!" More distractions for the poor mind!

The words were few, but the teaching was potent, remembers Michael: *Vasanas* keep their ever-present dance in our minds, urging us to hop helplessly from one thought to another.[18]

Mastering the Sexual Urge

An army officer had come to attend one of Swamiji's spiritual camps. He was hefty, young, and handsome. As the days went by, he started to look more ragged as well as restless.

At one *satsang* he asked Swamiji, "How does one control one's sexuality?"

Swamiji laughed: "You're asking *me* about sexuality!? What does a swami know about it?"

Then, in a more serious tone he said: "It's very difficult to control one's senses: seeing, hearing, touch . . . Even one single sense is very difficult to control, even one sense at a time. Look, sex involves all the senses at once: touch, sight, smell . . . that's why it's the last one to go. It's natural that that's the most difficult urge to master."[19]

UNDERSTANDING THE SPIRITUAL LIFE

Bharat Bhushan Gupta recalls how Swamiji gave advice to a householder who was thinking about moving into the life of a renunciate:

Readiness for *Sannyasa*

Swamiji was invited for *bhiksha* at the residence of a local devotee, who was a prosperous businessman with a large family, all living together in a spacious house. After the dinner was over, the devotee, about sixty-five years of age, said:

"Swamiji, I have worked all my life and established my business. Now I wish to take rest and retire. What is the age at which one should take *sannyasa*?"

After some moments, Swamiji answered, "When you find that your duties are over and your sons are capable of looking after the business."

"But, Swamiji, my sons don't let me. They keep asking for advice even when they don't need it. They just don't want me to leave the business," the host asserted respectfully.

Swamiji had a hearty laugh: "Never mind," he said. "In that case your daughter-in-law will certainly make you leave one of these days."

The subtle message of *vairagya* had been delivered with wit.[20]

Recognizing Your Divinity

Swamiji was telling us that when the guru first tells you that you're *Brahman* and not the body, you don't quite believe him. He expanded on this idea with a story from his own experience:

One day, Swamiji was walking down a path near Rishikesh. It was so hot that not even "a decent crow" was out at that time.

"Eh, Swami!" a female voice called out, but he paid no heed. He had just recently taken *sannyasa,* and his station was new to him. He didn't realize that he himself was being addressed. When he finally realized it was he the woman was addressing, she invited him to have *bhiksha.*

"In the same way," said Swamiji, "you need time to get used to the idea that you are in essence the pure Self — *Atman, Brahman.* It takes practice."[21]

Not a Part-time Religion

Once a young man asked Gurudev in a *satsang,* "How is it that in Christianity the followers of Christ attend church compulsorily every Sunday? Why do Hindus have no such rule?"

Pat came his reply: "Our religion is not a part-time religion."[22]

Vedanta in a Hurry

Swamiji described a young man in a hurry. While boarding a bus that was about to start, with one foot on the footboard, he asked, "Swamiji, what is Vedanta?"

> Swamiji said that for such a man in a hurry, the reply must be short and to the point. What was the reply Swamiji gave? "Detach the mind from the world and attach it to the Lord."[23]

In other versions of the same story, Swamiji gave the reply in even shorter form: "Detachment—attachment!"

DISCIPLINE

We have to become masters of our minds if we are to realize the pure Self within us, Gurudev taught us. In fact, he said, *"Discipline of the mind alone leads to Self-realization."*

He himself was the picture of discipline on all fronts: always punctual, his *dhoti* and *kurta* freshly washed and pressed, the few belongings that traveled with him from place to place always neatly arranged. Although a devoted assistant or two was always at his side to help him pack and keep his room in order, it was obvious that the neatness that surrounded him was largely the result of his inspiration. Even his desk, though covered with piles of letters and various categories of documents, still spelled immaculate order.

Especially in the early years, punctuality was, above all, the hallmark of his discipline. A meaningful stare, sometimes a roar, sometimes deafening silence met a late straggler into the lecture hall. He himself was always exactly on time.

No Distractions Allowed

Some twenty or thirty minutes into the lecture, Swamiji had already succeeded in lifting our minds into a subtle space quite different from the one in which we had just roamed around before the talk began. The usual mental clamor had already subsided a little, and the tense lines in our faces began to relax. The university hall, with a bank of gradually elevated rows of seats, was very quiet, with only a muffled cough now and then disturbing the silence.

A slight crack and squeak at the back diverted our attention from Swamiji's words. Some heads turned backward to see the cause of the noise. A young man had just entered the hall and was walking slowly down the steep bank of stairs, finally edging himself into a row somewhere toward the front of the auditorium. During his excruciatingly long descent down the stairs, Swamiji said not a word and followed his every movement with his eyes — as we all held our breaths. By the time the man sat down in his chosen seat, the message of the deafening silence around him must have reached its mark, for his face was quite red as he settled his body into the seat.[1]

Punctuality

Back in the early 1960s in India, when Gurudev happened to arrive a few minutes early at the site of the *yajna* [in India, usually in an open-air meeting place], he used to wait in the car and at exactly the time announced for the beginning of the talk, he would begin the *Omkara* [*Om* chanting], marking the start of the *yajna*.[2]

Alarm Clock Discipline

A small group of new devotees in California were making the first arrangements to sell Swamiji's books in the United States. Several of them set up a communal living situation, so that they could do Swamiji's work and also practice their *sadhana* together. They were all very energized, doing their work with great dedication and fulfilling their daily *sadhana* with enthusiasm, including early morning meditations.

However, as time went on, they became a little lax in following through with their daily meditation discipline. Correspondence continued with Swamiji, but no word was said about the state of their daily spiritual practice. One day, one of the workers received a package in the mail with a return address of someone in India whom no one at the house knew. They opened the package and found a small traveling alarm clock.

"Strange! They must have made a mistake!" they said to each other.

No news came to clarify the contents of the strange package, but they continued to have a peculiar feeling about the happening.

Then Swamiji arrived from India for his next lecture series in California. Swamiji and one of the local workers were riding together in a car, Swamiji in the front seat, she in the back. No conversation was taking place.

Finally she broke the silence to say: "Swamiji, a funny thing happened a while ago: I received a package from a stranger in India with an alarm clock inside."

A long silence ensued.

Then Swamiji said three words in a very deep voice, "I sent it," followed by yet another long silence.

"I sent my feelers out to your house in California," he finally added, "and everyone there was asleep."[3]

The elaborate *abhisheka* ceremonies, the ritual bathing of the 40-foot idol of Sri Hanumanji at the Sidhabari ashram, have been organized every five years with the help of R. Krishnamoorthy, who recounts how Gurudev's attention to detail and insistence on discipline accompanied every step of the preparations:

Doing the Job Right

For more than three months preceding the 1987 *abhisheka* ceremonies, I wrote letters to Gurudev and received prompt replies with his comments. By this process, a minute-to-minute program was fixed and approved by Gurudev. A list of more than a hundred items required for the *abhisheka* rituals had been reviewed by Gurudev in great detail, to the extent of him pointing out that I had left matches off the list!

The *puja* proceeded well on the first day. On the second day, some confusion ensued among the donors, and some devotees tried to overrule me and sit near Gurudev's chair, although in the drawing that had been submitted to Gurudev earlier for approval, the seating positions of all donors had been clearly demarcated. When I went to call Gurudev to the prayer site, he saw the few dozen devotees sitting around his chair. He looked at me hard and said, "Go and get the drawing!"

Being very engrossed at that point in the details of planning, I blurted out in confusion, "What drawing, Swamiji?"

Promptly came the reply, "The seating arrangement, *buddhu!*"

Fortunately, I had the file with me and showed Gurudev the pertinent page. He pointed out his chair and the empty space around it. He looked at me and looked at his chair. No words were said.

I said, "I am sorry. Just give me two minutes." He looked at his watch.

I went running and pleaded with the devotees to move back into the positions allocated for them. They didn't know that was Gurudev's order, nor did I tell them so. Somehow, with folded hands, I managed to convince them to move and rushed back to Gurudev. With a beaming smile he walked tall and sat down in his chair.

Later, when complaints were made to him about the readjusted seating arrangements, he replied, "He was only doing his job. Don't blame him!"[4]

Following Gurudev's directives precisely was very wise, as many of his devotees found out only after the fact. Those who didn't question the wisdom of his instructions had a large pay-off:

Following His Directives

Uma Jeyarasasingam had wanted to visit Uttarkashi and expressed her desire to Swamiji, but he said, "No. I'll tell you when to go."

During one of her trips to India, Uma found out that one of the young swamis in Chinmaya Mission had arranged a trip to Uttarkashi for her, without letting her know in advance. When she found out, she said to him, "No, I can't go yet. Swamiji has not given me his directive."

The next morning, the young swami called her and said, "It's a good thing you didn't go: There was a major landslide in Uttarkashi."[5]

Many times over the years we witnessed many instances of our guru's disciplinary action, and those of us who continued to be at his side learned quickly that punctuality, orderliness, and cleanliness were at the top of Swamiji's list of musts for a spiritual student. Yet, Swami Tejomayananda remembers, Gurudev's discipline "was not dry or harsh, but accompanied by compassion."

Admixture of Compassion and Rigor

Once, during one of the training courses at the Sidhabari ashram, Swamiji had told all the students to start the practice of doing three *japamalas* three times a day [reciting a mantra during three turns of the 108-bead rosary].

On the first day, practically no one had followed his instruction. The next day, after the forenoon class, Swamiji dropped a bombshell:

"How many of you have not done *japa* today?"

Several hands went up, timidly and hesitantly. Swamiji never opened his eyes (thank God!) and continued:

"Those who have not done *japa* will not have their lunch today!"

The students were unhappy over what they had done, yet happy that they were being made to do some *prayascitta* [compensatory act]. To undergo a discipline — and that too, upon instruction from one's guru — was a joy.

Time passed. The hands of the clock showed 3 p.m. Hunger was gnawing mercilessly at the vitals of the students. They looked forward to evening tea like a prisoner anticipates release after serving a long sentence. The "fasters" were the fastest to the tea table that day.

A strange sight met their eyes. There on the table was arranged a variety of delicious-looking snacks. Upon inquiry, the students learned that they were there because of Swamiji's instructions:

"I don't want my children to starve. I am happy they fasted for what they did. Now let them eat!"[6]

Swami Purushottamananda also recalls his guru's strict discipline: "Once, we were chanting the *Siva Mahima Stotra*, but my voice did not reach Gurudev's ears. Gurudev said, 'Today you won't eat lunch until I hear you chant properly.' From that day onward, my chanting improved."

No Prayer, No Supper

At Sandeepany Sadhanalaya in Mumbai, the students always chant a prayer before meals. One day, Swamiji did not hear a prayer being chanted.

"OK, no supper for them tonight," was his directive. "He gives you everything, and yet you don't even have time to thank Him."[7]

Broken Rules

During the brahmachari course at Sandeepany Sadhanalaya, some eight brahmacharis left the ashram while Swamiji was not there in order to hear a talk by J. Krishnamurti in the city. Swamiji's directive was that no one must leave the ashram grounds without permission. These young students had not

even told the manager about their plans. However, the manager found out and kept their names on a list.

Swamiji was to give talks at Surat, and the plan was to have the group of brahmacharis from the course join him there, providing a good break from the routine of daily classes at the ashram. When plans were underway to leave for Surat, Swamiji took out the list and said, "Hm," and read off the names of the eight brahmacharis who had taken their unapproved "break." "You stay back. You won't be going to Surat."[8]

To Fast or Not to Fast

Once during a camp, the ashram cook complained about the brahmacharis. Gurudev scolded the brahmacharis and gave the instruction: "You are not having lunch today."

All of them fasted through the lunch hour, but they were not sure if they could have dinner. So one of the brahmacharis was chosen to go to Gurudev to inquire: "Swamiji, none of us has taken lunch. May we have dinner?"

Gurudev agreed. As the brahmachari was approaching the door to leave, Gurudev said in a loud voice, "All but you! You come back."

The brahmachari was hungry but had no choice. He told the other brahmacharis that they could have dinner and then went back to Gurudev. Gurudev gave him some work, which the brahmachari performed.

Later, a woman devotee went to the brahmachari with fruits and milk, but he refused the offer, saying that Gurudev had not given him permission. The woman explained that Gurudev had sent the food himself. The brahmachari was confused and went to Gurudev and asked what was to be done with the fruits and milk.

Gurudev said lovingly to him, *"Buddhu!* I told you that you must not take dinner, but I did not tell you not to take early breakfast! It is now past 12 midnight!" (Gurudev was still working at his desk at 12 midnight, though his usual time of rising was 3:30 or 4:00 a.m. . . .)

The next morning, the cook apologized to Gurudev and explained that a misunderstanding had occurred. Gurudev later told the brahmacharis: "I can punish my children, but how can I punish the cook?"[9]

On at least one such occasion of disciplining his students by withholding a meal, Gurudev also observed a fast — in sympathy for them.

Hard Lesson

After the morning session was finished during a *yajna* in Jamshedpur, Swamiji was met by a brahmacharini who had arrived from a far-away town. She prostrated to him.

"What are you doing here?" asked Swamiji.

"Swamiji, I came to seek some advice on something," she answered.

"You should not have left your post," said Swamiji sternly. "You should have stayed there and telephoned me with your question."

He then gave instructions to the organizers to book her on the next available train to return to her town. To the brahmacharini he gave another instruction:

"Call me with your question when you get there."[10]

When Gurudev's discipline took on extra-strong coloration, the objects of his discipline suffered mightily. Hurting badly, with egos crushed, some even swore to leave him forever, only to return within hours or days, cleansed of the inner dross of which they themselves had been unaware.

Guru as Potter

A devotee had just been sent into a tailspin by Swamiji's latest administration of discipline. He looked at the person in deep compassion and said in a tender voice:

"A guru has the most unenviable position. He is like a potter. He supports the clay from the inside with one hand and molds if from the outside with the other, now and then giving it a slap."[11]

At times, people other than his students became the targets of his disciplinary tactics.

Leaders Are an Example

At a *Gita Jnana Yajna* in India, all the dignitaries but one had already assembled on the dais and Gurudev was ready to start, but the Governor had not yet arrived. When he finally did, Gurudev remarked sternly:

"If you, Governor, come late, what do you expect the people who look up to you to do?"[12]

6 a.m. Class

Once, in Bangalore, the morning classes by Swamiji were announced to be at 6:30 a.m. Some people living in a slightly distant area of the city urged the secretary of the local Mission center to request Swamiji to make it 7 a.m. instead. The young man, rather inexperienced, went to Gurudev a day before the whole program started and conveyed the demand. Swamiji listened, paused, and then, in a tone of utmost consideration, said, "All right, make it 6:00 a.m.!"

That was it. Surprisingly, the group that wanted the session moved to 7 a.m. were at the class every morning before 6:00, before most of the others![13]

No Complaining Allowed

Someone had just written to Gurudev complaining that a local Chinmaya Mission worker had refused to give him Swamiji's address; on Gurudev's instructions, for the time being his whereabouts were to be kept unknown except for those transacting Mission business. His response:

> *If I say "no address" to anyone — as an organizational instruction for everyone — you too will have to respect it. It is not right for any member of the organization to grumble, murmur, complain. This means that such members are not fit for the organization, and I have no compunction to rip such people away to keep the organization trim and disciplined. . . . the members must learn to live in the discipline of an organization. Must. Or else work cannot proceed smoothly, efficiently.*[14]

MEDITATION

"Greetings from the banks of the Ganges, right in the lap of the Himalayas," Swamiji wrote in a letter in 1968 while at his guru's erstwhile residence, Tapovan Kuti, in Uttarkashi. And he went on to say:

> *The meditative peaks are looking over my shoulders at what I am typing for you. I cannot keep those peaks away, because they just barge in uninvited, not only into my room, but right into the bosom, screaming:* "Meditate. Meditate. Meditate!"
>
> *In the heart of the Himalayas lies the Sanctum of Reality. To discover and contact this Sanctum, you will have to become the Himalayas. The girth, the height, the width, the mass of the Himalayas are constituted of motionless vibrancy — life hushed in stone — and every square inch of it is pulsating with life. Yet it itself is the sustainer of life — rock and soil, tumbling one over the other, as it rises into the clouds and stands majestic and still!*
>
> *Sit down and become the Himalayas. You be an actionless mass, spreading all over and completely motionless. Let Life and its activities emanate from you, on your surface, and get reabsorbed into you — as the forests of Himavan. If you can stay thus for ten minutes, you become the Himalayas! And in your core is the Sanctum of the Self.*
>
> *From the heart of the Himalayas flows the eternal Ganges, gushing perpetually in its sacred waters. Realize the center and let activities for the welfare of all others flow out of you into the world around you.*[1]

Every moment of our centering was, no doubt, as dear to the teacher as it was to the student. Many have hinted, quietly, about the joyous discovery they made of Swamiji's recognition of their deeper states of being. Any time he knew that one of his students had merged a bit deeper with the peace of the pure Self, he was there to support the moment, sometimes to acknowledge it in silence, other times, differently.

Energy Explosion

At a spiritual camp at Humboldt State University in California, a young man was sitting in morning meditation. He was in the front row, sitting on a cushion on the floor, right in front of Swamiji.

As he meditated, the young man had his eyes shut. At one point, he experienced an inexplicable feeling that prompted him to open his eyes and look at Swamiji. Swamiji was staring straight at him. Something — it felt like energy — shot out from the third-eye region of the young man's head, and the same thing happened from Swamiji's third eye, and the two energies met with an explosion in the middle, sending the young man into a very deep meditative state. He stayed in that deep state for some five hours afterwards, alone and totally quiet.[2]

In many ways and on many occasions, Swamiji took the opportunity to remind us that the sublime states that he used to call "mind at meditation" are beyond the usual constraints of the physical plane, be it time or space or convention or any other boundary one might want to superimpose:

Beyond Time

I remember asking Swamiji one time in the early years, "Swamiji, I've been trying to meditate. Sometimes the mind is obedient, many times not. What is your instruction: how long should I meditate each morning?"

He looked down at me from his seat at the writing desk, crossed one hand over the other in his lap, and smiled down at me where I was sitting cross-legged and full of expectation on the floor by his feet:

"Don't try to ascribe any time to something that is beyond time."

I remember feeling a little disappointed then. I had wanted a specific instruction, tailor-made for me, hopefully couched in a long series of sentences for detailed guidance on the path. All I got was one simple sentence. Yet, over the years, I've learned the fullness of the wisdom in his simple response.

Many of his responses were like that, utter simplicity, whereas our minds may have yearned for something complex and dramatic and personalized. He shot through all of our ego-fed yearning with utter, naked, unpretentious simplicity.[3]

However, Swamiji's answers to his disciples' questions were never exact replicas of each other. He also spoke of meditation as an uninterrupted 24-hour state of mind, as he described it in a letter:

> *All our experiences, joys and sorrows, successes and failures, pains and pleasures, honor and dishonor are His* prasad: *Let us accept them all in humbleness and gratitude. If we orient our life's plans on this essentially divine basis, we need not sit for meditation — all life will become one meditation.*

Twenty-Four-Hour Meditation

Many years back, before Swami Tejomayananda was himself a swami, he asked Swamiji in Uttarkashi, "How long should I meditate?"

"Twenty-four hours" was Swamiji's reply.[4]

Meditation, Swamiji told us, cannot be an activity divorced from the rest of life. If one leads a life filled with agitation and negativity and selfishness day in and day out, one cannot expect to sit down for meditation and, on command, glide into blissful peace. Fulfilling one's duties within the family, working with selfless motives in the world, and spending time with spiritual writings to help still the mind all help in preparing it for that special time in the meditation seat.

In a letter, Swamiji gave instructions on how to use the little book called *Hasten Slowly*, which he wrote to help new meditators in their practice. He said in a letter:

> *These lines are to be read in a whispering tone, and the meditator must consider that these words are the advice given by his own intellect to his own erring mind and undisciplined body. This is an inner sermon heard by one's own mind and body.*

And again:

> *Each day before meditation read one* You Must *[another small book of his] chapter. After your meditation, instead of immediately allowing the mind to explode into the fields of activity, allow it to glide slowly into the vigor of daily routine. After meditation, read again the same* You Must, *as before, in a whispering tone. I have found this to be very helpful for a majority of early meditators.*[5]

Not on Drugs

At a spiritual camp in Canada, Swamiji's meditation classes started at the usual time, 5:30 in the morning. As he did many times in many different camps, he prodded the meditators to leave the meditation hall quietly, to abstain from talking as they stood in line for their morning tea, then to take a quiet walk by themselves and continue sustaining the subtle mood created during meditation. Some managed to keep silent, others could not. However, the meditative mood overall was exceptionally deep.

After the third day of meditation, he reminded the listeners once again to keep their walks quiet and solitary, to look at the leaves and the trees and note what they see. "And," he said, "remember, you're not on drugs!"[6]

A Whirl of Agitations

During meditation class one morning, Swamiji lifted our minds to great heights of peace. Then he said, "Try to hold this peace after you leave your meditation seat. Otherwise, before you have left the meditation hall, your mind will be back in its usual whirl of agitations."

After meditation, I walked over to Swamiji to prostrate to him, as I had done every morning after class. Since he always sat cross-legged on the platform in those days, his feet had not been available for touching, in prostration, so every morning I had used his *chappals*, placed on the floor directly in front of him, as a substitute for his feet. This morning, another devotee preceded me and removed the *chappals* from their position to place them near the stairs leading from the platform, so they would be ready for Swamiji when he left the stage after the lecture that followed meditation.

The object that I had used all these mornings as a symbolic focusing point for my feelings of love and surrender had suddenly been removed. Besides, it had been *my* self-appointed task each morning to change the position of his *chappals* to help ease his descent from the platform later! Now that opportunity for a brief act of service had been usurped.

I did my prostration and left the lecture hall for a brief walk before the morning's lecture. The utter peace I had known in meditation was beginning to be shattered by agitated thoughts — my reaction to the vanishing *chappals*. Then I remembered Swamiji's words of a few minutes ago: "Before you have left the meditation hall, your mind will be back in its usual whirl of agitations."

Immediately, I caught the vagrant thoughts and tried to disempower them by substituting others: "This must be the Lord's way of showing me that in one's devotion one should not become attached to any one object or activity. All creation is equally sacred." I consciously thought loving thoughts about the devotee at whose hands the *chappals* had disappeared. All traces of impending agitation in the mind vanished.

In the lecture following the meditative walk, Swamiji made sure that the lesson was complete: One wrong thought, he said, can become one's downfall from great heights of peace if only one lets oneself become obsessed with that thought. He said that if you let go of a ball at the top of a staircase, you can still catch it when it's rolling down the first few steps, but if you let it roll down further, the rush downward will gather new momentum with each step, making the ball irretrievable in its frenzied journey. The trick is to catch the ball — or the wandering mind — in its first downward hops.

I smiled inwardly. Yes, the teaching never stops. In one brief morning, my guru had taught me a lifetime's worth.[7]

Swamini Sharadapriyananda recalls her early years with Gurudev and the guidance he gave her in her meditative practice:

Not Physical Silence

My *manana* [reflection] commenced in Uttarkashi. We were taken by Sri Gurudev to Uttarkashi during 1968 and 1969 for the summer months, as he decided to stop all lecturing and spend some time in retreat. This way, we had more time for meditation. I sat for meditation often and tried to be silent. But due to my hearing defect, there was an incessant noise in one ear. However much I tried, I could not get beyond the noise. I was worried and desperate. Would I have no chance at all to reach that glorious state beyond all description because of this ear defect? Of what use was all the study and effort if I could never reach the goal?

One day, almost on the verge of tears, I approached Sri Gurudev and asked, "Swamiji, am I doomed forever? I can never realize the silence!"

Pujya Gurudev could feel my misery. He smiled and assured me, "Don't worry! It is not *that* type of silence you have to reach."[8]

No Gate-Crashing

In 1971, Pujya Gurudev decided to spend one month in Uttarkashi and wrote to me to join him there for one week. By that time, I had already been working in Bangalore for two years. Overjoyed, I left for Uttarkashi. I was determined to make utmost use of the chance to spend time in meditation and reach the Supreme before returning to Bangalore.

At that time, women devotees were staying in town, not in Tapovan Kuti [the ashram]. In early morning, I used to go to Tapovan Kuti for tea. The first day, I searched out an empty room for my intended deep meditation sessions. I found one small room under the staircase of the dining hall in which unused blankets were stored. I cleared it up to get sitting space for myself. As soon as tea time finished, I would sit there and meditate for hours and hours. My sole effort was to detach myself from body consciousness and explode into the Supreme. Afterwards, I would go to Sri Swamiji to prostrate at his feet and seek clarification about my *sadhana*.

Sri Swamiji divined what I was doing. Perhaps he felt that my restless, wandering nature was being somewhat subdued and told me to stay there for a full month. I was in seventh heaven. I pursued my meditation, driving myself hard to detach from the body. It was strenuous physical exertion on my part. One day, I somehow got rid of consciousness of the lower part of the body, but I was very conscious of the upper part. What was this state? Had I reached halfway through? I went straight to Sri Swamiji and asked him, "I got rid of half of he body. Can it be done this way, part by part?"

Pujya Gurudev must have had a hearty laugh within. Outwardly, he remained quiet and did not reply to me. Later on, we all gathered around him for *satsang* as he was reclining in an easy chair. He was talking to a devotee, and as if by way of an explanation to him, he said:

"Once I felt very bad about my meditation and asked my guru: 'I am stuck like this. What am I to do?' He advised me to go around and keep myself busy."

Sri Gurudev did not look at me, but I knew that his answer was intended for me. I was stuck in my meditation. Any more exertion would only exhaust me and not take me forward. I trotted back to Bangalore after the month, wiser with the understanding that I could not gate-crash into the realm of the Supreme without some more service in the field.[9]

Dry Spells

Several meditations in a row had been very deep and enlightening. Then a dry spell set in, a dry spell I remember experiencing a number of previous times after an intense tuning in with Gurudev. I remember asking him the question of why the mind goes so neutral after having been intensely tuned in to him for a while. At that time, he had said to me that when that happens the student always worries, but never the teacher, because for the teacher it means that intense *sadhana* is taking place in the student.

At the current spiritual camp, this strange sense of neutrality following upon the heels of intense spiritual experiences seemed especially puzzling and bothersome, because I had been so deeply tuned in not only to my guru but also my *Ista Devata* [chosen form of the Lord]. I asked Swamiji about it.

He said that when the mind grows sluggish in this way, the seeker must give it some *tapas* [austerity practice]: deprive it of food or give it a cold shower. The mind will straighten out and get back into shape, he said. I tried a cold shower the next morning, and, indeed, the results were good.

However, my question was not quite answered yet, and Swamiji knew it. He returned to the topic again in other discussions. He explained how devotees of the Lord, such as Mirabai, often sing of their anguish in having first glimpsed the Lord's face, then falling back into darkness, seemingly light-years away from His presence. The only thing for the devotee to do is to keep praying, meditating, and knocking on His door — until He lets you in. "You must not give up," said Swamiji.[10]

Rama's Grace

I was all the while feeling that I should do *pranayama* [breath control] and meditation. But *how* was the question. At last, I referred to the scriptures to seek guidance from them. I started doing *pranayama* as well as meditation in the morning after *puja*. After some time, I developed an unbearable sensation in the head whenever I uttered *Sri Rama Jaya Rama Jaya Jaya Rama*. I was disappointed with the development: I loved God so much and had an intense desire for meditation.

At this juncture, one young man with whom I had become acquainted offered me a few books written by Pujya Gurudev and Swami Tapovanam. Since that time, I began to feel that I should write to Gurudev and seek his blessings.

One fine morning on December 10, 1981, I wrote a letter to Gurudev to his 321st *Gita Jnana Yajna* at Tiruchy regarding my problem in uttering *Rama Nama*. I immediately received a letter from Gurudev advising me to undergo Chinmaya Mission's Lesson Course and then approach him again.

Accordingly, I commenced the study course. By the time I completed the course, the head-breaking sensation that I used to get while uttering *Rama Nama* had subsided, and I was very happy. I wrote to Gurudev about it. Promptly, I received a reply informing me that it was all Rama's grace and he was only a *nimitta matram* [acting as an instrument of the Divine]. Now I live peacefully centered in Him, who is in our own heart.[11]

A Taste of Bliss

At an early morning meditation class in Kuala Lumpur, I was reflecting on how the ultimate Reality, which is one homogeneous whole, could have different attributes such as "bliss" and "consciousness." It can't be both!

This thought stayed in my mind the whole day. At 4:30 p.m., a lady came to meet Gurudev and asked him a question about *vasanas* and how and when this world was created. While answering her question, Gurudev raised our minds from the how and when of creation to great heights of contemplation. He turned around and looked deeply into my eyes for a couple of seconds and then said to the lady:

"Hang on to Him only. . . . In meditation the 'bliss' that you experience is not you. It is His. He lets you taste it. The 'consciousness' that you experience is not you. Both 'bliss' and 'consciousness' are His. He lets you have a taste. Don't think that that is all or that you have reached the goal! Know that they are His and wait for Him.

"From here it is not for you to experience Him. When He wants, He will come and lift you up. Wait there for Him. Don't leave Him! Keep Him always with you!"[12]

Flower Meditation

During a *jnana yajna* in Nepal, as we were leaving for a *bhiksha*, Swamiji paused in the garden before a pot of brilliant, pendulous fuchsia blooms. He lifted a flower with its pale pink outer petals and scarlet central cylinder and asked, "Why does this flower hang down?"

At the moment, we all became intensely aware of the startlingly bright color against the blue sky.

Then he looked over his shoulder and said quietly, "Use that for your meditation!"[13]

Doing *Japa*

A new devotee of Swamiji's asked him to bless her *japamala*. He took it in his hands and said:

"Ah, *japa*! To do *japa* you must not be a wife or a mother or a daughter. You must be His alone."

And as he blessed the *mala* and gave it to the devotee, he said: "You continue with *Om Namah Sivaya*."

The devotee had not told him that *Om Namah Sivaya* was already her chosen mantra.[14]

TEACHERS AND TEACHING

Watching Gurudev at work meant learning at every step. "Gurudev was an ideal teacher," says Swami Purushottamananda. "He had in him the love of a mother and the discipline of a strict father. But he was also very unsparing where studies were concerned. He sent away a student who failed to learn by heart the question posed to the teacher in the *Mundaka Upanisad*. Yet he captured our hearts with endless love."

The breadth and depth of his teaching was immense. "He taught me the alphabet, and he taught me the grammar," remembers Dwaraknath Reddy of Tiruvannamalai, India. "After that, I could pick up the study myself." And he goes on to say, "We were dynamized into action — as well as quieted in the mind — by him."

Gurudev's methods of teaching were as various as the people who came to learn from him. Some he prodded gently and lovingly, some he blasted with strong words, others he teased, and yet others he brought to a state of surrender by allowing them to attend to him in his daily needs. And for the same person, his method of bringing a particular lesson home varied according to the state of mind of the student at that moment.

The young people who were currently studying, or had completed their studies, at one of his Sandeepany institutes of Vedanta received particular attention. He said in a letter to a devotee about his work with the brahmacharis who had begun their work of service and teaching after graduation from Sandeepany:

> *Sweepers go out and clean the street gutters, and in the process they themselves get dirty. Then they need to go home to wash themselves and their clothes. They are then ready to go out and get dirty once again. So it is with my brahmacharis and brahmacharinis. I send them out into the world, and they get dirty. They come*

back to me all dirtied up — and with a lot of patience, a touch of the whip, and a lot of love, I clean them up and send them out into the world again.

And so it goes on. All I can do is hope that one day they won't need to come back at all!

That is what Swamiji meant when he said, *"I'm not a mule guru."* He was always inspiring us, teaching us, cajoling us to raise our minds ever higher toward the Source of all life, but he refused to make pretenses about carrying anyone into God-realization on his back. In fact, over and over again, in many ways, he reminded us that he was but an instrument of the Higher and a catalyst for *our own* striving toward God-realization.

CONSUMMATE TEACHER

An Empty Drum by the Roadside

While sitting in *satsang* with Gurudev, as often happened in his presence, a deep peace overtook the assembled crowd and no one said a word, although many of us surely had saved up plenty of questions for him earlier, with every intention to ask them. However, especially after we were already some days into a *yajna* or camp and had slowly allowed the usual turmoil in our minds to abate a little, we often found ourselves simply sitting in *satsang* in silence. Gurudev focused his large, expressive eyes on our silent faces, drummed his fingers along the sides of his chair, and said:

"Come on! I'm just an empty drum by the roadside. Unless you beat on me, no sound comes out!"

So some listeners managed to summon up a question or two from the recesses of their minds — and drummed away at the always willing drum of the guru.

On another occasion he said:

> *The teacher can be of immense help to those students who have purified themselves and become ready for their spiritual unfoldment. Thus, the entire responsibility for our inner growth rests with us, the seekers, and not upon our teachers. They are always great; they are ever "on." But our own inadequacies cheat us of our deeper experiences.*[1]

Swamiji outshone many a teacher in knowing how to reach down to the level of the audience. The proof of the efficacy of his method was in the number of people who turned toward the spiritual life as a result of his words. He knew that if half or more of the audience came in ill-prepared to receive the highest teachings of the Upanishads in their pure form, he must find ways to bring that sublime message forcefully into his listeners' minds. He used stories, similes, jokes, charts — whatever means he could devise to reach past the tumult in many a mind.

Yet there were always some listeners in the audience who heard the message behind the stories and glimpsed the subtlety and simplicity of the eternal teaching.

Reaching the Listeners

A listener at one of Swamiji's spiritual camps became perplexed during a lecture because she sensed that the ultimate message of Vedanta was extremely simple and clear, yet Swamiji was as though embroidering it with many unnecessary details.

She wanted to ask him about it but was reluctant to do so in front of others, since she considered her question impolite and perhaps presumptuous. So she waited until everyone had left the *satsang* and approached him:

"Swamiji, why is it that the truth you give out to us is like a clean, straight line, yet you then proceed to put all sorts of embellishments around it. Why?"

Swamiji was looking out the window. He said, "That's because of what *they* need. They have a need to hear it that way."[2]

Another devotee has a somewhat similar story to tell:

The Teaching Beyond the Words

At one *yajna*, a listener tuned in to Swamiji's words in a particularly deep way. And the more she tuned in, the less important became the words — to the point where they seemed ridiculous. She looked at Swamiji on the lecturer's platform, and he seemed to be Shiva himself, dancing about in the form of Nataraja. She said to him in her mind: "How ridiculous that you keep talking on in words! It's so simple! It's all just Shiva's dance! The true teaching of

Vedanta is so far beyond any words that you or anyone else might utter!"

He looked across the many heads in the audience and straight into her eyes and winked meaningfully with both of his eyes as a smile spread across his face. She knew then that he had heard her inner cry and was agreeing with her.[3]

A Variety of Instruments

It was *satsang* time at the home of Neeru Mehta in Lucknow in the 1970s. A *sastri* [one knowledgeable in the scriptures], a senior professor of Sanskrit, had attended Swamiji's lecture and was now at the *satsang*. He had admired the lecture, but was perturbed about one detail and asked Swamiji about it, in Hindi:

"You give such good discourses on the *Gita*. So many educated people and youngsters listen with great discipline and interest. I don't understand why you don't speak in Hindi." (Swamiji had just been answering some questions posed by *satsang* attendees in Hindi.)

Swamiji was quiet. He looked at the professor with eyes full of compassion, smiled, and said, in Hindi, "*Sastriji*, the Lord has made this instrument (pointing to himself) for English-speaking seekers. He has a variety of *sastras* [instruments, weapons]. He uses them according to the necessity of time and place. Sometimes what a sword cannot do, the needle can do."[4]

Gurudev's teaching was tailor-made for each student, often creating what appeared to be contradictions:

One Question, Two Answers

Two devotees had both asked Swamiji a Vedanta question they had been wondering about. Both asked him the same question, but in private discussions with him received two different answers.

The two devotees got together and discussed this happening at length: Why two answers to the same question? How can that be? They continued discussing the dilemma for one year.

When Swamiji arrived again in the San Francisco Bay Area one year later, they said to him: "We asked you one question, Swamiji, but you gave us two different answers!"

"I didn't know you'd be talking to each other," said Swamiji. "I answered the question to suit each of you differently."[5]

Swamiji had an uncanny ability to relate subtle ideas by painting very graphic images that would cling to people's minds and remind them of the inner meaning of the teaching, as if to say, "I know that abstractions will go in one ear and out the other, but if I can paint a vivid picture for you, you're sure to remember!" One example:

Gruesome Immortality

"When the Upanishads say, 'You are immortal,' people generally think that means the body will be immortal," said Swamiji. Then he went on to describe the resulting scene:

"Just think: The swami keeps on living. One generation dies, the second generation dies, but the swami keeps on living. His body has shrunk a little, but he keeps on living. The body shrinks some more, but he keeps on living. He is immortal! Eventually, shrunk to a small size, he is put on the shelf. Then, one day, he becomes a toy for the cat!"[6]

He used this same principle in teaching young children. In fact, his sessions with children were so delightful and wise that many of us conspired to create ways to attend his talks with young listeners, although he often disallowed adults to attend his formally scheduled meetings with children. But when the chance was given to us, we sat in wonderment as we listened to him reaching the minds and hearts of the very young. G. B. Bhatia recalls:

Heavenly Birds

Gurudev would say that a spiritual teacher should be like a mother, giving out wisdom according to the digestive capacity of the receiver. A mother gives half milk, half water to a young baby and then reduces the amount of water as the child develops the capacity to digest milk. To a growing, active child she gives solid food, quite necessary for his growth and level of activity.

Once, a group of small children, some 5 to 8 years of age, had gathered in Gurudev's *kutiya*. Gurudev told them the following story:

There was a pair of heavenly birds who always flew above the clouds, not visible to the people on Earth. They were getting old and decided to have children. So they laid a cluster of eggs. The eggs were light, as all heavenly bodies are, but when the chicks inside them grew large and were ready for hatching, the eggs became heavy and started dropping toward the Earth.

Soon enough, small chick heads popped out of the eggs. Their mother told them, "You are heavenly birds. You have wings with which you can fly. All you have to do is:

Close your eyes.

Break the shell.

And spread your wings.

The chicks replied, "We are warm and comfortable in the shell. Only our heads are out, and they feel cold!"

Again, the mother advised them that it was for their own good that she wanted them to come out of the shell and realize their heavenly state by following the steps she had outlined:

Close your eyes.

Break the shell.

And spread your wings.

But the chicks would not listen and started falling faster and faster toward the Earth. Now the mother was full of anxiety, for soon the chicks would crash and die. So with full love and concern, she again pleaded with them:

Close your eyes.

Break the shell.

And spread your wings.

Among the group of chicks, two said to each other: "She is talking to us with so much love and concern. Let us try what she says!"

The two of them closed their eyes, broke their shells with a kick of their tiny feet, and spread their wings. Lo! They could fly in the sky! The rest of the chicks crashed to Earth and died.

Gurudev asked the children to repeat what the mother bird had advised the chicks to do. The children at his feet repeated in a loud chorus:

Close your eyes.

Break the shell.

And spread your wings.

Then he advised the children to obey their parents and told them that obeying their parents would always be for their own good.[7]

Many of us heard that same story — adjusted to our level of understanding but holding the same charm — repeated in lectures to adults, in order to bring home a powerful message about spiritual development: "Be brave enough to dash toward your inborn right to freedom!"

Gurudev took whatever opportunity he could to teach. Everyday, seemingly insignificant events became vehicles for passing on the message of the rishis [seers]:

The Burned Shirt

Gurudev was giving a *yajna* in Vancouver, Canada. One day, when it was Robyn Thompson's turn to iron his clothes, she somehow turned the iron on too high a setting and burned a hole in the front of one of his shirts.

Robyn felt miserable, thinking, "I have been given the privilege of ironing his clothes, and then I end up burning his shirt!"

Robyn recalls, "I thought to myself: It is always best to tell Gurudev about such instances right away, but one instinctively wants to delay. However, experience had shown me that it was always best to come out with the problem immediately, or else one would carry it all day as 'mental baggage' and not be able to see past that mental agitation."

Before Gurudev went to rest, Robyn summoned her courage and said quietly to him, "Swamiji, I burned your shirt: I am so sorry."

He roared a laugh: "The shirt may have gotten burned, but the swami did not! Never mind. What does it matter?"

For Robyn this became a powerful teaching about the immaculate nature of the Self that nothing can touch. She recalled how the *Bhagavad Gita* declares the Self beyond all destruction by material forces: "Fire cannot burn It, water cannot wet It . . ."

Says Robyn, "These words of Gurudev are ever in my memory and never cease to inspire me."[8]

We All Follow *His* Teachings

A new attendee of Swamiji's lectures, Michael Mayzel, had just finished his first lecture series with him and asked an older devotee for some advice:

"How do you thank a teacher?"

"Follow his teachings," was the older devotee's reply. When Michael was saying good-bye to Swamiji after the completion of the *yajna*, he said to his newfound guru, "Swamiji, I'll follow your teachings."

Swamiji smiled, "We *all* will follow *His* teachings."[9]

Gurudev made it very clear that the tradition of teaching he followed was uncompromisingly pure and serious. When he first came to the United States, he entered an environment of dynamic spiritual interest yet little discrimination among the hordes of potential seekers. In guiding us in our plans for arranging a *yajna*, he said:

> *I want in our publicity the full blast of our serious approach. Ours is not a cheap path: It is not catering to weak escapists, but meant for those of heart, head, and muscle! Please put it thick. We may not have thousands crawling into our halls, hoping for some miracle or some psychic tickling. I am not here in the USA to tickle people. We follow the ancient rishis — in their unadulterated, uncompromising, narrow path of self-evolution. This is not for all.*[10]

He scoffed at the idea that a simple exchange of mantra and money between teacher and seeker could bring an ardent lover of God any closer to realizing His true nature. He said in a letter in 1968:

> *There is no shortcut in evolution. Spirituality cannot be packaged and exchanged in the religion-market during a casual transaction called by the high-sounding, but empty, word "initiation," or* mantra diksa.

He was not shy about calling those who followed this process the *"large number of fools demanding an easy path to the Peak."* He went on to say:

> *The Royal Path of Vedanta is used only by a few lions among men. On our path there is no initiation; there are no shortcuts.*[11]

The Teaching Belongs to No One

When, under Swamiji's direction, we first began to lay the groundwork for starting a quarterly journal of Vedanta called *Mananam*, as its editor, I explained to Swamiji the need to copyright the material in order to protect it from plagiarism. But he was reluctant to do so: "No. This teaching belongs to no one. Copyrights are unnecessary." Finally, despite his resistance, I managed to convince him to allow the copyright to be registered, on the grounds that we sometimes reprinted materials already copyrighted by others, and our own copyright of the collected work would afford the other authors the appropriate protection.[12]

Lakshmi Reddy of Hyderabad had a similar experience. In 1976, she had written to Swamiji that after Chinmaya Mission had completed certain programs under their own umbrella, dozens of other organizations copied them in "plagiaristic mischief." Gurudev wrote back:

> *Chinmaya Mission's job is to initiate, pioneer, and propagate the true values of Vedantic life for humanity at large. India's hundreds of mystics, rishis, and* mahatmas *gave their best to the world at large. Why crib or monopolize? Let others copy and arrange more such programs. Stand apart and watch joyously. If others copy, glory in it, for they are also doing the same divine work. Silently congratulate them that our efforts have inspired other organizations. Our Mission's work is thus fulfilled.*

The full-time nature of a spiritual teacher's job was brought home in a short but telling exchange:

In Uniform at All Times

Swamiji had to go to a public meeting and asked a senior army officer to accompany him.

The officer said, "Swamiji, would you give me just a few minutes? I'll go and change out of my uniform. Then I'll be with you." (The regulations call for an army officer to be out of uniform when attending public meetings.)

Swamiji inquired, "Why? Are there certain things you're not supposed to do while in uniform?"

"Yes, Swamiji," was the reply.

"See that?" continued Swamiji. "That is why my guru said: Uniform at all times! So, even when I go to bed I wear my uniform!"[13]

GUIDING NEW TEACHERS

Swamiji never hesitated to encourage those who were ready to pass on the message of Vedanta to others. When a new devotee started her first study group, he wrote to her:

> *Jai Jai Jagadishvara! The Lord must be infinitely happy about your work. Ten students for you! This is Grace! Let us be humble and, surrendering unto Him in devotion, act on for His glorification. A new surge of confidence, a new flood of wisdom shall stream into you — and through you to others. The more the surrender, the thicker this beam of wisdom. Try! I am not exaggerating. It is our arrogant ego that clogs the streams of inspiration. Try!*[14]

And again:

> *Have you started independently helping five other Americans to get the lessons [the Chinmaya Postal Lesson Course] and to pursue Vedanta studies? This is the only antidote for the ailing nation that has reached now a stage of uncontrollable lust and passions, with nothing but threats of death and disaster thick in the atmosphere. The invigorating inner bliss of the Vedanta philosophy alone can refresh them and bring at least a look of sanity into those wild eyes of today's mad America. You now have a duty to perform to the people around you.*[15]

In response to a question from a study group leader who wondered how far one should go as group leader to guide others on the path, he said:

How much should we heckle and hackle, prod and bolster our group members? This problem has no rule-of-thumb. The law is we keep on helping others — the dull ones all the more lovingly. Never say, "I can't." Some of the dull ones open up finally as the best. Let them drop off if they want: You must with unabated enthusiasm encourage them. The fact that they come to the group shows there is something in them wanting to express itself. Om.[16]

And in a letter to a student who was just beginning to take up the task of teaching in a public lecture he said:

Each of you must thus burst into activity, [doing the teaching] as your own sadhana, *an offering unto the Self-in-all, a song of the depths bursting forth from oneself in spontaneous inspiration. Live Vedanta and just open the mouth and heart for its fragrance to spread. Live and then speak. Mere prattling will not help either the speaker or the listener.*[17]

In a letter to Br. Atma Chaitanya when he was about to go into the field to teach, he said:

If you are a real devotee of the Lord, you can do more service to the world than all the politicians put together.

Even the man who was to inherit Gurudev's mantle experienced vigorous early training as a fledgling teacher of others. Swami Tejomayananda, who became head of Chinmaya Mission worldwide after Gurudev's *Mahasamadhi*, remembers his own early days of training with his guru:

Rigorous Training

I also had the great fortune of learning from him. Many a time he would take me along to Uttarkashi. At that time, there was no regular Vedanta training course, so Gurudev used to teach *Vivekacudamani* and the *Gita*. While other Chinmaya Mission members would come and go, I was a nearly permanent student there. I used to sit right in the front. Actually, I felt that Gurudev used to teach me only.

Every now and then, he would ask questions, and if out of ten questions I didn't answer even one or I didn't answer quickly enough, he would say, "You don't know the answer" or "You are sleeping in class." Sometimes, he would speak and leave the sentence half-way and ask me to complete it. And if I spoke softly, Gurudev would ask me to go out on the banks of the Ganga and speak so loudly that the man on the other side could hear me.[18]

At his Sandeepany institutes of Vedanta, Swamiji encouraged the students to begin practicing public speaking in front of the group, training them slowly to become teachers in their own right. Also among householder devotees, he created opportunities for public-speaking practice:

Unexpected Instruction

The year was 1971. I was deeply involved in serving and motivating the study classes in Bombay. Being an ardent student of *Valmiki Ramayana,* I used to share the glories of the epic with small groups. I often quoted relevant examples from it in my study classes. The news of my inherent love for the *Ramayana* had somehow reached Gurudev.

One Sunday morning, when I went to Gurudev's *kutiya* to offer my *pranams,* Gurudev looked up with a smile and, to my surprise, commanded, "This evening you are going to give an hour's talk on the *Ramayana* in the temple hall."

Naturally, I became nervous, as this was to be my first public talk in Gurudev's presence! In the evening, I followed Gurudev up the temple steps, my heart beating unusually fast. The Jagadeeshwara Temple was packed to capacity, adding to my nervousness. Gurudev then bade me to sit on the *Vyasa Pitha* [literally, "Vyasa's seat," or the seat of the teacher]. When I hesitated, Gurudev raised his voice with a loud "Hmmm," and pointed his finger toward the *Gita.*

After prostrations to Lord Jagadeeshwara and Gurudev, I sat down, closed my eyes, and started the discourse with the recitation of the traditional verses.

I felt a strong and sudden surge of inspiration from within. I could not see Gurudev, as he chose to sit next to the *Vyasa Pitha.* The unprepared topic turned out to be *"Ramayana,* the Essence of the Vedas."

Gurudev was overjoyed. After offering affectionate words of appreciation and encouragement, he took off the gold chain with a rare gold-bound *rudraksa* that he had been wearing for years and lovingly put it around my neck.

He said with a smile and a pat, "Wear it always."

I felt blessed and overwhelmed with a deep sense of gratitude. A divine sense of fulfillment, resulting from the overflowing of the guru's grace, pervaded me.[19]

Later came additional instructions:

"Fire Off!"

In 1978 Gurudev instructed me to conduct my first *Ramayana Yajna* in Bangalore, India. Just around that time, Gurudev happened to be in Bangalore, but had to leave a day before the *yajna* was to begin. At the airport, before checking in, Swamiji sensed my anxiety on the eve of the first *yajna*. He turned toward me and said in a loud voice: "Mani, close your eyes and fire off!"

With the spiritual battery charged, that is what I have been doing all these years — as his instrument.[20]

Youngsters in Training

The youngsters of the Chinmaya Yuva Kendra of Chennai had arrived at the Sidhabari ashram during a spiritual camp there. The dining hall became vibrant, with them enthusiastically running about serving food. Not only that, but the evenings became more entertaining with the brilliant shows they staged. . . .

The best was yet to come. After one evening discourse, Gurudev stepped down from the dais and announced, "Today the youngsters will give you a talk on *Sri Rama Gita* from *Tulsi Ramayana*."

Three youngsters got up.

Gurudev said, "Up on my seat."

The youngsters crept up, dead nervous. And who would not be? Three hundred people all dressed in saffron robes staring at you, and add to that the Master of Masters himself sitting at the end of the hall to hear you speak!

A little of fumbling in the beginning and then . . . they fired off confidently. Each of the three speakers spoke for five minutes. All the listeners were impressed. Imagine the joy rising in the bosom of the Master as he saw his 35 years of hard work finding its fulfillment![21]

As new teachers began their work of teaching, they met up with various obstacles: For some it was too much vanity; for some, not enough courage; yet for others, too great an identification with the role of teaching. Gurudev had advice for one and all:

Brush aside pride and vanity and permit God to work in and through you.

When you speak, don't have the attitude that you are teaching others. You are only reflecting and thinking — aloud — on the problem at hand. Others are overhearing your thought parade. That is all. Surrender unto Him, and you will then be His instrument to serve all others around the world.[22]

When did the flute worry about the audience or have to judge what tune to play next? Be a flute in His hands. Only when you are acting with ego can you get upset emotionally, exhausted physically, and confused intellectually.[23]

No Introduction Needed

Before one of his annual *yajnas* in San Francisco, Gurudev asked me to give the introductory talk. I was honored, but also a little apprehensive about speaking in front of some two to three hundred people. As I was about to speak, Swamiji, who was sitting next to me at the podium, turned toward me and eyed me with piercing interest. I realized that speaking to an audience of hundreds was simple compared to speaking in the presence of one's own guru, for whom one yearned to be all-perfect. As I moved into my short talk, the paper in my hands began to shake, as did my knees and my voice. Though immersed in a favorite subject of mine, my guru, instead of soaring on flights of inspiration, I was instead drowning in nervousness. Swamiji interrupted me halfway through the ordeal, turned to the audience, and explained with a chuckle: "The swami needs no introduction. It's the students who need to practice public speaking." Then, turning to me, he said, "Go on. Relax, relax. Take your time. Relax!" The rest of the talk progressed easily.[24]

Teacher as Gardener

Swami Subodhananda recalls Swamiji giving him the following guidelines for teaching a new batch of students at Sandeepany (Himalayas) in Sidhabari:

"We are the gardeners; the students are the flowers. You, as teacher, can protect them from wild things, but you cannot make them blossom. Whatever color they already have will come out — *you* cannot make it come out. It will happen in its own time."

"I was appointed to be gardener here," says Swami Subodhananda of his responsibilities at the Sidhabari ashram. "Gurudev gave me the equipment and the job."[25]

In a letter to Luis Jauregui, a California devotee who had begun teaching Vedanta both in English and Spanish, starting with a *yajna* in English in 1975 in San Francisco, he wrote:

I admire your missionary zeal. Depend upon Him. Watch how He organizes your future and how He uses each of us. Yield to His will and act.

And in yet another letter, Swamiji reminded him as to Who was really in charge, Who was doing the work:

Learn to surrender unto Him in all actions and act as He dictates.

Wait and serve.

Watch and serve.

He shall reveal His plan to such an individual!

Similar reminders appeared in subsequent letters, as Swamiji implored the new teacher to keep the ego at bay and to surrender to the Higher in the work of teaching:

Surrender yourself and wish to serve the people ardently — the rest will flow out of you. Scrape off [any manifestations of the ego] if the ego arises and if selfish ideas spring up. These can clog the entire flow. Beware![26]

Gurudev always knew when each of his new teachers was ready for the next step. Some he held back from certain activities at a given time, others he prodded and pushed into action:

Best Timing

After the course at Uttarkashi was coming to an end, the student who was to become Swami Purushottamananda had developed a strong desire to visit Badrinath, a holy site relatively close to Uttarkashi. When he approached Gurudev for permission to go, he said, "No. First you go out into the field for two years. Learn to stand on your own feet and then you may go to Badrinath."

The brahmachari was quite disappointed, but obeyed his teacher, making a resolution that at the end of the two years he would definitely go on a pilgrimage to Badrinath.

At the end of the two years, the young brahmachari checked his calendar and found that he could make the much-desired trip. Fortunately, Gurudev himself was to be at Uttarkashi around the same time, so the brahmachari traveled to Rishikesh, from where he could choose to travel further either to Badrinath or to Uttarkashi.

"I was thinking of writing to Gurudev to seek permission again but was scared that he might refuse!" remembers Swami Purushottamananda. "On reaching Rishikesh, I found that all the buses going to Badrinath were full. Thus, I was left with no alternative but to proceed to Uttarkashi. Even then, I had decided that I would just offer my *pranams* to Swamiji and move on. The rest I left to fate and to Gurudev. If he said no, I would cancel the trip."

Once in Uttarkashi, the brahmachari offered his *pranams* to his teacher, who said to him, "You want to go to Badrinath immediately, don't you?" The young disciple was shocked that even after two years Gurudev had remembered and had read his mind without even the slightest prompting from him. Gurudev then asked Swami Vajreshwarananda to arrange for the ticket and show the young disciple how to get to Badrinath and what sights to see. Later, in Rishikesh, the brahmachari had to change buses. Even so, he got a seat and everything went smoothly. When he returned, he discovered that the earlier batch that had been traveling with him on the leg to Rishikesh was still there, waiting for their connection to Badrinath.

Concludes Swami Purushottamananda, "When you leave everything to Gurudev, it all comes out OK."[27]

One Meal a Day

Brahmachari Sudheer, later to be known as Swami Dheerananda, wrote to Gurudev seeking his permission to go to Uttarkashi for nine months after the completion of the Vedanta course at Sandeepany Sadhanalaya. "Since Sri Gurudev was in Uttarkashi with Sri Swami Tapovanji Maharaj for some years, I thought that I should be there at least for some months," recalled Swami Dheerananda later.

Some days after the brahmachari had sent the letter, Swamiji reached the ashram in Mumbai, looked at the young brahmachari-in-training, and exclaimed, "Nine months in Uttarkashi?! You will die there! Go for one month only!"

"Yes, Swamiji," was the brahmachari's quick reply. Then he added: "Swamiji, may I go for forty-one days?" Sri Gurudev smiled and agreed, "OK!"

In a few days, the brahmachari received a letter from his guru guiding him in his projected *sadhana* at Uttarkashi:

> *Eat one meal a day.*
>
> *Do 1,000* Gayatri Mantra japa *in the morning.*
>
> *Study in the afternoon.*
>
> *Contemplate in the evening.*[28]

Preparing the Disciple

When the young woman who later became Swamini Samvidananda took the course at Sandeepany Sadhanalaya, she did not complete the full two and a half years. She had previously been a professor, and Swamiji was determined that she complete her education.

"Get your PhD. Finish your studies. I don't want your parents to think they've lost you," he said to her, assuring her that whatever texts she may have missed studying at the Sandeepany course she may learn from him by attending his camps and *yajnas*. And so she did.

At some point thereafter, Swamiji instructed her to start teaching — passing on what she had learned at Sandeepany. "Call all your neighbors for a cup of tea," he said, "and start lecturing. If neighbors are not available, call together some students. If students are not available, call some servants. Make them sit and you start teaching. They may not be benefited by your teaching, but *you* will be!"

After her Vedanta studies were complete, she worked as a principal of a post-graduate college for seven years and then took early retirement. At this point she wanted to dedicate her life totally to Swamiji's work and was ready to do anything to support it, even sweep floors, if need be. She went to Sidhabari to meet him there and prostrated at his feet:

"So you've left the college?" Swamiji inquired.

"Yes, Swamiji."

"You're not going back?"

"No, Swamiji."

"So, you've left one college. I'm giving you 55 schools [the Chinmaya Vidyalayas totaled 55 at that time]!" Swamiji declared.

She felt a little nervous at the thought. He patted her with a consoling hand, "Don't worry. Come with me to Bombay. See all the files; then you'll understand what Chinmaya Vidyalayas stand for."

After she submitted her first report on the schools, Swamiji wrote: "I just finished reading your reports. I liked them very much: so precise! . . . "[29]

Gurudev's innovative suggestions for gathering together a beginning teacher's first audience re-echo his own early efforts in publicizing his talks:

Announcements by Bicycle

In the initial stages, there were no workers to publicize or promote the work Swamiji was doing. There was no money either for any kind of publicity. So Swamiji would himself cycle around the town with a megaphone in hand. He would wear a vest and a turban when he went about announcing his own talks. He would shout, "Come and listen to the Swamiji who has come from Uttarkashi and is giving good talks in English!"[30]

Keeping the Candle Lit

One of the brachmacharis working in India had been doing his Vedanta teaching work in the field for some three or four years when he wrote to Swamiji complaining that the workers who were once helping him had left him and that now fewer people came to listen to him. He felt bogged down in a morass of obstacles and felt no longer useful where he was serving.

Swamiji's reply was largely a story:

> *I have received your letter. Just forget all about it; such things happen now and then. Don't take anything to heart. You will regain your place in time. Now you listen to this story:*

> *"Once a blind swami was visiting another swami in his* kutiya *in Uttarkashi. While they were talking, night slowly descended in the valley, but both were unaware of it.*
>
> *"By and by the guest got up to leave, but before he parted, the host swami gave him a coconut shell with a lighted candle in it.*
>
> *"Naturally, the departing guest protested, 'What's the matter with you, Swamiji? You know I'm blind. To me night and day, darkness and light are the same. So why have you given me this lighted candle?' 'No, no,' explained the host. 'This light is not for you, Maharaj. It is for others — that they may not crash into you.'*
>
> *"Satisfied, the* sadhu *left, carrying the light.*
>
> *"As the blind swami proceeded in the light of his prodding stick, cautiously moving forward, suddenly someone coming from the opposite direction bumped into him. 'Haven't you eyes, my man? Can't you see the candle-light? How careless you are!' cried the blind swami. The man merely said, 'Your candle has gone out in the breeze. There is no light in your shell.' And he walked away."*
>
> *Brahmachari, now you retire to a quiet place nearby and live for three weeks in study,* japa, *meditation, and one meal a day. Keep* mauna *[silence]. Learn again to smile within. The candle has no light now. It is only a shell that cannot help others.*[31]

Because all brahmacharis and brahmacharinis did not follow a continuously smooth trip upward on their own evolutionary ladder, observers at times expressed doubts to Gurudev about the quality of teachers that Sandeepany Sadhanalaya had produced.

Different Kinds of Disciples

In the late 1970s, a devotee asked Gurudev in a letter:

"Swamiji, are all the students of Sandeepany Sadhanalaya coming up equally well? Where are they all now? We hear of only a few brahmacharis. What about the others?"

Swamiji replied:

> *All of them are really good and up and coming, and they are at different stages of their unfoldment. Some take a longer time to shed their ego, and so for a length of time they suffer under its inner tangles and inhibitions. Some surrender their personal ego too quickly, explode into blinding brilliance, and then again recrystallize for themselves a new ego built laboriously on their own little successes. To break it they need constant help from us at Sandeepany, from time to time, for years.*
>
> *As the ancient masters say, disciples fall characteristically into three prototypes: (1) those who impart Vedanta* sastra *[scriptural] knowledge to others, efficiently and eloquently, (2) those who maintain and administer our various organizational activities, and (3) some dreary rice-bags and hapless clothes hangers. These are in every institution the world over, in any walk of life, especially, I must admit, in all spiritual and religious organizations . . . .*
>
> *In fact, it is almost axiomatic to declare that every teacher must recognize that his disciples are a mixture of the poor, the fair, and the good types. The poor disciple utilizes the teacher's influence and benefits by it; the fair disciple admires and even reveres the teacher's kindness; the good disciple alone can thrive and grow under the teacher's strict discipline, and himself become a teacher.*
>
> *Now I am sure I have replied you exhaustively. If you had written to me to discourage me, you have certainly failed. I am closely observing and anxiously reviewing the performance of my boys and girls who have left or who are with us still at Sandeepany Sadhanalaya. There is no point in hurrying anyone. Growth is effective and enduring, beautiful and enchanting only when it takes place at its own leisurely pace and in its own natural rhythm. Watch a flower opening. Look at the dawn and the sunrise, the dusk and the sunset. No hurry! Let it happen — at His gracious pace!*[32]

You Know More Than You Think You Know

A devotee of many years had led many study groups and helped in various ways with Chinmaya Mission's work, but had seldom had the chance to be an assistant to him in his daily correspondence. Finally, during a trip in which she joined him overseas, there was a blessed chance to participate, together with another devotee, in the daily duties of preparing his clothes, straightening up his room, and helping him with his correspondence.

One day she was sitting at his feet as he was sitting at his desk. She was sorting through the letters he had just received and passing them on to him for reading. As was his habit, he commenced to read some of the letters out loud, slurring over some words, then punctuating others with great emphasis or a cascade of dramatic intonations. One letter was of particular interest to the devotee. It asked a question about a fine point of Vedanta pertaining to the relationship between *jiva*, the individual soul, *Isvara*, the Lord, and *Brahman*, the supreme Reality. She couldn't wait to see what answer Swamiji would write to that particular letter, since she, too, wanted to know the answer.

She proceeded to take down dictation for all the letters in the pile, but no answer came to the letter that had peaked her interest. When she was about ready to leave his side to type up the just dictated letters in her own room, Swamiji handed her the letter with the question about *jiva-Isvara-Brahman*:

"Here," he said. "You answer it. I'll sign it."

She was in shock. But she didn't know the answer! How could she follow his instruction? But she trusted his action and kept quiet.

Once in her room, she proceeded to type up her notes for all the letters he had dictated. Finally, she had to gather the courage to write the answer that was entrusted to her. She prayed to her guru in her mind and searched for the right words deep inside her. Miraculously, they came.

When she took her letter to Swamiji for signature, he read it quickly and, without making one mark of correction on it, signed it.[33]

NATURE

Gurudev was at times heard commenting that his own guru, Swami Tapovanam of Uttarkashi, was finely attuned to nature, but he himself, not being as fond of walking over great expanses of countryside as his guru had been, was less of a nature lover. However, his devotees remember otherwise. Although he was not given to long nature walks, there is little doubt that his connection to nature was very strong and very deep.

Beauty — His Expression

Swamiji was resting on a verandah in Nairobi, Kenya. With him were three long-time devotees, Anjali Singh, Asha Kamdar, and Neeru Mehta. Swamiji was admiring the nature around him and the clouds moving gently in the sky.

"*When* do they move and change shapes we do not know, but they *do* move," he said.

Looking at the clouds, Neeru said, "They are like *jagat* [the world], moving and changing patterns without us knowing how they all change."

"Yes," said Swamiji.

Neeru remembered how, at another time, while Swamiji was in transit on an airplane, he had said: "I am the midday sun. You can see in its light, but you cannot see *it*. You can only see the rising and setting sun."

He had continued, "You can see all objects in the light of the sun, even yourself and the swami, but you cannot see the sun — the subject."

Thus, deep in reflection, the small group sitting with Swamiji in Nairobi became quite still.

Swamiji said, "In moments like this you see things very clearly, but you cannot stay there. You return, because the customs officers there are very strict" [referring to the fact that glimpses of an egoless state are possible now and then, but our habit patterns pull us back into the world as we have known it].

"This natural beauty," added Swamiji, "also gives *santi* [peace]. It is *santam, sivam* [auspiciousness], *sundaram* [beauty]. If beauty is seen as His expression, it gives *santi* and is *sivam*."[1]

Gracious Like the Sun

The Master sat out in the open [at his ashram at Sidhabari], his disciples sitting all around him. He looked up at the mountains and smiled, "Mother Nature is shy: She is dressing up the mountains behind a thick curtain of clouds."

Such informal *satsangs* became more frequent. Gurudev would come out every evening and sit out in the open. We sat around him, as he spread peace, joy, and laughter. Sometimes he looked up at the mountains, and with his sharp vision peeped behind the curtain and informed us that the "manufacturing" of the snow was going on well. We waited impatiently to see.

At other times, he would look toward the setting sun and say, "Look how graciously the sun sets. This is how you must grow old — graciously, majestically."[2]

One *Sannyasin* Among a Thousand

In January 1980, Swamiji was being driven from Sidhabari, where work had just begun on the ashram. Two cars were in the entourage on the way to Jammu to catch a plane there. Swamiji's car, as always, was ahead, going fast. The second car lagged behind and soon was out of view. Seeing a beautiful spot by the road, Swamiji said, "Let's stop here and wait for the other car to catch up with us."

The hillside beyond was covered with deodar trees. In the middle of the mass of green was one deciduous tree, resplendent in bright autumn colors. Bedecked in bright orange, it stood out among the mass of green.

"See?" said Swamiji, "among the trees also — one *sannyasin* among a 1,000 trees!"[3]

Stories abound about how Swamiji related to animals — and they to him.

Obedient Peacocks

Once, during a *yajna* in Andhra Pradesh, a lot of peacocks were screeching during Gurudev's talk. After some time, Gurudev said in a very loud but affectionate voice:

"Murugan, Murugan, go!" Thereafter, the peacocks were silent.

According to the *Puranas*, Murugan [also known as Karttikeya] is the son of Lord Shiva, and his *vahana* [vehicle] is a peacock.[4]

A Snake in the Audience

During a *yajna*, while Swamiji was expounding Chapter XI of the *Gita*, "The Cosmic Form Divine," a small snake wriggled into the hall. Naturally, some devotees became restless, and one of them picked up a stick lying nearby.

"What is it?" asked Gurudev.

"Swamiji — a snake!" the devotees said in explanation.

"Leave it alone," Swamiji said. "How do you know which *jiva* comes in which form to see the *Visvarupa* [cosmic form] of the Lord?"[5]

A Hen's Circumambulation

At a *yajna* in India, after the talk was finished on the last day of the lecture series, Gurudev was doing *japa*. After the *japa*, when he was about to get up from his chair, a hen was seen walking gracefully up the platform and toward Swamiji. Swamiji sank back into his chair and watched the hen quietly without blinking an eye. The hen walked past Gurudev, went for a *pradaksina* [circumambulation] around Swami Tapovanji's photo, and walked down the ramp. Only then did Gurudev get up to leave the dais.[6]

Conversation with Birds

During one stay at a devoted couple's home, Swamiji's hosts noticed that every time he left the house the birds would start chirping very loudly, even shrieking. The shrieks were especially loud when he was walking toward the car to go to the airport to travel to his next destination.

"Yes?" he said, turning to the sound in the trees. "I shall return. I'll be back!"

Swamiji actually did come back sooner than anyone had expected, for his schedule was changed to include a previously unscheduled stopover in their city.[7]

Swamiji used to bring plants from around the world to Sidhabari to be replanted on the ashram grounds — redwood saplings from California, cherry trees from Australia, still other plants from elsewhere. All his plants and flowers received intense and loving care from him.

Young Ones Need Extra Care

One year Swamiji brought a small blossoming cherry plant from Australia to his ashram in Sidhabari. He called the gardener and showed him the exact spot where he wanted the sapling to be planted. Then, as the gardener was doing the planting, Swamiji stood by his side and watched. He instructed the gardener that a small wire cage, draped with cloth on the sides as well as the top, be placed around the plant and that it be watered regularly.

During the course of the spiritual camp that was then in session, every day Swamiji went to inspect the plant, instructing the gardener to open up the enclosure and see how the little sapling was doing. First, he instructed the gardener to lift the cover in the morning but to put it back before noon to protect the plant from the scorching sun. With each passing day, the cover was left off a little longer until finally, a few weeks later, as the cover over the sapling was opened up, Swamiji said:

"Look! Now you don't need to cover the sapling anymore. It's strong enough already. Even a storm won't affect it now." He paused, looked at the tiny tree and the devotees gathered around it and said:

"In the beginning you have to protect a plant from the scorching sun and the rain and the wind. It's the same with spiritual seekers. In the beginning, they need protection and support, but as they grow strong, they can stand on their own feet."

By the time the camp was over, the plant had just the wire mesh around it, no cloth. It was well on its way to making Sandeepany Himalayas its permanent home.[8]

"My Arms and Legs"

Swamiji received a call from someone saying that Jairam Jaisinghani, the ashram manager, was cutting down trees at Sandeepany Sadhanalaya. Swamiji called the ashram to give his directive:

"No more cutting of trees. These trees are my own arms and legs. You cut my trees, and I'll cut *you.*"

As it turned out, only one branch needed to be cut that was scraping against Swamiji's *kutiya*. So Swamiji authorized the work — but with his warning in place.[9]

Talking Trees

At Krishnalaya during the 1992 spring camp, Swamiji had been asking for several days that four tall evergreen trees in front of his residence be trimmed back: He wanted a "wall" of trees created, he said. The trees looked too "undisciplined" for an ashram, he explained to the staff. Though puzzled by the instruction, members of the Krishnalaya staff began to call the various tree-pruning establishments in the area, and every one of them said: "What?! Pruning in May? This is the wrong time for pruning! If you prune now, the trees will die!"

Discouraged by the experts, the staff hesitated and kept postponing the action, but Swamiji persisted. Finally, it was agreed that two feet would be trimmed from each of the trees — and it was done. Swamiji inspected the job and was satisfied, indicating that the trees will be all right, that we just needed to give them a bit of extra water for a few days.

That afternoon, an unseasonable rain fell to bless the freshly trimmed trees. (And years later, the trees are still standing tall and healthy.)

As Swamiji stood near the trees, inspecting the trimming job, he chatted with a few people about the proceedings. One person offered recently heard information about the messages that plants send to one another via chemical substances transmitted through the air. By this means, it seems that plants can truly communicate, just as some traditional tales tell us. Then Swamiji proceeded to tell several stories to elaborate on the theme:

Sometimes, he said, people in India play out a drama in front of a tree that is not producing fruit, in order to induce it to produce. For instance: A fruit tree was not producing fruit year after year, so father and son walk out to it one day, and the father wields his ax, ready to cut the tree down. The son pleads, "No, father, don't cut the tree yet! Wait for one more year. If in one year the tree produces no fruit, then you can cut it down." The father relents. Before the year is out, the tree has produced the first crop of fruit.

Then, from his own experience Swamiji told the following story:

At Swamiji's ashram in Mumbai, Sandeepany Sadhanalaya, he had instructed his workers to plant some creepers near one of the buildings. From year to year the creepers showed no sign of blossoming. Then came time for some remodeling of the nearby buildings and Swamiji instructed the workers, "These creepers haven't blossomed once. Cut them down when you begin the remodeling work."

Then he left for a two-week lecture tour in South India. When he returned, the creepers were in bloom. And, of course, they were spared.[10]

A Healing Touch

In the winter of 1991, Swamiji was again at Sidhabari, and was once again inspecting his plants and trees. One small redwood tree, which had traveled there from northern California, was obviously ailing. He called the gardener and said, with concern and tenderness in his voice:

"How come this tree is ailing?"

He asked the gardener to cut two of its dry branches and then held his hands against the tree trunk for a while. For the next few days he repeated the action, holding his hand against the tree trunk while saying words of encouragement: "It's OK. You'll be all right."

The tree still stands there today, strong and healthy.[11]

Water Discovered

Swamini Sharadapriyananda was planning to organize a social welfare project that came to be known as Chinmayaranyam. She had chosen a site among the poorest of the poor in the state of Andra Pradesh in India. The land was very undeveloped, with no apparent source of water, although many attempts had been made to dig a well on the land.

The swamini invited Gurudev to the site to show him where she was planning to set up the new ashram. A *bhiksha* had been arranged for him there. After the meal was concluded, he took some water in his mouth to rinse it out and then spat it out on the bare ground near him.

"Who said there is no water here?" he said, laughing.

The swamini noted the exact spot.

After Gurudev left, she located that same spot and had the workers dig for a well there. They found water at that exact spot, even though earlier they had dug in the same area, but with no success.

Today, the site holds 60 acres of newly forested land.[12]

Stories abound about how Gurudev's presence influenced the weather:

Last-Minute Sunshine

In March of 1982 a *yajna* was being planned in New Delhi. For seven days it had been raining, but the organizers — recalling the many times that nature seemed to have adjusted herself to Gurudev's needs — said, "The rains will stop when the *yajna* starts," but inauguration day arrived and it was still raining.

Then, just half an hour before the official inauguration was to commence at 6 p.m., the rains finally stopped, and the sun peeped out for a short while before setting. That night, after the lecture was over, a downpour came once again. However, for the remaining days of the week-long *yajna*, not a drop of rain was to be seen.[13]

Many stories are told about how, with Gurudev's blessings, nature was coaxed into submission at the site that houses his Sandeepany (Himalayas) ashram in Sidhabari:

With Hanumanji's Help

When Chinmaya Mission obtained a piece of land donated by a devotee in Sidhabari, Himachal Pradesh, India, Gurudev planned for the construction of an ashram there. He called for the engineers and construction crew to begin the work. Once the contractors had reached the place and actually commenced the work, they found that it was completely inappropriate, even impossible, to build on the site. The land was on a small hillock overlooking a vast open plain skirting the high Himalayan peaks. Strong hurricane-like winds could lift entire buildings away.

Sri Gurudev was passing that region one day and visited the site to evaluate progress. The contractors plainly told him about the impossibility of the project.

Gurudev remained long in meditation at the site. When he opened his eyes, he said, "We will have an ashram here. But first let us bring Sri Hanumanji. When the father sees his son, Vayu Bhagavan will calm down." [Vayu, Lord of the Wind, is Sri Hanumanji's father.][14]

They learned that the patch of land was known to all surrounding villagers to be uninhabitable because of the strong winds. No one had ventured to build a house there.

Taming the Winds

In the beginning, the Sidhabari ashram had only four buildings. Then some barracks were built with corrugated metal roofs as temporary housing. The winds were so strong that sheets of metal would occasionally fly off the buildings across the ashram grounds. People would have to hold hands to walk across the grounds without being toppled by the winds.

Many a devotee asked, "Swamiji, how can you build an ashram where it is so windy?"

"Don't worry. When Hanuman comes, the winds will stop," was Swamiji's reply.

And so it happened. Once the 40-foot Hanuman idol was installed, the winds stopped.[15]

Rain Not Invited

The inauguration of the Sidhabari ashram, Sandeepany (Himalayas), was fixed for April 23 and 24, 1981. It had been raining heavily for the past ten days. It was now April 21, and we were wondering how the function would be held.

Param Pujya Gurudev arrived on April 22. He looked up at the dark, clouded sky and said in a loud voice: "I did not invite you!" — as if ordering Lord Indra to withdraw.

The rain stopped, and we held our inauguration in bright sunshine.

At noon on April 25, when we were dismantling the inauguration set-up, showers returned with a vengeance.[16]

The *Devas'* Celebration

It was the eve of the first Hanuman *Abhisheka* at Sandeepany Himalayas in Sidhabari, on October 9, 1982. Around 4 p.m. it started drizzling. The devotees were anxious.

"Why worry?" said Swamiji. "He is Vayu Putra [the Son of Vayu, the Wind God]. The *devas* [deities] also want to celebrate His birth. Vayu is their friend."

A light shower continued for about ten minutes. Then the sky cleared, with not a speck of cloud anywhere. Snow caps could be seen on the Himalayan range beyond the ashram. The sky had been cleared for the big rituals the following day.[17]

Waves of Rain

In 1992, a video recording was being created of Gurudev's *Vivekacudamani* lectures at the Sidhabari ashram. A heavy rainstorm set in, and the rain made so much noise against the roof of the hall that the sound at times drowned out Gurudev's voice. Gurudev told Shubhra Tandon, who was overseeing the videotaping, to hold up her hand as a signal to him to stop talking when the sound of the rain began to drown out his voice.

Although Shubhra was feeling reluctant to use this method to stop Gurudev's lecture mid-stream, the next time the sound of the rainstorm drowned out his speech, she gathered up her courage and raised her hand. He stopped talking.

He asked one of the devotees to sing a *bhajan*. During the *bhajan*, he stretched out his hands across his knees with palms upward. His eyes were closed, apparently in prayer. The first *bhajan* finished. The *bhajan* singer waited to see what Gurudev's next directive would be. It was still raining very hard.

"I'm sending an appeal," he said, pointing upward. "Sing another one."

As the second *bhajan* began, Gurudev returned to his meditative state. The rain tapered off, then again blasted down with great noise. After a little while, the rain tapered off once again and finally died down altogether. Meantime, Gurudev was still in meditative prayer. Then he nodded his head, smiled, and started talking.

Every afternoon, Shubhra used to review the videos taken in the morning class. The taping had been done using two cameras, one focusing on close-up views. She now had a chance to see, close up, what had transpired during the time Gurudev sat in prayer with palms raised upward. During the singing of the second *bhajan*, Gurudev's palms were first open. Then he folded his fingers back over his palms, forming loose fists. He did this several times, alternating between open and closed palms. When he unfolded his fingers, the sound of the rain was heard to be very strong. When he folded his fingers back over his palms, the sound of the rain tapered off.

Shubhra had not noticed this detail during the actual taping, but during her review of the close-up shots, she realized, in utter awe, that the movement of his hands exactly matched the surging and ebbing of the sound of the rain.[18]

Snow in the Summer

Whenever Swamiji conducted spiritual camps at the Sidhabari ashram, there was always snowfall on the mountains. One year, snow fell even in June, a month during which snow never falls otherwise. The devotees saw it as a sign that the *devas* were offering *vibhuti* [holy ash], in the form of snow, to Swamiji.[19]

Once Again, the Lord's Grace

After all the stories I had heard about how the very elements bowed their heads at the sight of Gurudev's divine work at Sidhabari, at the October 1997 Hanuman *Ahbisheka* at Sidhabari, we again witnessed that miracle continuing. It had been raining hard up until the day of the camp; then the rains stopped, and the camp, along with the filming that had been planned, proceeded in sunshine. Then, on the day of the *abhisheka* — when we formed long lines to take our turn at the "bathing" ceremony, and then as we sat down in front of the statue of Hanuman after the oblations were over — the sun mercifully hid behind a vast cloud cover, so that the heat would not strain us unduly. Just before the *arati*, a few drops of rainwater fell to bless the event. And, at the very moment the light was circled in front of Hanumanji, the sun peeped out between the clouds for one long minute and again disappeared from view.[20]

BEYOND THE BODY

Swamiji's relationship to his own body was the ultimate teaching on how to deal with the body's constant attempts to bind us. In May 1967, he sent a note to an early devotee in the United States:

> *Last evening in the discourse while on the stage I took slightly ill, and I have been advised to take a little more rest if I have planned to work a few more years. The body belongs to Narayana, and its repair and maintenance is entirely His responsibility. However, as the driver in charge of this vehicle, I am planning to give it some rest. And serve!*

In September of that year he wrote:

> *I am watching a tremendous change in myself. Now I want to retire for two to three years before I rush out for work. But can I? How can I get rid of the red monkey on my back? Mother Ganga commanded me some fifteen years ago to go out and serve. Let her clear my way to go back to quiet and rest. Om. Om. Om.*

The following month, October, he wrote:

> *You should not in the least feel worried that I am going into retreat. This is only a temporary phase. If, on a long pilgrimage, your vehicle is pulled up at a filling station for gas, you should not grudge the few moments that are lost; for without gasoline, the vehicle would get stranded. I am pulling up only for a refill. In fact, I am not even going to switch off. We will be putting the gas into my car while it's still running.*

In May of the following year, 1968, he wrote:

> *I have successfully done it all and here I am, after sixteen years of continuous work in the service of Narayana, back again in my Hut of Meditation on the banks of Mother Bhagirathi for a retreat of at least six continuous months.*

Here also it is not going to be a total retreat. I will have some thirteen students (full-timers) and their lessons will go on, both in the morning and in the evening.[1]

REPEATED CHALLENGES

Despite Gurudev's efforts to go into retreat, his body finally succumbed to the relentless pace that he had put it through. In early 1969, he suffered a massive heart attack that kept him relatively inactive for many more months.

"I Have Told Lord Death to Wait"

Many years ago, when I was still a brahmachari posted in Poona, Gurudev had his first heart attack in Mysore. Devotees around him panicked. On hearing the news, I went to Mysore. Everyone was worried. After two days, when Gurudev regained consciousness, he said, "I have told Yamaraja [Lord Death] to wait. I have lots of work to finish."[2]

In October of that year Swamiji wrote:

At New Delhi, the head of the Cardiac Department at the Indian Institute of Medical Sciences, Dr. Roy, is the authority. He examined me long. He is satisfied with my progress, though it is slow, as I am now running the sixth month after the attack — but it was a massive attack, indeed.[3]

By 1971 he had recovered more of his strength, but still some serious symptoms persisted:

I am feeling much better. My general health has very much improved, much more than what the doctors here ever dared to hope. But my complaints are still with me: (1) angina pains, (2) missing beats, and (3) waves of fatigue that overwhelm me. These I will have to learn to live with.[4]

That year, he was again back on the road, returning to the United States after several years of absence to hold a much-awaited *yajna*. Because of the persistent symptoms, he was advised by his doctors to have an oxygen tank near him at all times. So when we saw him entering the *yajna* halls in those days, an attendant always trailed behind him with a small oxygen tank in hand. The attendant then sat down in the front row, with the tank in her lap, ready to administer oxygen as needed. Gurudev generally took a whiff of oxygen before starting the lecture and then, immediately after completing the lecture, he would spend several long minutes once again inhaling oxygen from the tank; and, back at his place of residence, he would be on the tank for some ten minutes or more to help the body recoup.

Over the years, many devotees had the experience of being at Gurudev's side when his body was undergoing a health crisis. Shubhra Tandon, who met Gurudev while she was still in her teens in India, recalls one instance:

A Bout with Malaria

The plane landed at the Delhi airport. Swamiji was already suffering from high fever. The year was 1976. My sister and I descended the steps, wondering what would happen next. I was just a teenager and had known Swami Chinmayananda only three years. I had seen glimpses of his divine powers. I knew he was a master of the *Bhagavad Gita*, he was the most humane person I had known — the most witty, loving, and intelligent — and he pampered me and showered so much love on me. I just loved him! I cannot recall how the next hour unfolded, but we did somehow reach the house of our host. . . .

Swamiji was ushered into a huge room by the local devotees and bundled into bed. While a couple of his old devotees saw to his comfort and summoned a doctor, we speculated about the consequences of his blazing fever. Would Swamiji postpone or cancel the *yajna*? Or would he show us some miracle and be up and about to give another one-and-a-half-hour lecture? Would he skip today and be well enough tomorrow? What was wrong with him?

He looked very ill, almost collapsing, weak, and even seemed to be shivering. We got news that some of his devotees were flying down from Mumbai to take care of him. I was getting worried now. How bad was he? I had been put in a very small room just across from his bedroom. All I remember was that I was not allowed to see him once the Mumbai people arrived. They were busy tending to him, and the doctor was taking blood samples. Everybody appeared to be doing their duty, and here I was just left in solitary confinement in my room. My sister had already proceeded to her hometown.

While his senior disciples took on the *yajna* responsibilities, Swamiji remained confined to his room. The entire next day I sat in my tiny room, alone, trying to catch fragments of conversations to ascertain what was going on. I wanted to cry and just see him once so that I would know that he was going to be all

> right or not. I couldn't imagine my world without him, for he had taught me so much in so short a time, and he was always there for me. . . .
>
> Finally, after what seemed like an eternity, someone came to tell me that Swamiji was asking for me. I was overjoyed! A few people had been allowed to see him. I joined the small group. I could feel his strong presence as I entered the room. How powerful was his energy level, even though he was physically sick! Even the most intelligent human beings cannot emanate energy around them when they are in the best of health. I knew in an instant he was much more than ordinary. . . .
>
> He acknowledged the visitors and tried to smile at them. When my turn came, he motioned me to come close to him. I knelt down so that my face was quite close to his. The smell of the medicine overpowered me. He looked so feeble. I can still remember that moment. He spoke to me:
>
> "I know they didn't allow you to come and see me. Are you all right?"
>
> I nodded. Tears floated in my eyes, and I knew that within seconds I would be crying out loud. He looked at me with so much compassion and said:
>
> "Don't worry. I am not going to die. I will be all right."
>
> A wave of relief swept over me. I could feel all my tension and anxiety leaving. I smiled back as I tightened my grip over his hand.
>
> "You go and stay with your cousin and attend the rest of the *yajna*. I am going back to Bombay. I will meet you later."
>
> How did he have the strength to say all this? He kissed me on my cheek, and I felt as if I had gotten back the father I had almost lost. Everything was going to be all right now![5]

In July 1980, while Swamiji was conducting a *yajna* in Chicago, he experienced shortness of breath, fatigue, and angina pains, more than he was accustomed to. An EKG and stress test were performed, which were grossly abnormal. He was persuaded to go to Flint, Michigan, that same day and undergo a cardiac catheterization there, under the watchful eye of a devotee, Dr. Apparao Mukkamala of Flint, who was instrumental in making the arrangements. The test showed more than 90 percent blockage of three blood vessels supplying blood to the heart. The cardiologist who performed the catheterization was stunned that a person with such a diseased and weak heart could be working.

There was accumulation of fluid in the lungs due to the weak pumping action of the heart, which had decreased by 60 percent. With difficulty, the devotees in Flint persuaded Swamiji to consider bypass surgery. "After 24 hours of intense negotiation," recalls Apparao Mukkamala, "Sri Swamiji finally consented to be evaluated by Dr. Denton Cooley in Houston." Arrangements were made to go to Houston within a few days.

Auspicious Day for Surgery

At the Houston, Texas, hospital, after Dr. Denton Cooley had reviewed the angiograms prepared in Flint, Michigan, he strongly suggested that Swamiji undergo coronary artery bypass surgery.

Thinking that Swamiji was an Orthodox Hindu. Dr. Cooley asked him, "By the Hindu calendar, what is an auspicious day for surgery, Swamiji?"

Swamiji, with his usual sense of humor, replied, "As long as Dr. Cooley operates on my heart, any day is an auspicious day!"

The next day, Dr. Cooley himself performed the quadruple bypass on Swamiji's heart. He performed the surgery himself from beginning to end, which is rather unusual. It is customary that the assistants and the physicians in training perform at least part of the surgery, while Dr. Cooley does the most critical anastomosis.

Dr. Cooley also personally took the photographs of Swamiji's heart during the surgery. As a result, many devotees had an opportunity to see the actual physical heart of Swamiji after surgery was over.[6]

After the surgery, Gurudev gave Dr. Cooley a gift — a copy of his *Holy Geeta* (*Bhagavad Gita*), inscribed on the first page with the words: "You saved my life. This will save yours."

Before the operation, Swamiji had kept things light-hearted with his usual joking. An overpowering conviction that all would be well pervaded our minds. I remember holding Swamiji's hand briefly before he was wheeled away to the operating room and sensing the continuity of his life and work so powerfully that no doubt remained in my mind.

Nalini Browning, too, remembers it that way:

No Ordinary Patient

Those of us who were around Sri Swamiji were sure that if he consented to the operation, it would be successful. A strange kind of peaceful acceptance came over each of us. There was no anxiety. We knew he would come through and even be healthier than before. At the same time, we were keenly aware of the agonizing suspense that people were suffering around the world. *Pujas* were being conducted at all Mission centers, and thousands of people were chanting and praying for Swamiji's recovery. Before the operation, he talked about how the combined thoughts of many people do have an effect.

Up until the last minute before the surgery, he made us laugh. He carefully tied his beard and tucked it up under his chin. When they strapped him down to wheel him into the operating room, he said, "And what if I change my mind now? . . . O.K., never mind!"

Throughout the time at the hospital, one thought was consistently in my mind: "He is doing this for us! He has no need of the body. He has willingly submitted himself to enormous pain and suffering out of his great love for us."

To tell the truth, I was horrified at the thought of seeing Swamiji immediately after the operation. I had been told in advance about the tubes that would be attached to every possible part of his body, and my mind had projected such fearful images that I was secretly looking for excuses why I should not see him. I've always been squeamish about hospitals, and until now the Lord had spared me the necessity of having much to do with them. I wondered that of all of Swamiji's devotees how I ended up being there with him. One part of me was extremely grateful, and another part of me didn't want to see any of it.

But seeing Swamiji for the first time immediately after surgery was nothing like I expected. It is an image that will remain engraved in my mind forever. The tubes, although they were there, were not at all conspicuous. Swamiji wore a blue hospital gown, his beard was still tucked up under his chin, and his head lay placidly to the side. He looked as though life was just barely clinging to his body. Never have I been struck as powerfully by the Christ-like presence in Sri Swamiji as I was at that moment.

For days, Swamiji was as helpless as a baby. It was hard to imagine that great mind, that great spirit, contained within such a fragile form. He seemed just like any other sick patient, and I'm sure the nurses had no idea of what man they were placating, cajoling, and tormenting with constant demands. Nor, I am sure, could they understand why there was a constant influx of doctors from out of town and from the Houston area, who were continuously at hand, anxiously looking after Swamiji's slightest need. In fact, Dr. Anne, a devotee from Chicago, was allowed to watch the operation being performed by Dr. Cooley. It was not too long, however, before the hospital staff became aware that this was no ordinary patient.

From the moment he could even gesture with his hands, he was teasing and joking. In his helplessness, he was so loving, taking comfort from a familiar touch or presence. When he couldn't talk, he offered his hand as an expression of welcome and affection. Silently, in simple ways, he continued to teach us how God and his devotees are not separate, how God wants the love of his devotees as much as they need His love.[7]

Without a doubt, the hospital staff had begun to understand that this was no ordinary patient. Swamiji had left his loving mark on them, prompting them to show special care in supporting the guru-disciple relationship:

Swamiji's Family

Among the devotees who attended to Swamiji during his initial few days in the hospital in Houston, Texas, were Nalini Browning, Vilasini Balakrishnan, Dr. Anne, and part of the time, Rudite Emir. Later, after he was out of intensive care, other devotees arrived.

Hospital regulations required that only family members could be near him during the critical hours before surgery and also directly following the operation, when he was under close medical supervision in intensive care. Access to all visitors was severely limited. Nalini, Vilasini, and Rudite explained to the hospital administration the special characteristics of this case, and that for Swamiji, they were, indeed, family. Much to their relief, all three were signed in officially.

A deeply touching moment arrived a day or two days after surgery, recalls Rudite. "We had only brief minutes to be with Swamiji intermittently throughout the day, but the nursing staff had become keenly aware of how much we wanted to be in his presence. At one point, the nurses were apparently planning to transport him on a gurney from one room to another, and a message came to us in the waiting room: 'Have the Swami's family wait to greet him outside the Intensive Care Unit. They may want to accompany him down the hallway to his new room.'

"The Swami's family! — we hadn't realized how deeply those words would touch us. And, of course, we were there to be at his side as he was transported to his new room."[8]

Even during those critically ill days, Gurudev never stopped teaching. Vilasini Balakṛishnan, who served as his assistant for many years during his travels both in India and North America, recalls:

Teaching Inner Silence

Swamiji sacrificed his personal comforts many times for the sake of teaching his students. One striking example that had a great impact on me was when Swamiji was recovering from triple bypass coronary surgery at a Houston hospital.

A few days after the surgery, while still in the hospital, he was so weak that he gesticulated with his hands to communicate with us. Once he gestured for some water. He was apparently thirsty. In my nervous excitement to serve him, I rushed about the room to find the water and bring it.

Swamiji, who never lost an opportunity to teach, even now, while weak from surgery, chose to teach me a lesson. As I rushed over to him with his water, he tiredly waved it away. He turned away and sank back into bed with a look of resignation.

I heard his message loud and clear. He refused the water, which his body was craving, in order to make me aware of my agitation. He was pointing out to me the need for inner silence, to be in deep composure at all times. What people saw and heard when they sat for his discourses was amazing presence, a force of inspiring dynamism, an energy that crept into one's heart and opened it to greater wisdom. But one strong quality of Swamiji's that was not as apparent on the stage was his deep, penetrating, soul-stirring silence. This lesson he taught off-stage. It is this teaching that made him a living Upanishad. It is in this silence that the mind gets hushed and the joy lying within one's being comes forth. Swamiji was always in this silence. I became convinced of this while serving him. As far as I can tell, he never fell from this interior silence. And now he was taking the opportunity to teach me about it — from the hospital bed.

Inability to be always fully composed was a shortcoming of mine, for I had a habit of feeling anxious and thus trying nervously to be useful. I sat down on the floor and silently prayed, "Please, God, help me to sit here silently. Let me just serve in silence. If he needs something, let me silently get it. Any thought of mine will disturb him. He is teaching me to let go of my anxiety. For his sake, let me calm down."

With this prayer repeated like a mantra, I served. Next time he asked for some thing, I got it for him slowly and calmly. He accepted it and smiled. This lesson was one of the most valuable of my life.[9]

Others Come First

Swamiji had just come out of intensive care. The tubes had been removed from his throat, and he could begin to talk to us a little, although it was apparent that talking was difficult and his energy level was still extremely low. We could visit him two at a time. I went up to his bedside, took his hand, and said a quiet "Hari Om, Swamiji."

He then said his first words to me following the surgery: "How are the husband and children?"

Even then, despite his own pains and discomforts, he put others first — and he was teaching *me* to put others first.[10]

One's Arms and Legs

During the around-the-clock watch at the Houston hospital, especially after the initial intensive-care days, devotees were continually streaming through to offer their help. Swamiji was never alone.

We asked him, "Swamiji, do you ever get tired of having people around you all the time?"

Frail as he was, he roared back at them, "Only if there's hate in the heart does one get tired of people. Do you ever get tired of your arms and legs? Do you ever want them to go away? You may want to change your clothes, but not your arms and legs!"[11]

Post-Surgery Exercise

During post-operative recovery, Swamiji rested in Flint, Michigan. One day, Dr. Apparao Mukkamala suggested that Swamiji take a walk in the evening. To the doctor's amazement, Swamiji replied that he had just completed four miles of walking. However, the doctor was very puzzled, because Swamiji had not left the house all morning.

When Dr. Mukkamala expressed his surprise, Swamiji laughed and said that he had done all his exercise mentally![12]

With the bypass operation, Swamiji had, indeed, gained a new lease on life. But as the years went by and as he continued to drive his body relentlessly to meet the demands of his inner vision and the wishes and needs of his countless followers, the wear and tear on it began to show with ever-increasing ferocity. He had also developed diabetes, which required daily insulin shots and a strict diet, and, in time, left his feet without feeling and his legs seriously weakened.

Doctors estimated that he was left with less than 25 percent of his heart's capacity as he continued his grueling program of work until the final heart attack in 1993, which forced his body to succumb altogether.

MASTERING THE PHYSICAL

Despite all the challenges that his own body gave him, Swamiji continued to remind us, most of the time through his own example, that the body is *not* the master. "Rise above it," he repeated in a variety of ingenious ways, "just as you rise beyond your thoughts and emotions, to discover the real locus of your identify within the purity of the Divine Self within." His own mental and physical stamina — especially during the later years, despite all medical indications to the contrary — is, by now, legendary. However, that single-mindedness about the mind's superiority over the body was seen even during the very early years of his work:

No Excuses for Rest

The early devotees had many opportunities to travel with Gurudev to places such as Uttarkashi, where he had learned the Upanishads from his guru, Swami Tapovanam. Shakuntla Bindra traveled with him to that remote spot many times in the early years of his teaching, in the 1950s and later. In January 1957, after packing up the necessary provisions for a two-day trip, they boarded a bus for Rishikesh. They spent the night at Rishikesh and then proceeded on to Uttarkashi in a very small and uncomfortable bus. At Dharasu, a small village on the way, they had to leave the bus behind, either to walk on foot or travel on the back of a mule for the next 18 miles to Uttarkashi. Those who chose to walk, as did Swamiji, found that keeping up with him was quite a challenge, as he walked very fast, taking long strides with his long legs.

"I happened to be with Gurudev all the time," recalls Shakuntla Bindra, "going up and down little footpaths. On the way, at small wayside shops, he would order two glasses of tea and black *chana* [beans] to eat. At one place I felt tired and sat down. He said, 'Even you?' — so I got up and continued to walk with him. He gave strength to my body and spiritual food for my mind. We reached our destination."[13]

Those of us who traveled with him by car in later years discovered that 4 a.m., or even earlier, was his favorite time to depart, no matter what time he needed to reach his destination for his next engagement.

Mind over Matter

I was traveling with Gurudev in Kerala in the early seventies, sometimes by car and sometimes by plane. One morning we were to travel by car several hours to his next stop. Plenty of time was available to reach his destination in time for the projected talks; however, as was his habit, he announced that everyone should be ready to depart at 4 a.m. sharp.

We dared not linger and were ready to depart at the appointed hour. I sat in the back seat with another devotee; Swamiji was up front in the passenger seat. As we rolled over the dark countryside, I felt sleep overtaking me, closed my eyes, and started to doze.

A loud call of my name jarred me upright. It was Swamiji calling me.

"Mind over matter!" he said. "Always teach the body to obey you. Sleepiness is just a state of mind."

After that lesson, I dared not sleep for the rest of the journey. And many times when I feel sleepiness trying to overcome me at an inopportune time, I remember Swamiji's lesson that dark morning in Kerala.[14]

Another account from Gurudev's early years of teaching demonstrates his inordinate ability to be master over the material plane:

Despite Pain and Blood

Back in the early 1950s, when Gurudev was walking up onto the speaker's platform during a *yajna,* he had to climb up wooden stairs leading to the platform. One step had a nail protruding from it, but nobody had noticed it. Gurudev walked up onto the platform, sat down cross-legged, and gave his talk for one and one-half hours.

At the end of the talk, he would usually get up and walk out; only after his exit would others begin to leave. But that day, he did not leave first. Instead he said, "Hari Om. You can all disperse."

The listeners all looked at him and wondered what was happening, but they prostrated and walked off. Swamiji remained on the platform. Somebody went of up to him and asked, "Swamiji, what happened?"

He said, "I want to get up, but I cannot."

We all walked up to him to see what was wrong.

The whole side of his left leg was covered completely with blood. It was from the nail in the stairs.

Supported by others, he got up from his seat, saying, "I don't know what it is. It's paining."

The cloth of his garment was stuck to his leg; slowly, his attendees pried it loose. The blood had been oozing from his leg since the beginning of the talk; yet, he had continued the talk to the end. No one had been aware of any sign of pain or change in Gurudev during the talk. This is true nonawareness of the body![15]

Many years later, he wrote in a letter to a devotee:

> *I am a young fifty-five, not an old fifty-five. Age has no meaning for a seeker. You diligently learn to put your mind where your heart is, not where your body is. This is laying the foundation for the temple of your spiritual life.*

Yet, those around Gurudev who had grown to love not only his teaching but also his physical presence could not keep their minds from focusing on the ailing body of the guru. Because of his obviously frail health, devotees were constantly on the lookout for curing him with new methods or for pampering his body. Once when someone offered him an aspirin to ease some ache, he said, "So, all this time the body has been functioning without aspirin. You suddenly assume that aspirin is necessary for it to continue working?" And he slapped his thigh in glee as he roared his typical deep laugh. On another occasion he said, "I take medicines just to please everyone."

Up and Down

Sheela Kirpalani remembers a time when in the course of hosting Swamiji at her house in New York she was powerfully reminded of his adamant nonadherence to the demands of the body. It was the summer of 1990. Gurudev's health had become more delicate in recent years, and so naturally Sheela was concerned about the flight of stairs that led to the bedroom that he would be using. Climbing stairs was hard on his heart, as well as difficult for his legs to maneuver, which had over the years become quite numb from diabetes.

Upon his arrival, he went upstairs to his room. He then descended the stairs to take breakfast with many devotees who had come especially to see him. After breakfast, he headed upstairs again to answer the mounds of correspondence awaiting him.

Sheela recalls, "I became more and more anxious regarding the additional climbs and descents that he would be making on that staircase for the remainder of his stay with us, so I suggested to Swamiji that we serve him lunch in his room. He eyed me curiously and asked, 'Why?' I tried to explain that this would lessen the number of trips on the stairs, thereby putting less strain on his heart."

But Swamiji told her in no uncertain terms that he would be dining downstairs with all of his devotees.

Sheela remembers his exact words at that point: "So I'll go upstairs; then downstairs; then up . . . then down . . . up . . . down . . . — the ups and downs of life."[16]

Many wrote and spoke to Swamiji about their concerns for his health, yet he continued to demonstrate profound detachment from the workings of the body — through lavish joking, through total disregard for the strains his schedule put on his physical being, and, at times, through mischievous disobedience of the doctor's orders. Now and again, we caught him conspiring with a hostess to serve him a bowl of ice cream or some other sweet disallowed by his strict diabetic regimen.

A letter written to a devotee in Singapore in Spring 1992 shows how he viewed the role of the body within the larger scheme of things:

> *Made up of the five elements, the body is a nest of diseases and pains. To cater to its demands can be a twelve-month, twenty-four-hour job — and yet it will suffer. Use it as an instrument for* seva *of others. Trees give fruits to others; the tree eats none. The river never drinks, but its waters are meant for plants, animals, and humans. The sun, the wind — look around. In nature, man alone wants to live for himself and perpetuate! Leave it alone. Let the body run its course. Let us live our life peacefully in Him, the Bliss. Look after the body as a workman tends to his instruments.*

Letting the Pain Be

Swamiji was sitting in a chair and an American devotee was massaging his legs.

"Typical Christian," teased Swamiji. "She wants to take away the suffering from the legs. Let it be there. What's a swami without a voice? If the body has to suffer, let the suffering be in the feet!"[17]

"I Am Not the Body"

Bharati Sukhatankar was preparing the syringe for Swamiji's daily injection of insulin. He took the syringe and the alcohol-saturated cotton and dabbed his thigh with it, ready to give himself an injection. She found it painful to watch and turned her head away, looking out the window.

"Why are you looking away?" inquired Swamiji.

"Swamiji, it's painful for me to watch," replied Bharati. "Doesn't it hurt you when you do it day after day?"

Swamiji's reply was simple and direct: "When I say, 'I am not the body,' I am *not* the body!"[18]

A *Mahatma's* Diseases

At a *satsang* with Swami Akhandananda, the great exponent of the *Bhagavatam*, a devotee had asked why *mahatmas* become ill with terrible diseases.

"Do you want an honest answer or a dishonest one? The honest one will hurt you," said Swami Akhandananda.

"An honest answer, of course!" was the response.

"People bring us offerings of all kinds," said the Swami, "and we redistribute the wealth, but when negativities come our way, we can't distribute them."

"Is there any way that the devotees can help lessen the *mahatma's* disease?"

"Yes," was the answer. "If a group of devotees creates the *sankalpa* to take on the teacher's ailments — that will work."

On hearing this story related, Asha Kamdar decided she wanted to take on her guru's diabetes. She didn't say a word to Swamiji about her decision but spoke to other devotees about it, gathering together a small group for the task.

When Asha met Swamiji again, she still did not tell him about her resolve, but Swamiji insisted that she order a locket with a gold chain inscribed with the message "I have no heart trouble" on one side and "I have no diabetes" on the other.

On several occasions, he repeated his request that she have the locket and chain made: "I *told* you to get the chain made!"

Some time later, when Asha met Swamiji again at the Mumbai ashram, he asked if the chain was made. When she showed it to him, he put it on her wrist and said, "Now try!"[19]

"I Don't Travel"

Someone asked Swamiji how he can manage to travel so much. Doesn't he get exhausted, especially given his fragile health?

Swamiji's reply was: "*I* don't travel. Bombay comes, Bombay goes. Madras comes, Madras goes. *I* don't go anywhere!"[20]

Bliss Despite Pain

At one of the early camps in the United States, at Sonoma State College in California, Swamiji developed a severe tooth problem and had gone to see the dentist. Despite medication, he was still in severe pain as he chatted quietly with several of us in his bedroom. It was sunset, and the scene of the glowing sky was extraordinarily beautiful through the open window next to his bed. Swamiji sat on the edge of the bed in his orange undershirt and gazed for many long minutes at the incandescent sky. His face shone with an ecstatic, unearthly beauty, and the whole room was suffused with a quiet, yet almost unbearably potent energy. He kept gazing out the window, his profile against the red sky the picture of bliss.[21]

Many devotees recall valuable lessons learned from Swamiji on how to revitalize one's energy, as well as rise beyond the limitations of the body. He showed us how he managed to revitalize himself despite the severe demands on his organism:

An Energy Recharge

During one of Swamiji's springtime visits in California, with lectures at Stanford University in Palo Alto, I was invited to drive along with him in the car that was taking him to the lecture hall. I was crowded into the back seat with several others, just behind Swamiji in the front seat, as we drove the most scenic route through the Stanford campus. Swamiji and his driver continued with some of the discussions begun earlier at Swamiji's residence.

Just as we drove into Palo Alto, all of us in the car fell silent as Swamiji leaned back in the car seat. For me, his presence was even more powerful as he put his head back against the head rest and closed his eyes: Was he sleeping? praying? chanting?

The driver pulled up to a place near the building where Swamiji would speak and opened the door for him. Swamiji stood up quickly, as though entering into the very air, stretched as he stood there, then took in a few slow, deep breaths as he looked around him. A long row of trees arched over the sidewalk, and he seemed to engage with them with total attention. He was silent now as he walked along the sidewalk toward the door of the lecture hall, head lifted to the trees as though to receive their energy. He said not one word to those of us around him, continuing to be entirely at one with the natural setting, as though he were being recharged and was thanking nature for this gift of energy.

When he entered the building and was met by the organizers, he was, as always, vigorous and energetic, his own energy now being offered to those around him. His communion with nature seemed to be forgotten.

But I never forgot. When I become frustrated because I have no time for a vacation, a trip to the ocean, or a hike in the woods, I remember how Swamiji entered into that bit of forest between a parking place and a lecture hall as though it were a vast wilderness retreat — in silence, completely given up to nature and its beauty — and "came back" refreshed and invigorated.[22]

From Exhaustion to Exhilaration

It was during Swamiji's next-to-the-last spiritual camp at Krishnalaya. His physical condition was very weak. He did little walking, and now always with cane in hand, often swaying perilously as we all watched with apprehension. We drove him even the short distance from his residence to the lecture tent.

One day I had taken my turn to be at the wheel to drive him the short distance. We had already arrived at the entrance to the tent when someone rushed over to open the door for him. Sighing heavily, he unfolded his tall frame and heaved it out of the car seat. It felt to me as though he was using his last ounce of strength just to get himself up and out of the car. "How will he ever be able to make it through tonight's lecture?" I thought, my heart tearing at the sight of him struggling so.

He walked slowly onto the platform in his deliberate, majestic way, slightly bent at the shoulders now and leaning on his walking stick. He sat down, grimacing a little as he crossed one aching leg over the other, opened his copy of the *Bhagavad Gita*, took one look at the listeners, and began: "As we were saying yesterday . . ." The dynamism that poured forth from his being that night was incomparable even by Swamiji's standards, and in my eyes had no

> relationship to the body I had just witnessed emerging from the car. It was obvious to me that this man before us was fueled by a Source far greater than what we were used to witnessing in our lives. That night I realized what he meant when he said that God himself works through those who allow themselves to become His instruments.[23]

As his physical condition deteriorated, people often urged Swamiji to stay in or near large cities, not at remote places such as his ashram in Sidhabari in Himachal Pradesh. His reply to such entreaties was: "Don't people die in Bombay also?"

When devotees urged him to take extra rest because he looked tired, his reply at times was: "No. I'm always at rest." Or, at Sidhabari during a spiritual camp, when once again he was being urged to give his body a much-needed reprieve, he said, "Four hundred people are out there waiting for me — so *samasti* has to work." [Literally, *samasti* means "totality"; here, the One Reality functioning through the instrument, Swamiji.]

Against His Own Nature

> One time during a *bhiksha* at the home of my son, Dr. Manoj, Swami Purushottamanandaji, having been informed by Dr. Manoj that Gurudev's heart ejection was only 24 percent, inquired of the health condition of Pujya Gurudev. Dr. Manoj opined that Pujya Gurudev believes in nature and preaches for nature, so he would accept that the body is controlled by nature. Therefore, he should take rest.
>
> Swami Purushottamanandaji asked me to convey this to Gurudev. I narrated this conversation to Pujya Gurudev at the next Sidhabari camp. He did not reply, but three days later he became seriously ill. When I, along with others, was sitting at his bedside, Pujya Gurudev spoke to me, "Ghelubhai, convey to Dr. Manoj Patel that Swami Chinmayananda is lying in bed against His Own Nature."[24]

"Don't Ask"

Once, when Swamiji had just arrived at the airport, Swami Subodhananda asked him, "Swamiji, how is your health?"

"Don't ask," said Swamiji. "I'm using this as much as I can. If you ask, she [the body] will think she's important."[25]

Ever Young

Swamiji was resting in his drawing room when someone asked, "How is your health, Swamiji?"

Swamiji kept quiet.

"It's good that you're resting," the person then added.

"Yes," said Swamiji. "The body is resting, but the fellow inside is very young. He wants to remain on the move."[26]

Vedantic Medicine

I had gone to meet Swamiji at the ashram in California, Krishnalaya, to hear his talks on *Vivekacudamani*. Swamiji invited me to have breakfast at his table. It was heavenly! Dr. Pillai kept exquisite classical instrumental music playing in the background, and Swamiji ate in silence, moving one hand to the music, gesturing at a particularly satisfying passage or closing his eyes with pure pleasure.

Robyn Thompson, his assistant, came to the table with Swamiji's medicine: three or four tablets. He held them in the palm of his left hand, staring at them, his shoulders rolling in silent humor. We all stared at the pills also.

"These keep me alive," he said.

We all felt sad at the thought of our beloved Swamiji sustained by heart pills.

He kept them in his hand a moment longer. Then he pointed at them deliberately, one by one, whispering, almost in reverie: "This one is *Vivekacudamani*, this one is *Gita*, this one is the Upanishads."

We all closed our eyes, minds suddenly skyrocketed from the mundane — in the breathtaking presence of one for whom every thought and every experience was divinized.[27]

Besides the example his own life provided, also Gurudev's advice to us continuously provided guidelines on how best to relate to our physical existence:

"Let Her Eat What She Wants"

An elderly devotee of Swamiji's, Mrs. Advani, had asthma, and she suffered from frequent coughing attacks. The doctor had banned several items in her diet, including spinach, a difficult restriction to uphold in a Sindhi household.

One day Swamiji was eating together with Mrs. Advani at the same table. Swamiji's plate contained many varied foods, including spinach, but not Mrs. Advani's. He inquired about the reason. "Gulu [the woman's son] told me," was her answer.

Swamiji looked to the left, looked to the right, and said, "Gulu is not here. Eat!" Mrs. Advani ate the spinach, with not one sign of bad after-effects.

Later, Indra, her daughter-in-law, and Swamiji had a discussion about her mother-in-law's diet. "What's this?" inquired Swamiji. "You're not allowing her to eat certain things? Why are you troubling her? How many years does she have left? Let her eat what she wants!"

After that, Mrs. Advani ate spinach and other restricted foods with no negative after-effects.[28]

THE FINAL YEARS

Expanded Heart

Years back, a cardiologist had diagnosed a "heart enlargement" in Gurudev. On hearing this, we promptly wrote to Gurudev at Uttarkashi, referring to the ailment and extending our prayers for speedy recovery.

Promptly came the witty reply: *"All these years I have been trying my best to expand my heart to accommodate all! Now the doctors say it is also an ailment!"*[29]

Swamiji wrote similar letters to other concerned devotees:

The doctors have now suggested that my heart is slightly enlarged. (They don't know that this is what I have been trying all through my life! This is between us, let not the doctors hear!)[30]

So Gurudev continued to expand his heart and expend his precious strength — until, in the early 1990s, it became apparent to many of us that he was still with us in body through pure miracle only. For years, doctors had been saying that his heart was functioning at a quarter of its needed capacity, and the percentage appeared to be decreasing as the days progressed. Critical heart episodes continued to plague him, but his characteristically high spirits continued without faltering, often interlaced with a touch of humor. He said in a letter to two devotees:

Thank you very much for your letter and the card full of signatures of loving thoughts wishing me recovery. I am not sure if I am not wishing for yet another attack, because of the joy of knowing that so many sincere, devoted hearts in their love for me are praying so ardently. It doesn't matter if I suffer a bit if it makes you all pray so sincerely![31]

Several particularly grave crisis points in his health occurred in Sidhabari, the site of his beloved Sandeepany (Himalayas) ashram. Dr. Kshama Metre, the resident doctor in charge of the Project serving the local village communities near Sidhabari, recalls how she "pretended" to be the doctor attending Gurudev. "I could only pretend to be a doctor next to him," she says. "How could I be a doctor for him who was everyone's doctor?"

Yet, she went through the motions of attending to him during a number of health crises:

Obstinate Patient

During one of his stays at the Sidhabari ashram in the early 1990s, Gurudev's blood sugar level was in a very erratic state. Dr. Kshama Metre was taking Gurudev's vital signs. A cardiologist also arrived shortly, as well as other doctors.

It was decided among the doctors that Dr. Metre must tell Swamiji to be more regular about his diet to help control his diabetes. Just then he was watching television with several people gathered around him. Dr. Metre took his pulse and blood pressure. She looked up at him and said, "Gurudev, your blood sugar is getting erratic and Gurudev should not be eating fried *pappadam*."

Gurudev suddenly turned away from the television screen and shouted in extreme anger:

"How dare you tell me this? Who told you to tell me this?"

Dr. Metre remained calm, praying to him. Others were trying to calm the situation, "It's OK, it's OK."

Gurudev said, "I can eat whatever I want."

The following morning Gurudev was having breakfast. Dr. Metre was waiting to give him his insulin injection. Gurudev addressed one of the devotees at the breakfast table:

"You know, yesterday I screamed at Kshama."

Dr. Metre approached him to give him the shot. She had just barely done her *pranams* when he began to give her a big hug.

"So what were you saying yesterday?" he asked her.

Then Dr. Metre explained everything to him in medical terms. He listened very silently with a sweet smile on his face. Dr. Metre recalls: "The feeling I had is indescribable — how much he blessed me. It transformed me completely. When the Lord scolds you, take it as *prasad*: It transforms you completely."[32]

In May 1991, a major health crisis hit in the middle of a spiritual camp at the Sidhabari ashram. Shubhra Tandon recalls:

"I'll Be Back"

The night was dark, hot, and humid. I felt restless and decided to leave my room and go toward Swamiji's *kutiya*. We were three weeks into the *Gita* and *Mandukya Karika* camp at Sidhabari. It was May 1991. Swamiji had been a little unwell since a couple of days, and we had requested him to take some rest and asked if we could curtail the number of visitors for *satsang*, as there were too many people crowding around him, making it difficult for him to breathe — a strain on his heart. Instead, he chose to sit outside now, and he seemed to have caught a chill. . . .

My mind flashed back to fifteen years earlier, to Delhi. That time it had only been malaria. Things were different now. Swamiji had more heart problems now. More years, more strain, and more physical weakness, in spite of his boundless energy. . . .

The army ambulance pulled up near his *kutiya* gate. Only a few devotees had come out, the rest were oblivious to what was happening in the ashram. Two men walked in with a stretcher. Was he that unwell? Would he even go on the stretcher when he could be heard talking loudly? My heart was pounding hard. I was hoping his condition wasn't that critical, and that this was not the last glimpse I was going to get of him. Even with all the knowledge and instruction he had given us, this was a hard pill to swallow. I stood next to the *kutiya* door. Suddenly, he appeared in sight. I saw and heard him say something with an irritated look as he waved the stretcher aside. I remember he had often said, "I'll be carried on two sticks only once!"

He walked with measured steps. He looked very tired. I couldn't gauge the extent of his condition, but I had been told it could get really serious. I clutched the door handle and held the door open for him. I thought he wouldn't notice me, as it was dark and I had pressed myself against the wall. He stopped. He gave me a piercing look straight in the eyes, and touched my hand very gently:

"Don't worry. I'm not going yet. I'll be back."

I stood absolutely still, numbed for a moment. He had read my mind again. The door of the ambulance closed. I was told that as he got into the ambulance, he just fell onto the stretcher waiting there.[33]

Dr. Metre also vividly remembers the details during that particular crisis in Gurudev's health:

Others First

Dr. Kshama Metre was called to Swamiji's *kutiya* in Sidhabari. He was going into heart failure, and was given some Lasix. It was obvious that he had to be transferred to the hospital immediately (Military Cantonment Hospital near Sidhabari).

Ten minutes later the ambulance arrived. A crowd had gathered outside his *kutiya*. Dr. Metre gave Gurudev some injections and said, "Swamiji, please don't move" — but he was already out of his bedroom, marching toward the door.

"Gurudev, we have to take you out on a stretcher!" Dr. Metre implored.

"I'll die with my boots on," was Swamiji's reply.

He then climbed the two steps into the ambulance vehicle. Once he was inside, she sat next to him, holding his hand, tears rolling down her cheeks. He stroked her hand consolingly, "I'll be fine."

When they reached the hospital, Gurudev was carried by stretcher through a dark corridor to the Intensive Care Unit. Dr. Metre was at Gurudev's side, holding his hand. In the dark, she didn't see a crack in the floor and fell down hard, but he held on to her hand and pulled her up. No one else was aware of what was happening, only Gurudev and she.

By midnight, the emotional strain of the day had taken its toll on her. Feeling extremely exhausted, she said to Gurudev's assistant, "I'll just lie down for a minute." After a while, she got up with a start from deep sleep and walked up to Gurudev's hospital bed, thinking that he's asleep.

Then she heard his voice: "Is your leg all right? Did you have a good sleep?" She had told no one of the sprained ligament in her leg.

Always, no matter what his condition, Gurudev put others first.[34]

After his hospital stay in Sidhabari, Gurudev was transferred to a hospital in Mumbai. Dr. Apparao Mukkamala of the United States and Laju Chanrai of London flew to Mumbai to meet Gurudev there and take him to the United States to be seen by the world-renowned cardiologist, Dr. Kanu Chatterjee, of Moffitt Hospital in San Francisco. The cardiologist examined him, said that further evaluation was needed, and strongly advised Gurudev to stop all work.

However, Gurudev had already made plans to hold a Marathon *Gita* Camp at Krishnalaya that June. In thirty days, he planned to expound all eighteen chapters of the *Bhagavad Gita*, a session that was to be videotaped by professionals. Thus, despite his grave physical condition, Gurudev conducted the *Gita* camp as planned, holding his lectures in the intense glare of lamps stationed next to the video cameras.

In October of that year, he was once again back at Sidhabari, where another crisis hit. Asha Kamdar of Mumbai and Dr. Kshama Metre of Sidhabari were both witnesses to much of what transpired during that health crisis:

Heart Failure in Flight

It was October 17, 1991. Gurudev had just finished a *yajna* in Kanpur and had gone to Delhi on his way to Sidhabari. The previous night he had gone to bed without dinner. All night, the light in his room was on. At 4:30 a.m., the light was switched off. At 7:30 a.m., he appeared in the doorway:

"What are those little white tablets you take for fever?"

"Crocin."

Gurudev took one-half a tablet. His fever was up to 102°F by now, and the doctor was called, who urged him not to go to Sidhabari.

But Swamiji's answer was: "Ah, I'm going to my own home," so plans proceeded for him to go to Sidhabari, accompanied by Asha Kamdar, who originally had no place reserved on the sixteen-seat aircraft.

Swamiji was wheeled out in a wheelchair to the airport, with Asha taking charge of his respirator, medicine kit, briefcase, and suitcases. In the airplane, his face looked very grey and ashen. His body was trembling with fever. Asha supported his head with her hand throughout the trip.

Gurudev finally arrived at Sandeepany (Himalayas) and was received with the traditional *Purna Kumbha* at the ashram. The people who received him knew that he was unwell, but they had no idea how very grave the situation was.

He was transferred to a nearby military hospital and stayed there for three days in intensive care, attached to intravenous drips and heart monitors.

At one point during his three-day stay, Gurudev told Dr. Kshama Metre that he wanted to go to the bathroom. She told him that he must not get up from bed, but he insisted. They argued back and forth for a while. Then he started getting out of bed, pulling the intravenous tubes out, toppling the oxygen tanks, and yelling to Swami Subodhananda, who was nearby: "Get me the wheelchair!" — and he went to the bathroom as he had intended. An orderly was asked to stand at the door of the bathroom, which had been left ajar. When, after what seemed like a very long time, Swamiji finally came out, he sat down on the wheelchair and grinned like a child.

Meanwhile, pandemonium had broken out in the hospital at the sight of what Swamiji had just done. The nurses and doctors were hysterical, screaming and scrambling. Once Swamiji was back in bed, it took them half an hour to reconnect all the tubes properly. The attending doctor came to his bed, held his hand, and said, "Please cooperate with me, Swamiji. For twenty-four hours, no getting out of bed. Please!"

"OK," Swamiji relented.

"Good boy," the doctor smiled in relief.

Twice during this hospital stay, including two days before the bathroom incident, Gurudev's clinical functions stopped. The heart monitors showed ventricular fibrillation. Clinically he was no longer alive, but the doctors administered some medicine, and he revived. When he had recovered he said, "Twice I was gone, but more work needed to be done, so I came back." However, he *did* concede enough to his body's grave condition to cancel his next two *yajnas*.[35]

Meditative Miracle

While Gurudev was in the Intensive Care Unit in the Sidhabari hospital in October 1991, at one point Dr. Kshama Metre saw that he was moving into very serious heart failure: He was turning blue. She called the doctors and nurses to prepare his injections, but feared that this was the end. He seemed not to be conscious, at least not awake. Suddenly, he sat upright in bed and assumed a meditative pose for several seconds. Then he collapsed back onto his bed. The doctors then knew that he would come out of it somehow, and he did.[36]

People around Gurudev were continually using the physical body as the frame of reference for life. He was using another:

What Body?

During his hospital stay in Sidhabari, two nurses came into his room with bathing equipment and said, "Sir, it is time for your sponging."

"I am immaculate!" he said.

Nurses, thinking that he had not understood, explained, "Sir, we need to wash you up now."

"I am pure," Swamiji replied. "I am immaculate!"

They still thought that he had not understood them and explained again that they needed to wash him.

Finally Gurudev relented, "Never mind. You can wash this body now."[37]

Despite his frail condition, in November 1992, Gurudev returned once again to the United States, this time to conduct a tour of major American universities, including the University of Michigan, Stanford, and the University of California campuses at Berkeley and San Diego. He was intent on forging relationships with scholars in the West to encourage collaborative study of the world's religions, India's ancient literature, and the Sanskrit language. He encouraged them all to pursue such study at his recently established Chinmaya International Foundation near Cochin in the state of Kerala in South India.

And so he completed his tour as planned, giving in to physical constraints only so far as to allow more liberal use of a wheelchair than before.

"He was not relating to his body at all," Dr. Metre recalls from those last years when his physical frame was becoming weaker by the day. He would say to the cardiologist examining him, "OK, have you finished the examination of this body? What did you find?" — but he said it in all compassion, explaining in a gentle way that he was not the body.

As we watched him smile through his grueling schedule, it became ever more obvious to all of us that Gurudev's point of focus was far, far beyond the body and our own usual locus of experience: It was securely centered on the immaculate Self. How else could he have done what he did?

LAST GOOD-BYES

It was Swamiji's last camp at Krishnalaya, just a few weeks before he dropped his body, or attained *Mahasamadhi*. We had just finished a *Paduka Puja,* worship of the guru's wooden *padukas*, or sandals. Traditionally this worship is performed on the guru's feet, symbolizing the reverence the devotees feel for the foundation of spiritual knowledge on which the teacher stands. However, toward the end of his life Swamiji's feet had been made vulnerable by diabetes, and we chose to perform the worship on his *padukas* instead. The air was charged with intense energy. We watched Swamiji walk off the stage, his tall, majestic frame wobbling slightly as he moved toward the opening in the lecture tent. He always walked with an unhurried, majestic stride, but this time he was walking especially slowly, almost lingeringly. Many of us were overcome with an incredible sadness as we watched him.

Only later did we realize that something in us must have known that this was to be the last time we witnessed him leaving that stage.

The following morning, the camp delegates gathered around Swamiji's car at 5 o'clock in the morning to bid him good-bye. Some were crying; others asked their last questions and gave their last good wishes for the journey. One young teenage girl was bidding him good-bye with tears in her eyes. He said to her:

"Be strong, be strong, be strong! Your guru is always with you."

Then he turned to her younger brother, who was wearing a T-shirt with Swamiji's image on the front: "Don't wear your guru on your tummy. Wear him on your back, so he can be there to protect you!"

Many devotees remember the last, poignant moments they spent with Gurudev, even though at the time they didn't know those moments were to be the last. Asha Kamdar of Mumbai and Padmashree of Bangalore, both of whom were assisting Gurudev with his preparations for his last flight to the United States, recall how he made a point of remaining with them for a long chat before his midnight flight, even though his usual habit would have been to rest for a few hours before the flight. He told them, "When I come back again, I'll come back empty."

Just days before Gurudev's *Mahasamadhi,* Michael Fantus had an overpowering first meeting with him:

An Unusual Aura

An unusual aura permeated the air around the cottage as I drove up. I wasn't really sure why I felt what I was feeling, but it seemed that everything around me was feeling it, too. It wasn't just the fact that it was quiet, but a feeling of order, that all was well, permeated the place. I walked up the steps and entered the cottage, careful to deposit my shoes at the door.

The cottage had a screened-in porch area that one entered before stepping into the house proper. As I ventured further into the house, the feeling I had experienced outside grew even stronger. As I entered the main room, I was somewhat startled to see about thirty people sitting on the floor. They were perfectly still, focused. I looked around and saw the object of their affectionate stares. I then realized the source of my earlier feelings of tranquillity.

Seated at a table with three or four others was Swamiji, eating his breakfast. To see him and hear his voice was — miraculous. I felt as rooted to the spot as the others seated on the floor must have felt. He was definitely the source of that warm, quiet, joyful wave that was washing over the place. He asked me to approach the table.

I felt my body move toward him as my mind stayed focused on him. He gave me some of the food off his plate. I then turned away from the table to find a place to sit down.

After Swamiji finished eating, he left the table, seated himself in the middle of the room, and asked everyone to gather around him. My teacher, Vilasini Balakrishnan, had encouraged me to come to this retreat to meet the man who had been so important in my spiritual growth. She began gesturing to me to come closer to where Swamiji was sitting. When I got closer, Swamiji leapt up out of his chair and hugged me close.

He told me how pleased he was that I had discovered Narayana, and that I should let others know about what I knew. He said that knowledge was a fire and that "fire needs fuel."

Being so close to Swamiji was to feel totally at rest, totally accepted, totally loved. The very air around him was charged with his unlimited compassion. At this time, Swamiji was much advanced in years, so he left the gathering after a short while to rest before his morning classes.

Three days later, I learned that Swamiji had suffered a major heart attack, which within another few days was to take his life. The doctors had estimated that the flow of blood to his heart had been approximately 25 percent of what it should have been. I was not only thankful that I was able to meet the most influential being in my life, but also amazed. For a man who was in such a frail state of health, he frolicked about with an excitement and enthusiasm for his students that truly could have come only from the Divine.[1]

A good many years earlier, Anjali Singh had experienced a powerful lesson in understanding the true meaning of the guru's presence. He seemed to be saying: "You can experience the vast calm of the Existence that I am — at all times, in all places":

Immortal Existence

After his first ventricular failure, he made me a solemn promise, "I promise I will never leave you. Remember that!"

Two years later, after more ventricular failures, I reminded him of that promise on a small note I sent to him while he was in an adjoining room, as I did not have the emotional strength to talk about it face to face. He put his reply down in writing on my own note:

"If I leave you, where is 'you'?" I am the very Existence — *sat* [the all-pervading Existence of *Brahman*, the supreme Reality]."[2]

A Disciple's Need of the Guru

During a *satsang*, Swamiji remarked, "The guru lives as long as the disciple needs him."

On hearing this remark, one devotee expressed her unsurpassed joy, thinking that the comment meant that Swamiji would certainly remain on the earthly plane for some time to come yet.

Noticing the devotee's interpretation of his words, Swamiji quickly added an additional clarification:

"I said as long as the disciple *needs* him, not as long as the disciple *wants* him!"[3]

About a week before his final heart attack in July 1993, Swamiji told a devotee in Washington, D.C.:

"The Lord has been calling me, but all these people won't let me go. I feel like a rope being pulled on both ends."

Despite obvious signs that his heart was not functioning — he was skipping some twenty beats per minute and experiencing palpitations and pain — he insisted on continuing with his planned program and proceeded to fly to San Diego. When questioned about going, he said, "What — do you think I'll collapse?"

In San Diego, his heart finally succumbed to the point where he had trouble breathing, and he was taken to the hospital. The doctors did not give much hope, but the only hope they could provide was through heart surgery. Despite all efforts by the medical staff and the nonstop prayers that continued by the devotees who had set up a chapel in a hospital conference room, Swamiji attained *Mahasamadhi* on August 3 at 5:45 p.m. Pacific Standard Time.

An Extraordinary Patient

During the hours preceding surgery, the hospital staff realized what an extraordinary patient they had in their ward. They bowed to the devotees' wishes and allowed us to line the hallways and chant the *Mrtyunjaya Mantra* as Swamiji was being wheeled from one room to another. When time came for him to be transported to another hospital for the surgery, we again lined the hallways, and again chanted.

During the second hallway chanting we saw a blonde woman none of us knew standing by one side, obviously deep in prayer as she listened to the chanting. Later we found out why she had been there: Her mother had been admitted to the hospital at the same time as Swamiji and had been critically ill. The woman was a student of metaphysics and apparently clairvoyant. She said that with

> Swamiji's presence in the hospital, she sensed very fine and high energies there. When Swamiji was scheduled to leave, she understood that he had been there so her mother could pass from this life in a blessed state. The mother had already passed on when Swamiji was being taken by ambulance to the second hospital. From her perspective, the deceased woman's daughter said, the purpose for Swamiji being at the same hospital was so that he could guide her mother to liberation.[4]

After the surgery, when Swamiji was being taken into the operating room for some minor surgical procedures, a surgeon who was checking the availability of rooms saw Swamiji being wheeled by on the gurney. He said to someone there: "That is a holy man. I can feel the power of his presence."

Swami Chidananda, head of the Divine Life Society and Swamiji's *gurubhai* [disciple of the same guru] since the time they had both studied together with Swami Sivananda, visited Swamiji in the hospital. He said of him:

> Swamiji is *Brahman*. It is *Isvara Darsana* to see him. He is beyond the body. He has dived into and merged with the Self.

He went on to say:

> Swami Chinmayananda's life has been the life of ten masters. It would take ten people to accomplish what Swamiji accomplished in his own lifetime.

DEATH DOES NOT MATTER

Watching Gurudev's body going through impossible demands over the years, many of us would pass through phases of being anxious about the length of his stay on this plane.

Death Jokes

> At one point in the seventies, thoughts about the possibility of Gurudev's passing from this plane became a bit of an obsession with me. I couldn't get them out of my mind.
>
> One night we were at a radio station in California, where Swamiji was about to be interviewed. Several of us were sitting in a waiting room together with

Swamiji, chatting informally with him. At one point, he leaned back, gave me a meaningful look and said, "And then they'll carry the swami off in a coffin!" And he laughed loud and hard, slapping his hands against the sides of his chair.

His light-hearted joking about death managed to drive all obsessive thoughts about death from my mind.[5]

Whether with jokes or otherwise, Swamiji had endless comments to give about the inconsequence of the body's passing:

A Falling Leaf

At the end of a camp in Canada, Veronica Hausman was in a sad mood, since this was the first time she saw Swamiji sitting in a chair, not cross-legged on a platform, as had been his style for so many years. No doubt it was a sign that the pain in his legs had become too severe for them to be crossed now. Thoughts of her guru's mortality overcame her and her eyes flooded over with tears.

Swamiji looked at her and said: "What does a tree care if one leaf were to fall?"[6]

A Place to Rest

During the early days of Sandeepany Himalayas in Sidhabari, before Swamiji's *kutiya* was fully built, the *kutiya* stood on a sloping hill, with no pathways around it, as there are now. One day Swamiji came out of the back of the *kutiya*, stood in a commanding pose, swept his arm across the expanse in front of him, and said to the gardener:

"Make a rose garden there, so I have a place to rest."

Before his *Mahasamadhi*, the rose garden behind Swamiji's *kutiya* was the place where people frequently brought his chair for outdoor *satsang*, thinking that is what he had meant by "rest." Only later did they realize that it was to become the place of his *samadhi*, the memorial built after he left his body.[7]

Rose Garden Transformed

Swamiji was walking around the grounds behind his *kutiya* in Sidhabari. With him was Krishanlal Chopra, who later served as head of the training programs (in sewing, weaving, and other skills) for village women at the Sidhabari Project.

"Chopra," said Swamiji, looking at the roses in his beloved rose garden. "You see, they're growing so beautifully here, not knowing for what purpose this place is."

Later, that became the very spot where Swamiji's *samadhi*, his memorial, was built.[8]

THE TRANSITION

Many signs indicate that Gurudev was well aware of what would transpire in 1993 — that the time would arrive for dropping the body. Swami Tejomayananda, who became head of Chinmaya Mission worldwide after Gurudev's *Mahasamadhi*, recalls:

Transition Directive

I was in the United States from 1989 to 1993. [Whenever Pujya Gurudev came to North America, I traveled] with him to all his spiritual family camps. On the last day of the 1993 Washington, D.C., camp, the last camp he ever conducted, he told me:

"You will now have to go to India and take up the organizational work, and you will have to go to every Mission center. And there will be some problems and difficulties that you will have to solve, but you don't worry. It all comes as God's will, and God will take care of it."

This is the last statement he made to me.

[Now,] whenever I see any kind of difficulty, those words come to my mind: "But you don't worry . . ." This is one statement that really gives me strength.[9]

"Internalize Me"

The *tulabhara* ceremony [ceremony for making offerings to the guru] was being planned to take place in Mumbai, a ceremony for raising funds for Chinmaya Mission's projects on a grand scale. Radhika Krishnakumar read the announcement that anyone who donates a minimum of 4,500 rupees would receive small silver *padukas* as thanks. "For no philanthropic reason," confesses Radhika, "but only to receive those *padukas*, I sent in my donation of *exactly* 4,500 rupees." She put the *padukas* on her altar, at which she prayed every day.

One day, she saw that the *padukas* had suddenly disappeared. Following the disappearance, at the beginning of every meditation, she heard within her the following words repeated: "Internalize me" — as though Swamiji were talking to her.

Twelve days later she received news of Swamiji's *Mahasamadhi*. He had been preparing her for the passing of his bodily form.[10]

Chandan Tilaka

Shobha Joshi used to put flowers by her photograph of Gurudev, but never placed a *chandan tilaka* on the photo, as many others do at their home altars. One day, when Gurudev was severely ill in San Diego, she felt as though he was telling her, "Put a *chandan tilaka* on my forehead. I'm in much pain." So she did.

Since her granddaughter's birth, she had not meditated for several months. Now, she started meditating again, as though urged. At one point during meditation she felt as though something came out of every cell of her body. Her entire body felt swollen. After the meditation, she looked in a mirror to check what had happened, but nothing at all was visible.

Later she found out that exactly at that time Gurudev had passed away.[11]

A Voice from Beyond

Many of us were with Gurudev during those last days in the hospital and, after the *Mahasamadhi*, we remained in San Diego to keep vigil in the memorial chapel until the time arrived for Gurudev's mortal remains to be taken to the plane heading for India.

On the evening of his passing, while I was still in San Diego, my husband was sitting in the living room of our home many miles away. Suddenly, he heard Gurudev calling in a very loud voice, persistently. My husband said to him, "You're looking in the wrong place! You don't want *me*. Rudite is not here. She's in San Diego!" The voice persisted for some ten minutes, he said. This experience happened to a man who, though having met Swamiji many times over the years, never became a devotee.[12]

A long-time devotee, Anjali Singh of New Delhi, took many photographs of Gurudev during camps and *yajnas* as she traveled to many sites around with globe with him. She has an extraordinary story to tell about the early signals she received from Gurudev about his leaving this plane:

Rare Photographs

During the *Vivekacudamani* Camp in Sidhabari in September 1992, I received a message in my room that Swamiji wanted to see me. This was a bit unusual. When I went up to him, he was sitting in his *satsang* room with a few devotees near him. On seeing me, he looked for a letter he seemed to have kept aside for me to read. It was an invitation for him from World Vision 2000 for their function in Washington, D.C., on August 7, 1993. They had expressed their wish to recognize at their meeting of world religious leaders the outstanding services to humanity rendered by Swamiji.

After reading the letter, I was even more baffled, because Swamiji used to receive invitations like this many times, and many times he had received citations and awards. Moreover, the honor that is accorded by society is a matter of course to great *mahatmas*, and they do not think of it as anything special. I said the news was wonderful, but my mind was definitely puzzled. He was talking about his program, which included a lecture tour in the United States spanning several months. The World Vision 2000 function would have fit in the middle of his already defined program.

He said, "Before that, I have to come to New Delhi for a day because there is a function at Tirupati." After that function, he would have had to return to the States again to complete his projected lecture tour.

"Goodness!" I said. "Such a long journey for just one day? Won't that be very tiring?" — meaning, why accept invitations that involve so much exertion?

He replied, "What to do?"

He then had someone bring his personal itinerary and in his own hand noted down the changes in it to accommodate the conference in Washington.

For the next two hours I could think of nothing else except: Why had Swamiji especially called for me? Was it just to show me this letter? It just did not make sense. There had to be some other reason. I continued to think about it. Then it dawned on me that it was his way of hinting that I could accompany him after the Delhi function back to the United States, so that those who would be going with him at the beginning of his American tour in June would not have to do the journey twice.

So I quickly went back to him and said, "Swamiji, may I go with you on this trip to Washington? And please promise that I may sit next to you all the way!"

I had worded this request carefully in my mind before asking, because on an earlier occasion someone had offered to accompany Swamiji on a flight *only* if nobody else was going, and she had felt Swamiji would be needing her. He had remarked on it later, "There is no *need*." We did not understand that the need was ours, not his. We are the ones who need the *mahatmas*, and by service to them our minds become purified.

I waited for Swamiji's answer. He lifted one eyebrow a little and said, "You're welcome!" I remember his expression very well as he paused and said, with a glint in his eye, "You will have rare photographs to take on that day. Yes, some rare photographs." He also agreed to let me sit with him throughout the flight.

Months later, at the end of February 1993, during a train journey from Hyderabad to Vizag, a few of us were waiting in the compartment with Swamiji. He said so many wonderful things that day. Afterwards I wrote down eleven points in my personal diary, among them:

"You are still identifying with the mind. Even a quiet mind is still a mind. Identify with That which is the Knower of the quiet mind."

One of the entries in my diary was about a bet I was arranging with him regarding the August 7 function. I had asked him if I could have his flight itinerary, as I would be going with him from New Delhi to Washington in August.

"I'm not going to Washington from here," he said.

"But that's what you said in Sidhabari. It was decided then that I would go with you," I said.

"I didn't say that. My itinerary is Orlando-Washington-Orlando [Florida]."

"But didn't you say you had to come to New Delhi for a day? That is how the whole plan was made. Otherwise, why should I be assuming for so many months that I'll be going with you?"

"I never said that."

"You did . . . you *did*, Swamiji! I'm 100 percent sure! I can't have heard wrong. You even said I would have rare photographs to take at the August 7 function. You said I could sit next to you in the plane. It wasn't for Orlando-Washington — that's such a short flight!"

I was bewildered that he could have forgotten something like this. "Let's have a bet, Swamiji!" Many times I would bet with him. (It's probably a past-life instinct.) It was usually one-sided, his participation being tacit. Whenever I won, which was 90 percent of the time, I would extract a "boon" from him. He would protest and say, "Look what happened to Dasharatha!" I would say that I wanted a Nachiketas type of boon. Usually I would bet only when I was 100 percent sure of winning, as I was this time. I even had proof!

"All right. Let's have a bet!" said Swamiji. I got excited, because Swamiji was showing an unusual interest and was actively participating.

"But how will we prove who won?" he asked.

"You wrote it down in your itinerary at that time. It will be written there!"

"And what is the bet?"

"Whatever you say."

"Ten thousand rupees!" he said.

"That is, if I *lose*! And you have to give *me* a 'boon' if I *win*, which is — a breakthrough in meditation. As it is, you owe me seven boons. This will be the eighth!" I answered.

"There has to be a limit to stupidity!" was Swamiji's reply.

His itinerary was then passed to him. He opened it, relishing each moment. We were both so sure of winning. In the itinerary was written "Orlando-Washington-Orlando" — and he showed it to me with a victor's smile.

My face fell. I was quite disappointed, because all my plans for the summer and for sitting with him in the plane got smashed in one stroke, along with it my boon and the breakthrough.

Seeing the crestfallen look on my face, he said, "All right. Out of compassion, I give you back half."

I just kept looking at him, thinking as if losing five thousand fewer rupees was going to make up for all those losses. He again said, "You need not give ten thousand; I give you back five! Remember, it is out of compassion for you." And a third time he again repeated, "I give you back half."

When one doesn't understand a thing fully, it keeps ringing in the mind, especially all those repetitions. I still couldn't understand how for so many months I had been under the impression that I was going with him when he had never said any such thing.

In April 1993 in Mumbai I asked him if I could go with him in the beginning of his tour since I was not to go in August, but he said, "There is no need."

On June 7, after a camp at Sidhabari, we arrived at the Delhi airport. Swamiji had to wait two hours in the airport lounge before he could change flights. I said, "You did not allow me to go with you, yet you said I would have rare photographs to take on August 7."

"Yes," he replied. "You will have rare photographs to take."

When Swamiji passed away on August 3, my daughter said, "How come Swamiji said you would have rare photos on August 7, when it should have been August 2 or 3?" It was only after her remark that I understood that "rare" referred to the condition of his physical equipment, not to so many *mahatmas* under one roof at the World Vision 2000 Conference.

"That's because his remains are to arrive here on the 6th," I said.

It so happened that even though it was first announced in the newspapers that Swamiji's remains would be arriving on the 6th, they actually arrived on August 7, due to a delay. Swamiji had called me to his room in Sidhabari eleven months ago and found a way to impress this date upon my mind.

When his mortal remains were to arrive, I took it as his command to me to take photographs even though I was not emotionally prepared to do so. I had been taking Swamiji's photos for so many years that he must have wanted the job completed. To all those who opposed my attempts, I kept saying that it was for the sake of historical documentation. Truly speaking, I was just doing what I thought he had wanted me to do. I requested the organizers to allow me to take pictures before the long queues of devotees were allowed inside. They gave me only two minutes, during which time I took eleven pictures. While taking them, I spoke to him in my mind:

"You lost the bet, Swamiji. You said you were not coming to New Delhi."

"I didn't really come, did I?" I imagined him saying.

"But you didn't fully win, did you? In fact, you made us all lose!"

"No! That is why I said I give you back half."

"So! What I had heard in Sidhabari was correct! You made me feel so stupid. At least you owe me half a boon, half a breakthrough?"

"There is a limit to stupidity! Remember, it is out of great compassion for you that I'm giving you half."

"I understand."

I had erroneously understood that his body was what he had meant by giving back half. It was only weeks later when I saw the printed photographs that I realized it was not his body he had been referring to when he said he gave back half. It was his real Self, even though "invisible"! We just didn't have the eyes to see him.

In the first photograph, his true presence expresses itself in the form of a single shaft of blue light going toward his eyes. In the second, a double shaft appears from both sides. In another, clouds of blue light are present. In yet another, he looks like Shiva sitting by Mount Kailas. Then there is a close-up of the mountains with blue light. Then comes a series of pictures with various hues of pink and mauve, as if an artist had painted in streaks of watercolor. A halo appears behind his head.

Whatever photographs were taken outside of those two minutes, even from the same angle and under similar conditions, do not hold the same magic. In those eleven two-minute photographs one can see his presence. He did this out of great compassion, to let us know that he is still with us. The room where his body was kept had no blue shafts of light, and I am told by professional photographers that if light had been leaking from my camera, it would also have appeared on his face.

Eleven months in advance, he had promised me rare photographs on August 7, 1993, and he had now supplied them with his own technical skills. He alone knows how he made that happen.

As for his second promise, that he would let me sit next to him on that journey, the organizers realized rather late that they needed a chair to support his back [as the body had been embalmed in the lotus position]. Since my house was the nearest to the Mission Center, they asked for one of mine. The chair is now back with me, next to me. It has a small dark-brown mark on it that was not there before — probably from crushed roses. The chair will be a constant reminder of his presence next to me for the rest of this life's journey. He did promise I could sit next to him for the entire journey![13]

A Vision of Light

Three days after Gurudev's *Mahasamadhi*, Sheel Dewan's daughter's friend lost her father-in-law. The friend asked for someone to chant the *Gita* for his last rites. They tried to find someone but didn't succeed. Then the friend asked if Sheel herself would be able to do it, but she was feeling very sad and lost because of Gurudev's *Mahasamadhi* just three days earlier and didn't feel up to it. However, she finally agreed.

The house she had to go to was just across their own home. She walked over there, but when she reached the building, she realized that she had completely forgotten her way: She no longer knew where the entrance was, or the lift, or any other detail. She just stood there, looking around. Then she saw that everything around her was transformed in light — the doors, the buildings, the garden. Everything was beautiful beyond description.

Then the beautiful light disappeared, and her memory returned. She again remembered how to reach the home of her daughter's friend.

Today she wonders, "Was it Swamiji trying to encourage me to recite the *Gita*?"[14]

AFTER THE PARTING

The Persistent Flame

After Gurudev's *Mahasamadhi*, Nalini Browning, who has a residence at Gurudev's ashram at Krishnalaya, Piercy, California, spent much time in Gurudev's bedroom, tending to the flowers and candles set out there, meditating, remembering. One day she noticed that the candle at the altar had almost burned down to the end and she was about to change it to a fresh one when she thought, "No, let it burn down all the way."

She returned to the room four hours later: The candle was still burning! And so it continued to burn for another day and night. At the point when she realized that something extraordinary was happening, Nalini stayed in the room for many hours, feeling that a message was being sent. Finally she said to herself, "I'm very sleepy; maybe I should go to bed now."

At that moment, the candle began to flicker. It went on and off for a long time and then died.[15]

The Miraculous Rose

The orange-blossomed rose bush bloomed whenever Gurudev came to Krishnalaya, California, even in the cold season. It grew just outside Gurudev's residence, next to the living room window where he held *satsaṅg*. It soon came to be known as "Swamiji's Bush," because of the bright orange color of its blossoms. Even after Gurudev's passing, whenever the buds began to form and then burst into full bloom, some significant event would occur.

It was Christmas Eve at Krishnalaya after Gurudev's *Mahasamadhi*. A Christmas tree was set up in the living room of Gurudev's residence. Nalini and Bill Browning, their family members, and a few others who had known Gurudev had gathered there. The curtains were drawn on the window facing the rose bush.

They had looked around the property for a flower to place in the room but had found nothing, as even in California the winters in the northern part of the state can be quite severe, leaving no blossoms in sight.

One family member had still been standing outside the house and just then entered the room. "The rose bush is blooming!" she exclaimed in surprise.

Nalini opened the curtains to the window facing Swamiji's Bush. There it was: one bright orange rose blossom looking through the window into the living room. The lights of the Christmas tree reflecting against the window formed a ring of light around the rose.

That one solitary blossom bloomed for a very long time.

In April 1997, Nalini Browning saw that the bush was again about to burst forth in orange blossoms. She wondered, "I wonder what will happen this time?"

On Sunday morning, before the weekly *satsang*, she had gone into the living room and found a rather stale and musty smell there. She brought in a camellia blossom and set it next to the chair where Swamiji used to sit in *satsang*. She lit the lamps in his bedroom and adorned the small altar there with some azalea blossoms. Then came time for *satsang*, which was held in a back room of the house.

After *satsang*, she opened the French doors to the living room and was hit by an overwhelming fragrance of roses. No windows were open, nor were there any roses in the room, just the camellia by Swamiji's chair, a flower that has little fragrance.

She then walked toward the bedroom and already in the hallway leading up to it she felt an overpoweringly strong, sweet fragrance meeting her. When she opened the bedroom door, the fragrance that met her was so powerful it engulfed her completely.

Nalini then beckoned others from the *satsang* to verify her impression, to make sure that she was not just imagining things. The others, too, detected the inexplicably strong fragrance and were at a loss as to how to explain it. They felt as though Swamiji was using the sweet fragrance to beckon to them, "Come! Come!"[16]

Teachings that had begun while Gurudev was still in the body continued after he had left his physical form. Some dreamed dreams in which Gurudev appeared to give advice on business; others were reassured through powerful dreams of Gurudev's continued love for them.

Three-Day Sorrow Cure

After Gurudev's *Mahasamadhi*, Anjali Singh was going by train to Sidhabari, feeling very sad. She remembered a similar trip, together with Gurudev, some years before:

She was feeling very sorrowful — as she had been feeling for many years, as long as she could remember. When they were alone, he asked her about a sarcastic remark she had made, seeking to find out what sadness had motivated her to say it. She began to spill out all of the reasons for her sadness, until her voice caught and she stopped.

"Everything's OK," she said. "It's nothing." Then no more was said.

In the taxi to Sidhabari she cried the whole way, still feeling very sad. Swamiji said nothing.

In Sidhabari, Swamiji offered her strawberries with cream, which he knew she loved very much. This continued for three days. At the lectures, she felt her sorrow starting to fade away, feeling Swamiji's love and compassion and the fulfillment of knowledge in her intellect. At the third day's lecture, Swamiji said:

"Why are you expecting happiness from the world? The poor world has no happiness to give you. It's like looking for water in the desert. The desert has only a mirage to offer."

Although Anjali had heard such statements before, this time the truth of it penetrated to the core of her being. She felt her sorrow lessen to a good one-half of what it had been before.

Now it was after Gurudev's *Mahasamadhi*, and she was once again going to Sidhabari, again feeling sad. She remembered the train trip with Gurudev and remembered how he had helped her get over the worst of her sorrow then. She told her companion that she knew everything would be all right again in three days, just like before.

On the third day she was still feeling miserable and thought, "Why hasn't it happened yet? It's almost the end of the day." Then, at *arati*, a deep peace overcame her and her sorrow melted within seconds. Both her previous left-over sadness and her new grief disappeared permanently. After that, she never again felt sorrowful about Gurudev's leaving the body. She realized that the initial lifting of sorrow had ended her expectation that worldly things could bring joy, and that the second lifting was to let go of her expectation that her guru would always be around to hold her hand through all difficulties.[17]

Sleepyheads Awakened

In 1996, a young man came to visit Krishnalaya, California, from out of town and arranged to spend some time there. He was a total stranger to Swamiji's teaching.

While at Krishnalaya, he started reading Swamiji's books — and loved them. He also watched the *Gita* videos, together with some old-time devotees. He became very connected to Swamiji through his books and tapes.

One day they were watching Swamiji expound the second chapter of the *Gita*. At one point, the visitor began to feel a little sleepy.

Just around that time, Swamiji was explaining a concept he called "electricity yoga" on the tape. At the very moment he said those words, the lights in the room started flickering on and off. The television picture remained unaffected, but the sound was gone. The phenomenon jolted the sleepy listener into full alertness once again.

The long-time listeners of Swamiji remarked to the visitor that, had it been a live talk, Swamiji might very likely have stopped talking to get people's attention and to jolt the sleepy ones into alertness once again![18]

Dream Savior

Tina Bedi of New Delhi had never met Gurudev while he was alive, but she had seen his photos and felt drawn by something inexplicable.

At one point, her life had become very troubled, and she was in great psychic pain. One night she saw a dream in which she was standing in a large body of water with no shore. It was a dark, rainy night. Then she saw a speck of light in the distance trying to catch her attention. When she finally came near it, she saw a man in a boat with an oar in one hand and a lantern in the other. He put down the oar and pulled her up.

On the boat was a little *kutiya*, where Gurudev was sitting in meditation. She sat down next to him. Gurudev instructed the man who had pulled her out of the waters to take care of her. Then the dream ended.

When she saw Swami Tejomayananda for the first time giving a lecture, she thought she remembered him from somewhere, but could not say where or when. Then Swami Tejomayananda sang "God, take my boat to shore," and she realized that she had seen him in her dream: He had been the one who had pulled her up out of the dark, shoreless waters.

Within a week, all her troubles and pain faded away.[19]

Instructions from Beyond

In a dream, Radhika Krishnakumar was watching Swamiji from the doorway of a house she had never seen before. He looked very ill. He was sitting in a bed, obviously convalescing from an illness. She went up to him and bowed her head at his feet. Tears were flowing copiously. Swamiji took a maroon pen, which had the word "Chinmaya" engraved on it, and gave it to her. She took it with a grateful heart.

The following day, she received a letter posted from Boston from Swami Tejomayananda asking her to become involved with the development of the Chinmaya Vision Program, a program that aims to apply Gurudev's vision of education to complement academic learning in schools. She is now actively working on the program, disseminating Gurudev's educational vision throughout India.[20]

Lost Book Found

During Gurudev's visit to the United States in the summer of 1993, Uma Jeyarasasingam conferred with him about the youth camp she was planning to hold at Krishnalaya in Northern California in 1994.

"What is the theme for the camp?" asked Gurudev.

"Lord Shiva."

"Good," he said.

Some months after Gurudev's *Mahasamadhi*, Uma was preparing a publication for the camp, working on her computer late into the night. She needed a reference book she had used before to locate a story about Shiva, but could not locate it in her home library. She finally gave up and went to bed.

That night, in a dream, Uma heard Gurudev say to her, "The book you're looking for is on the shelf in your *puja* room."

She immediately got up from bed, found the book on the shelf just where Gurudev had indicated it would be, and went back to bed, thankful and happy that her guru was still there to support her in her efforts, as always.[21]

Help from Beyond

A devotee from India had been pursing her Master's degree in another country since early 1992, supporting her studies through a financial loan. Gurudev knew all the details. Although now abroad, she longed to meet Gurudev regularly, just as she had grown accustomed to doing while living in Mumbai. They exchanged many letters.

One day she received a letter from Gurudev which, among other things said:

> *We will meet again — Where? How? These are for Him to decide. We wait in prayer and strive as best as we can in the field in which He has kept us.*
>
> . . .
>
> *Congratulations! You are now on the staff of the university! Some money must be coming in. Good. I will also try to send you some from here to help you hold on. Intelligently spend and live joyfully fulfilling His will as best as you can. This in itself is an intense* sadhana. *Live in the present, without wasting your time and energy trying to relive the past!*

She recalls: "His words [about our future meetings] kept me hoping that he would come through his hospital admission. He always kept his word, as he had shown me time and time again, so I was sure we would meet. . . . The last paragraph where he says that he will try to send me some money completely overwhelmed me. After his *Mahasamadhi,* I used to think to myself: How will he pull this one through? I knew he would do it, but I was extremely curious to see how he would. He had not received my letter in which I had told him not to do such a thing, so I knew somehow he would come through . . ."

He did. Swami Swaroopananda had his first full *yajna* in her city in early 1994. He stayed with a family that was not at all known to Chinmaya Mission. The young student ended up staying with them during the *yajna* so that she could lend them a hand. During that time, she grew very close to them. She ended up making them her local parents, and they came to her graduation that year. Afterwards, having become a permanent resident in her new country, she was working toward repaying her loan.

The devotee recalls: "One day they had a chat with me and asked me to live with them: After all, they were 'my parents,' they said. They told me I would not need to pay any rent or anything toward the food expenses. They told me that this way I would save money and repay my loan more quickly and be able to return to India. I only had to pay for my overseas phone bills and car costs. I was taken aback and discussed the situation with my mum, Swami Tejomayananda, and Swami Swaroopananda. It was decided that it was OK to move in."

She concludes, "I see this as my Gurudev working through them. He promised me support, and he did it in every possible way — and is still doing it! . . . He has shown me exactly how he works, and I know there is more to come. This to me is the guru literally looking after each and every need of the disciple!"[22]

Gurudev Revisited

It is February 1998 and I am in Sidhabari, three and a half years since my last visit. The *samadhi* is now complete. . . . It is strange and great being back here. Strange, because the excitement filled with anticipation of seeing Swamiji in person is not there. Great, because his presence is very much there. I feel happy as Bella [Salerno] and I walk toward our room. This is Bella's first visit to Sidhabari. She's known Swamiji since 1972.

The brown mountains and the snow-covered mountains behind them look so majestic — the Dhualadhar range of the Himalayas. They skirt one side of the ashram. My heart is filled with joy. I have so many memories of growth and chiseling, of laughter and silence here.

I enter the *samadhi* for the first time since the new structure has been built. It looks very beautiful from outside and from within. The Himalayan mountains stand behind in mute testimony. The entire interior is brown granite. In the middle is a square, raised platform on which is a brass statue of Swamiji in seated posture. They've dressed him in orange clothes, a shawl for winter and a *rudraksa mala* and garlands.

At first glance, it is hard to imagine his presence crystallized in a statue. The statue is not exact perfection. The face is not really Swamiji. I can't pinpoint exactly what it is. But his spirit is very present. He is there. His presence pervades the entire shrine. It is an intense experience.

The chanting starts. I look up. Swamiji is looking directly at me. This feeling remains for about five minutes. I have a very deep and powerful meditation.

After the *arati* everyone leaves. A brahmachari stays back. He turns all the lights off and sits in one corner. I sit down again. The sun has not peeped out yet. Tears flow down my cheeks. I am overwhelmed. I feel a hundred emotions. I feel I transcend time and am one with Swamiji. I pray hard. I pray to surrender all my negative emotions — my anger, my extroversion. I feel him so acutely; it is not my imagination, but reality!

This morning again I see it — Swamiji's face is distinctly visible on the brown mountain, one of the two peaks facing the back of his *kutiya* and the *samadhi*. High up on the mountain, a little below the center of the peak, his face manifests itself clearly — the face, the eyes, nose, mustache, and beard. It is he.[23]

Missing Soap

Shivaram, Swamiji's long-time attendant at the Mumbai ashram and later at Sidhabari, has been evoking Swamiji's presence every day since his *Mahasamadhi*. He is the guardian and caretaker of Swamiji's residence there. Every day, he rises at 3:30 a.m. to prepare tea for Swamiji, clean Swamiji's bathroom, and make his bed. When the weather gets cold, he puts an extra blanket on the bed.

One time Shivaram gave Swamiji's soap to a visiting devotee who needed it. The next morning, when he went to Swamiji's bathroom to clean it, he heard Swamiji's voice asking, "Where is my soap?"[24]

Was this Gurudev's way of encouraging his devoted disciple to continue with his spiritual discipline?

Several people recount how even after Gurudev's *Mahasamadhi*, he still protected them:

No Pain

Sheel Dewan of Mumbai went to Sidhabari in October 1996 to see Gurudev's *samadhi*. It was raining as they arrived. As she was walking to her room, she fell and fractured her patella. She could feel the bones parting.

An orthopedic surgeon was called, but it was already too late in the evening; he could come only the following morning. That night, she had terrible pains in the back due to the position she had to sleep in, with several pillows propped under her knee. Dr. Kshama Metre stayed with her during the night. Around 1 a.m., the pains grew very severe. The doctor said, "I'll take out the pillows one by one." But before she could do that, Sheel Dewan said to her, "Look! The bones are back in place! It's a miracle!" Dr. Metre slowly removed the pillows. All signs of pain had left; she could even stretch out her knee straight. "What has Gurudev done?" she asked in wonderment. "Thank God the doctor didn't come!"

Still, it was decided that an X-ray should be taken. After the X-ray, she was diagnosed to have a fractured kneecap, and the doctor told her she needed an operation. To reach Mumbai for her surgery, she traveled first to Delhi — thirteen hours by jeep over rough terrain, but she felt no pain whatsoever, despite

> the many jolts. From Delhi she flew to Mumbai for the surgery. Her doctors in Mumbai could not believe that she was suffering from no pain at all.[25]

When a *mahatma* leaves the body, he never truly leaves those devoted to him. As Gurudev himself had written to a young boy who wondered when he'd see him next:

> *Whenever you need me, close your eyes and look into your heart — and I will be there!*

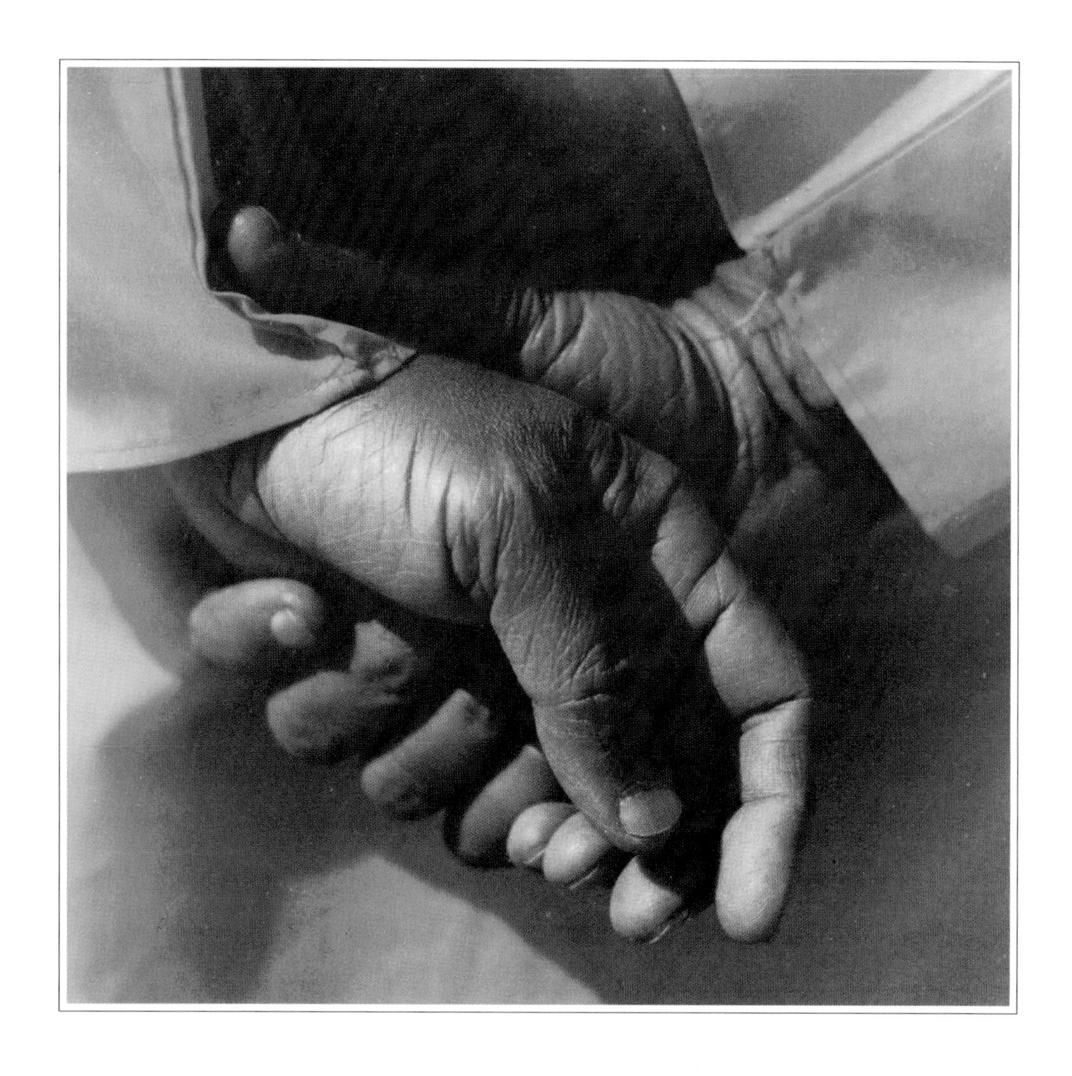

The vision
of an indescribable thing
must necessarily
be indescribable.

WHO WAS HE?

Devotees viewed Swami Chinmayananda as a manifestation of the Lord Himself; many saw him as a great World Teacher (*jagat-guru*); and yet others saw him as nothing more than a charismatic, highly intelligent, and entertaining personality. The truth probably is that he was *all* of those manifestations. Whatever the person in front of him evoked, that he was: He was a mirror with which to see ourselves more clearly. Yet his devotees never stopped marveling about one aspect of his being: that, no matter how closely they had grown to know him, he always remained utterly unpredictable.

Swami Chidananda of Chinmaya Mission moves into a meditative mood at the very thought of Gurudev:

> Gurudev is immeasurable and unknowable. What we saw of Gurudev is only the tip of the iceberg. As the *Purusa Sukta* says about the supreme Being: "One-fourth is seen in the world; three-fourths are up in the heavens!"
>
> Until the last moment of life in his physical body, he was so creative that nobody knew what his next plan or project would be. Again, from the Vedantic point of view, he is the Self and not the name and form that we "knew." With no attachment and identification, he revels in the Truth of his being. That is unknowable, indeed!

Gurudev himself was heard to remark on a number of occasions: "People will know who I was 20, 30, 50 years after I'm gone."

Swamiji's life and work was led by an inner charter difficult to conceptualize for a typical person immersed in a desire-ridden life. Where we may be drawn by the promises of a successful career or the beauties of a geographical locality, his "attractions" were of a different nature. He said in a letter during his early years of teaching in the West:

No part of the world attracts me. It is the people who attract me. I am not a traveler who is traveling for pleasure . . . I am neither interested in places nor things. I am interested in man; therefore, I go searching for people to talk to them, to understand them, and, if possible, to exchange ideas and give my own thoughts to them.[1]

Some were fortunate enough to attune themselves to him to such a degree that at times his being became so resplendent to the inner eye that they could barely view him with their physical eyes. Yet other listeners saw only the surface drama, as some Americans in the 1960s who came to hear Swamiji as just another interesting phenomenon from the East. Gurudev had just finished a scintillating talk at a Unitarian Church in California, when ladies from the audience were heard discussing the talk in the hallway: "Wasn't he a charismatic speaker!" they exclaimed. Had his charisma blinded them to who he really was under the seemingly magnetic and entertaining surface? Was the true teacher hidden from their view?

And hide he did, sometimes behind his charisma, at times even literally, in clothes that tried to conceal his real identify.

Disguised Swami

During one of his early *yajna* tours to the United States, as we had gathered at the airport to receive him in California, we all suffered a shock. Instead of the familiar orange robes that our eyes were straining to see, we beheld Swamiji dressed in a black pants and a Nehru jacket!

When we asked him later why this change in attire, he said, "When I'm in my orange robes, the passenger next to me invariably asks, 'Excuse me, sir, are you a sw - a - a - a - mi?' This way I can hide. Others leave me alone."[2]

Gurudev showed himself to us in many moods — and ever unpredictably:

Paradox and Unpredictability

At one of his spiritual camps, I had the unfortunate requirement to leave a day or two early, before the close of the camp. On the morning of the day I was to leave, I went to meditation, determined that it be good and deep — a proper ending to a sublime experience at the camp.

The meditation class was good, but my mind, unfortunately, stayed surface-bound. I walked out of the hall a little disappointed, and headed toward Swamiji's *kutiya*, where I was to join the meeting of a group of workers at Krishnalaya. As I walked slowly past the trees lining the walkway, I took in the beauty of the morning — the trees, the slowly lifting fog, the fresh air sweeping past my body. Suddenly, my mind took a deep dive, settling in a spot of quiet, solid, peaceful beauty and poise. What I had so valiantly sought in meditation class now arrived totally unannounced and unsought.

I walked into Swamiji's room, and the minute my prostrations were over I knew that Swamiji (of course!) knew. Seeing his deep, glowing look sent me even deeper into the peaceful state of mind that had chanced upon me. Others arrived for the meeting and gathered in a semicircle around Swamiji's desk. Various points of discussion were brought up: "What do we need to do to the property to secure it against fire, so that insurance companies would be willing to sell us fire insurance? Shouldn't we install fire extinguishers every few feet on each building? What improvements shall we make on the fence around the swimming pool to ensure that small children cannot maneuver their way through the gates and endanger their lives?" — and so on.

But Swamiji's mind was not to be tied down with practical matters. He was soaring in spaces that had little connection with insurance or liability or legal suits. He kept looking at me, obviously overjoyed to see the state of my mind, relishing the moment, dancing in joy. Instead of paying proper attention to the serious questions being presented, he kept throwing out one preposterous suggestion after another: "If all these many years our buildings haven't burned down, why should they burn now? If Lord Narayana wills it, let them burn! We will build them anew!" — and so on.

I couldn't believe my ears, yet my mind was dancing along with his, and the game continued. He pranked and laughed through the whole meeting, and so did I. At the edge of my mind, I felt a twinge of guilt for seemingly wasting everyone else's time, but it didn't deter the joyous game. Besides, *he* was in charge, and he was the one playing it. Although many in the group spent long minutes discussing the intricacies of insurance liability, little of practical value got accomplished. But what did get accomplished was getting a powerful taste of the unpredictable, paradoxical, yet sublime state of mind that a man of deep wisdom can exhibit, a state that may make no sense at the level at which we usually function.

> Sometimes his mind remains in the *sattvic* [serene] state, sometimes in the *rajasic* [dynamic] or *tamasic* [inactive], and at others, beyond the

> three *gunas* [thought textures]. Sometimes he appears as a worldly person and at others as one who roams in the streets of [the city of] Vedanta. But the sage whose ignorance has been dispelled by the teachings of his teacher never gets deluded.
>
> Sometimes he is silent, and sometimes he is engaged in discussions; sometimes he laughs out loud (without words of explanation), reveling in the bliss of his own Self; and at others he observes closely the behavior of the people around him. But the sage whose ignorance has been dispelled by the teachings of his teacher never gets deluded. (*Jivanmuktanandalahari* 11-12)

That day, Gurudev showed us how playfully he could sport through life's problems as his mind soared in spaces where seemingly serious earthly concerns became but a small twist in a vast, delightful game.[3]

There were times when Gurudev appeared to relish just being simply a man — a man who slaps his men friends on the back, discusses politics, and jokes about everyday things. Whether he was playing but another role to mirror the desires and interests of the people he happened to be with or whether he truly enjoyed the respite from the constant adulation and devotion bestowed upon him, we cannot judge. It is true, however, that at least on one occasion when a devotee's attempts at devotion became overbearing, when she practically followed him into the bathroom to serve him, he was heard to shout angrily: "The tyranny of devotees is enough to drive a swami mad!" Of course, once again, he may have simply been relaying a lesson that someone needed to hear.

Many tried to fathom the true swami, to define who he really was. As they attempted to do so, some had unforgettable experiences:

Unspoken Question Answered

During the time when the Sidhabari ashram was still partially under construction, Gurudev used to review the construction of every building, inspecting all work in minute detail. Three devotees followed him wherever he went during those construction reviews. Sometimes Gurudev would take a walk even after others had already gone to sleep. Still, the three would follow him at a distance wherever he went.

At the end of his late evening walks, Gurudev would approach the steps of his *kutiya*, turn around, and look at the three of them as though saying good-bye. Then Shivaram, his personal attendant, would open the door for him, and he would disappear into the darkness.

One night the three devotees were again following Gurudev. They walked in pin-drop silence; only the sound of his *padukas* could be heard. His tour finished, Gurudev approached his *kutiya*, went up to the steps as on previous nights, turned, stopped, looked at the three with a look that seemed to look right through them, and said:

"I'm Shiva, I'm Krishna, Jesus, Devi, Buddha, Muhammad — and much, much more." Then he walked into his *kutiya*, and Shivaram closed the door after him.

The three devotees went to their rooms, speechlessly. The next morning they compared notes about the previous night and discovered that each of them had had the identical question in mind the night before — "Who is he, really?" — but had not said it out loud. Though unspoken, the question had been answered by Gurudev.[4]

The site chosen for Sandeepany (Himalayas) adjoins the plains where the ancient sage Kapila Muni is said to have lived around 500 B.C. Kapila was the founder of Sankhya, one of the six systems of Hindu philosophy, which uses a very rational, analytic approach to unfolding the nature of existence. A small temple now stands over the spot where Kapila is said to have meditated in a cave more than 2,000 years ago. Memories of Kapila resurfaced one day during an inexplicable event at the Sidhabari ashram:

Slate *Padukas*

One beautiful evening Gurudev was sitting outside his *kutiya* at his Sidhabari ashram. The sun was just about to display his glory. A lady devotee came with great excitement and showed Gurudev what she had found:

"Gurudev, I was walking along the bank of the creek, and look what I found," she said, showing a stone slab shaped like a *paduka*.

"What good is one *paduka*?" said Gurudev. "Go find its mate."

So the devotee returned to the creek and before long found a second *paduka*-

shaped slab and hurried back to Gurudev's side. "Swamiji, look! I found the other half of the pair," she said with great excitement.

Gurudev smiled and said, "When I was Kapila, I wore these with a rope . . . and then threw them away into the river. . . . then Kapila's mother jumped into the river. . . ."

Everyone began laughing, but as the lady placed the *padukas* under the feet of Gurudev, to the amazement of all, the *padukas* fit both his feet perfectly.

Everybody sat in silent wonderment. He smiled.[5]

"I Am His Radha"

Swamiji had gone to a shop in Jaipur to purchase an idol for the Chinmaya Mission's Deenabandhu Temple in Bangalore. He wanted to purchase a brass Krishna idol, but the shopkeeper wanted to sell the idol only as a pair, together with Radha. The conversation continued for some time, but no progress was made in reaching an agreement. Time was running late, as Swamiji had to catch a plane soon.

"I want this Krishna," he said to the shopkeeper. "I am His Radha. I don't need another Radha. There is only one Purusha [the Absolute; the transcendent Self]."

The shopkeeper looked at Swamiji with astounded eyes and, without a word, let him have the Krishna alone.

"Mahatmaji," he said, "Whatever you want, just tell me. I'll let you have it."[6]

Narayana Himself

In May 1993, Gurudev had come to Hyderabad for a *yajna*. One day he had returned exhausted from the talk, as he had just recovered from a severe illness. Walking straight to his bed, he lay down on it. Ramesh and I were anxiously hovering by his bed. He was lying down with his eyes closed. He opened his eyes after a while and asked feebly, "How was the talk today?"

In all truth, I had not really given much attention to Gurudev's talk that day because of my anxiety over his health, but I had heard Gurudev's secretary Balan remark earlier, "Today it was not Gurudev whom I saw on the dais; it was Narayana Himself in all His glory! In my long association with Gurudev never have I seen him like this before; verily, he was Narayana Himself!"

With alacrity I therefore replied, "It was very good, Gurudev. Nobody guessed that you were not well."

"Yes," agreed Gurudev, "that was because it was not I who spoke," he said in a deep voice.

With half-closed eyes, looking at our confused faces, he continued, "There was one beside me who came and spoke." He indicated with his hands the shape of a photo frame.

We understood immediately that he was referring to Tapovan Maharaj, his own guru [whose likeness, in a frame, always appeared next to Gurudev's podium during his talks]. He smiled gently and, looking intently at me with the most tender expression in his eyes, said, "See that! All his life, he never spoke or gave lectures, and now, after his death, he is speaking so much, guiding all!"

I understood: The guru lives beyond his death! He continues to guide! He works through people who have totally surrendered to him.[7]

"I'm Right Here!"

In a *satsang* in India, someone asked Gurudev a question. He replied with unfathomable force:

"I'm right here! You don't see it! It's right in front of you!"

Then he went back to his usual tone. Everyone sat aghast.[8]

In many and different ways, people asked Swamiji if he was Self-realized. His answers varied. In a radio interview in 1975 he said:

I honestly confess that I have not realized. I am on the verge of it. I will not realize until you, too, my listeners, come with me. I am waiting for company. Alone I do not want to go.

At another time he said in answer to the question "Are you realized?"

That is for you to decide!

His words remind us of the vow of a *bodhisattva*, a person in a highly evolved state who deliberately chooses to inhabit a body again so that he can continue to serve the world and lead others to God-realization. Gurudev himself was the most eloquent exponent of what it means to live merged with the Truth of the Self, as in his response to someone's question, "Why does a realized person work?"

When one realizes the Truth, one becomes irresistibly vibrant with life. In divine spontaneity, activity gurgles through him. The physical equipment is generally too frail a reed to stand the blazing gush of love and work; therefore, such prophetic masters generally fold up in a blinding flash of brilliant service to mankind, carried on for a short duration of perhaps twenty or thirty years.

Your question is "Why should he work?" Can you tell me why the sun is illumining everything around it? Why fire is hot? sugar sweet? oceanic waters salty? Why birds fly? flowers bloom? mirrors reflect? air moves? earth revolves? . . . . Are they not expressing their essential nature? Can any one of them remain without their essential property? The realized saint is not responsible for what he is doing. He is one with Life. And Life expresses itself in action.[9]

Swami Chinmayananda is no longer with us in body, but his presence remains. As he himself spoke of his guru, Swami Tapovanam, so we now use Gurudev's own words to describe him:

The particular form that the great Lord took in the name of [Sri Swami Chinmayananda] has dissolved, and he has gone back to merge into his own Nature. He has now become the Essence in each one of us. Wherever we find the glow of divine compassion, love, purity, and brilliance, there we see but Sri Gurudev with his ever-smiling face. He has left his sheaths. He has now become the Self in all of us.

GLOSSARY

In most cases, the international transliteration style is used for Sanskrit words, but without diacritical marks. Where another, more commonly employed style is used, the international transliteration appears in parentheses. In the Glossary, as also within the text, Sanskrit words appear in italics, except in the case of words, such as guru, *which have become anglicized and therefore appear in roman type. Proper nouns of Sanskrit origin appear in anglicized spelling.*

A

abhisheka (abhiseka) Also called *Kumbha Abhisheka*. Ritual bathing of an idol.

acharya (acarya) Teacher.

amma "Mother." Used by many renunciates as a form of address toward all women.

arati "Light." The circling of a light before a deity or a holy person. A brief form of a worship ceremony that is traditionally performed at sunset.

ashram The residence and teaching center of a spiritual teacher, which often includes lodgings for his or her students.

Atman The pure Self, Consciousness, the immanent aspect of the supreme Reality. This same Consciousness, when regarded as transcendent, is called *Brahman*.

B

Balavihar Within Chinmaya Mission, a gathering of children for learning the immortal values expounded in the Vedas and the *Puranas*.

Bhagavad Gita Also spelled *Bhagawad Geeta* and *Bhagavad Geeta*. "Song of God." A major scriptural poem in eighteen chapters, contained in the epic *Mahabharata*. It is a dialogue between Lord Krishna and Arjuna, his friend and disciple, on the battlefield of the dynastic war between the Pandavas and Kauravas.

bhajan	Devotional song.
bhakta	A devotee of God; one devoted to the guru.
bhakti	Devotion. The path of devotion, one of the main paths to liberation. Also known as *bhakti yoga*.
bhiksha	A meal prepared as an offering to the guru.
brahmachari (m.) (*brahmacari*) brahmacharini (f.) (*brahmacarini*)	A seeker of the knowledge of *Brahman*; one who has taken the first monastic vows. The first of the four stages of life, the other being the life of the householder, the life of retirement, and the life of renunciation. The abbreviations are Br. (male) and Brni. (female).
Brahman	Pure Consciousness, the transcendent, all-pervading supreme Reality.
Brahmopadesam	"Learning about *Brahman*." Initiation into the *Gayatri Mantra*.
buddhu	Fool, often used as an endearing form of address.

C

CCMT	Central Chinmaya Mission Trust, the central governing body of Chinmaya Mission, located at Sandeepany Sadhanalaya, Mumbai, India.
chandan	Sandalwood.
chappal	Sandal.
Chennai	A name for Madras, South India.

D

darshan (darsana)	"Vision, sight." Beholding a holy person or place with the wish to receive a blessing.
deva	A deity, often associated with the forces of nature.
dhyana	Meditation.
dhoti	Male garment in the form of a long cloth tied around the waist.
diksa	Initiation.

G

Gayatri Mantra	Famous Vedic mantra that addresses Savitri, the Sun as Creator.
Gita	See *Bhagavad Gita*.
gopi	"Milkmaid." The *gopis* were devotees of Lord Krishna, exemplifying the most intense divine love.
grhastha asrama	The life of a householder. The second of the four stages of life, the other being the life of the celibate student, the life of retirement, and the life of renunciation.

guna	Thought quality or texture. The three types of *gunas* are: *sattva* (pure and serene), *rajas* (passionate and agitated), and *tamas* (dull and inactive).
guru	Spiritual teacher.
Gurudaksina	Offering to the guru as thanks for his teaching.
Guru Purnima	A day dedicated to the worship of the guru, celebrated on the full moon day of July.
guru-sisya	Guru-disciple.
Guru Stotram	A song in praise of the guru.

H

Hanuman	The disciple of Sri Rama, the epitome of the perfect disciple.
hatha yoga	One of the yogas, dealing primarily with the control of breath and culture of the body through a system of physical exercises and postures.

I

idli	Small, steamed cake make from *dal* and rice, a favorite food in South India.
Ishvara *(Isvara)*	The Lord, God.

J

jagat-guru* or *jagat-acarya	"World teacher." In 1986, the World Religious Parliament of New Delhi named five world leaders who were most active in spreading the spiritual teaching of the Vedas outside India; among them was H. H. Swami Chinmayananda.
japa	The training imparted to the mind by concentrating on a single line of thought to the exclusion of all other thoughts. It generally consists of repeating one of God's names, a mantra, with the help of a rosary.
japamala	Doing *japa* with a rosary; the rosary (*mala*) itself.
jiva	The individual soul.
***jivanmukta* (or *jivanmukta purusa*)**	A person liberated while living.
jnana	Divine knowledge, wisdom. The path of knowledge, one of the main paths to liberation. Also known as *jnana yoga*.
jnana yajna (Gita Jnana Yajna)	Also spelled *gnana yagna*. A series of lectures dedicated to the teaching of Vedanta. Used by Swami Chinmayananda to describe a series of lectures on Vedanta in which the seeker's ignorance is sacrificed in the fire of spiritual knowledge.

K

karma	The sum effects of past actions; a sequence of cause and effect on the moral plane. Action, work.
karma yoga	The path of action. This path is most fitting for those of mixed temperament — whose head and heart are equally developed. The seeker performs selfless activity, dedicating all his actions to a higher ideal and giving up all sense of agency.
karma yogi	A person who practices *karma yoga.*
kirtan (kirtana)	Devotional singing and dancing in praise of God and/or the guru.
Krishnalaya	The site of one of Swami Chinmayananda's ashrams, located in northern California, USA.
Kumbha Abhisheka	See *abhisheka.*
kurta	Shirt worn over pants or a *dhoti.*
kutiya	A small hut or residence; used to describe the residence of a spiritual teacher.

L

lila	Divine play, in which God enacts all the roles. The whole Universe is said to be God's *lila.*
lingam	See *Sivalingam.*

M

Mahasamadhi	The dropping of the body of a highly evolved person or enlightened being.
mala	Prayer beads; rosary, often make of *rudraksa* seeds.
mahatma	"Great Soul." A monk or highly advanced master.
manana	Reflection on and careful analysis of the knowledge gained from the teacher and the scriptures to render that knowledge free from doubt.
mantra	A chosen name of God that a seeker repeats to himself to purify the mind.
mantra-diksa	Initiation of a seeker with a chosen mantra assigned for meditation practice.
Maya	Illusion; ignorance or nonapprehension of Reality. It is described as an inexplicable power inherent in the supreme Reality, as heat is inherent in fire.
Mumbai	A name for Bombay.

N

namaskar (namaskara)	Traditional verbal Hindu greeting, accompanied by palms joined together and held in front of the chest or raised to one's forehead.
Narayana	A name of Vishnu, one of the three main Hindu gods.

P

Pada Puja	Worship performed on the feet of a spiritual teacher, symbolizing reverence for the foundation of spiritual knowledge on which the teacher stands.
paduka	Sandals of the guru, the traditional icon of the spiritual teacher.
Paduka Puja	Worship performed on the *chappals* (sandals) of a spiritual teacher. See *Pada Puja*.
pappadam	A crisp, flat bread made of *dal* (lentil) flour, often deep-fried.
***pranam* (*pranama*)**	A reverent greeting, usually with folded palms and bowed head, or a bowing of the entire body at the feet of a revered person.
pranayama	"Breath control." Part of the discipline of *hatha yoga*.
prarabdha	The principle of destiny. That portion of our past karmas that is being lived out in the present life.
prasad (prasada)	An offering to a deity or a spiritual teacher, or the remnants of such an offering returned as a blessing to the worshipper. A divine gift; sacrament.
prayascitta	Compensatory act or act of atonement.
puja	Worship; rite of worship performed at home, in a temple, or at a shrine.
Purana	"Ancient." Any one of the eighteen books of stories, attributed to Vyasa, in which Vedantic ideas are objectified and dramatized in the lives of saints, kings, devotees, and divine incarnations.
Purna Kumbha	A decorated vessel (*kumbha*) filled (*purna*) with water and held in front of one's body with both hands while receiving a *sannyasin* with chanted prayers. Symbolic of the fullness or completeness of a Self-realized person.

R

rajas	See *guna*.
Ramayana	An ancient epic poem in Sanskrit written by the sage Valmiki, highlighting moral values through the life story of Sri Rama.

rishi — Sage, seer.

rudraksa — "Eye of Rudra (a name of Shiva), red-eyed." Reddish-brown seeds that are used to string prayer beads.

S

sadhana — Any spiritual practice, such as reading the scriptures, meditating, distributing one's wealth to the needy, or withdrawing one's mind from worldly pursuits.

sadhu — A person dedicated to the search for God.

samadhi — "Tranquil mind." A state of absorption or thoughtlessness in which a person experiences his identity with the supreme Reality. Also, the memorial monument of a great saint.

samsara — The endless cycle of births and deaths that human beings experience before they realize their identity with the supreme Reality.

Sandeepany Sadhanalaya — An institute of Vedanta in Mumbai, India, where Chinmaya Mission swamis teach students an intensive two-and-a-half-year course in Vedanta.

sankalpa — "Will, determination." A declaration of purpose, a powerful thought, especially by an enlightened master.

Sankhya — One of the six systems of Hindu philosophy, which uses a very rational, analytic approach to unfolding the nature of existence. The founder of Sankhya is said to be Kapila Muni (circa 500 B.C.)

sannyasa — Renunciation, the monastic life, the last of the four stages of life, the other being the life of the celibate student, the life of the householder, and the life of retirement.

sannyasin — A renunciate; one who has taken the monastic vows.

santi — Peace.

sastra — Scriptures, including both those considered to be revealed by God (*Sruti*) and those written by sages (*Smrti*).

sastri — One who is knowledgeable in the *sastras*, the scriptures.

satsang (satsanga) — "Good company." Maintenance of contact with the higher values of life, either by association with noble persons or with inspiring writings and ideas. A devotional gathering.

sattva — See *guna*.

seva — Service done in a spirit of selflessness.

sevak **(m.)**, ***sevika*** **(f.)** — Someone who performs *seva*, service.

Sidhabari — The site of one of Swami Chinmayananda's ashrams, located in Himachal Pradesh, India. Also the site of his *samadhi*, his memorial monument.

sisya — Disciple.

sloka	Stanza, verse.
Shiva	God in the aspect of Destroyer, one of the Hindu Trinity, the other two being Vishnu and Brahma.
siddhi	Power; usually used to describe extraordinary powers of yogis or saints.
Sivalingam	"Mark of Shiva." An elliptical shape, usually set on a circular base; the simplest and oldest symbol of Shiva; the Godhead beyond form.
swami (m.) **swamini (f.)**	The respectful title of a Hindu monk (nun).

T

tamas	See *guna*.
thali	A large plate fashioned out of steel.
tilaka	In Hindi, *tika*. A mark made on the forehead with ash, sandalwood paste, or clay.
tulabhara	A ceremony for making offerings to the guru.

U

upanayana	A youth's formal initiation into Vedic study; investiture with the sacred thread. *Upanayana* is regarded as a second birth, and those who have undergone the ceremony are considered "twice born."
Upanishads	The final, philosophic portion of each of the four Vedas. Upanishads constitute the quintessence of scriptural truths. In all, 108 Upanishads have been preserved.
upasana	Worship.
upma	A breakfast food made out of cream of wheat, vegetables, and spices.

V

vairagya	Dispassion; indifference to worldly things.
vasana	Inborn disposition or motivating urge deep in the unconscious; the impression formed in the personality when one acts in the world with egocentric desires.
Vedanta	"End of the Vedas." One of the six systems of Hindu philosophy, evolved from the Upanishads, the end portion of the Vedas. As the word *veda* means "knowledge," *Vedanta* can also denote "the end of knowledge" or "the most profound knowledge." Vedanta teaches that the purpose of our life is to realize the supreme Reality as our own true nature.

Vedas — Four ancient scriptural textbooks, compiled by the poet-sage Vyasa from prophetic declarations handed down from teacher to taught over many generations. The four books are the *Rg Veda,* the *Yajur Veda,* the *Sama Veda,* and the *Atharva Veda.*

vibhuti — Holy ash; also used to describe supernormal powers.

viveka — Discrimination between the ephemeral objects of the world and the eternal Principle of life.

Vivekacudamani — A text written by the great Vedantin Adi Shankaracharya expounding, in detail, the basics of Vedanta.

Y

yajna — "Sacrifice." Used by Swami Chinmayananda to describe a series of lectures on Vedanta in which the seeker's ignorance is sacrificed in the fire of spiritual knowledge.

yajnasala — The venue for a *jnana yajna* lecture series.

yatra — Spiritual pilgrimage.

Yuva Kendra — The youth organization of Chinmaya Mission.

ENDNOTES

INTRODUCTION

1 Sheela Sharma, *Chinmaya Mission New Delhi News Bulletin,* November 1995
2 *Tapovan Prasad,* May 1994
3 Vilasini Balakrishnan, Silver Spring, Maryland, USA

LIFE

1 Lakshmi Reddy, Hyderabad, India
2 Solange Berg, San Francisco, California, USA
3 Rudite Emir, Los Altos, California, USA
4 Solange Berg, San Francisco, California, USA
5 Viji Sundaram, El Cerrito, California, USA
6 Bharati Sukhatankar, Belgaum, India
7 Letter to Veronica Hausman, Fremont, California, USA
8 Lolita Lodhia, Palo Alto, California, USA
9 Letter to Rudite Emir, Los Altos, California, USA
10 Letter to Rudite Emir, Los Altos, California, USA
11 Padma Gupta, New Delhi, India
12 Letter, anonymous
13 Radhika Krishnakumar, Chennai, India
14 Letter to Solange Berg, San Francisco, California, USA
15 Letter to Solange Berg, San Francisco, California, USA
16 Letter to Solange Berg, San Francisco, California, USA
17 Letter to Solange Berg, San Francisco, California, USA
18 Letter to Solange Berg, San Francisco, California, USA
19 Uncle Mani (Anant Narayan), Mumbai, India
20 K. B. Shroff, Mumbai, India
21 S. Subramanian, Mumbai, India
22 Anil Sachdev, New Delhi, India
23 Christine Grimmer, Sydney, Australia
24 Swami Purushottamananda
25 Isabel Taylor, Washington, D.C., USA
26 Rudite Emir, Los Altos, California, USA
27 K. Rajaram, as reported in *Tapovan Prasad,* August 1994

28 Christine Grimmer, Sydney, Australia
29 Anjali Singh, New Delhi, India
30 Letter to Rudite Emir, Los Altos, California, USA
31 Anonymous
32 Srichand Krishnani, Mumbai, India
33 Pranji Lodhia, Palo Alto, California, USA
34 Solange Berg, San Francisco, California, USA
35 S. V. Acharya, Mumbai, India
36 Letter to Solange Berg, San Francisco, California, USA

WORK

1 Swami Brahmananda, as retold by Prafulla, Bangalore, India
2 Rudite Emir, Los Altos, California, USA
3 Brni. Sadhana
4 Reprinted from *Tapovan Prasad*, January 1967
5 Letter to Solange Berg, San Francisco, California, USA
6 Sulochana Menon; reprinted from *Tapovan Prasad*, November 1966
7 Letter to Rudite Emir, Los Altos, California, USA
8 Anjali Singh, New Delhi, India
9 Brni. Robyn Thompson
10 Bina Patel, Vienna, Virginia, USA
11 Rudite Emir, Los Altos, California, USA
12 Letter to Rudite Emir, Los Altos, California, USA, June 1973
13 Jairam Jaisinghani, Mumbai, India
14 Kalidasan, Mumbai, India
15 G. B. Bhatia, Mumbai, India
16 K. C. Patnaik, Mumbai, India
17 Letter to Solange Berg, San Francisco, California, USA
18 Letter to Solange Berg, San Francisco, California, USA
19 Reprinted from *Tapovan Prasad*, June 1978
20 Reprinted from *Tapovan Prasad*
21 Anonymous
22 Barbara Gee, Menlo Park, California, USA
23 Letter to Rudite Emir, Los Altos, California, USA
24 Reprinted from *Tapovan Prasad*
25 Barbara Gee, Menlo Park, California, USA
26 Anonymous
27 Swami Subodhananda
28 Anonymous
29 Veronica Hausman, Fremont, California, USA; Pranji Lodhia, Palo Alto, California, USA
30 Viji Sundaram, El Cerrito, California, USA
31 Anonymous
32 Rudite Emir, Los Altos, California, USA
33 Narain Bhatia, Mumbai, India
34 Dwaraknath Reddy, Tiruvannamalai, India
35 Shubhra Tandon, Woodstock, New York, USA

36 K. C. Patnaik, Mumbai, India
37 Narain Bhatia, Mumbai, India

LOVE

1 Letter to Rudite Emir, Los Altos, California, USA
2 Jamna Batra, Mumbai, India
3 Anonymous
4 Lee Prosser, Springfield, Missouri, USA
5 Nalin Vissanji, Mumbai, India
6 Christine Grimmer, Sydney, Australia
7 Rudite Emir, Los Altos, California, USA
8 Rudite Emir, Los Altos, California, USA
9 Anjali Singh, New Delhi, India
10 R. Krishnamoorthy, Secunderabad, India
11 Anonymous
12 Isabel Taylor, Washington, D.C., USA
13 Sarv Singh, Los Angeles, California, USA
14 Gopal Sarma, Groton, Connecticut, USA
15 Asha Chakrabarty, Mumbai, India
16 Krishna Varma, New Delhi, India
17 Shobha Joshi, Mumbai, India
18 Rudite Emir, Los Altos, California, USA
19 Anonymous
20 Srichand Krishnani, Mumbai, India
21 Rose Ann Blau, Chicago, Illinois, USA
22 Padmavati (Pat) Loganathan, Buffalo, New York, USA
23 Joyce Smith-Gindlesperger, Bay Point, California, USA
24 Retold by Prafulla, Bangalore, India
25 Swami Dheerananda
26 Neeru Mehta, Ahmedabad, India
27 Nalini Browning, Piercy, California, USA
28 Krishna Varma, New Delhi, India
29 Prarthna Saran, New Delhi, India
30 Rudite Emir, Los Altos, California, USA
31 Shobha Joshi, Mumbai, India
32 Rudite Emir, Los Altos, California, USA
33 Brni. Robyn Thompson
34 Gaurang Nanavaty, Sugar Land (Houston), Texas, USA
35 Bharat B. Gupta, reprinted from *Tapovan Prasad*, May 1994
36 Bharat B. Gupta, reprinted from *Tapovan Prasad*, May 1994

MEETING THE GURU

1 Anonymous; reprinted from *Tapovan Prasad*, May 1994
2 Shakuntla Bindra, New Delhi, India
3 Rudite Emir, Los Altos, California, USA
4 Somesh Shah, Hong Kong; reprinted from *CMW News*
5 Kshama Metre, Sidhabari, India
6 Anjali Singh, New Delhi, India

7 Anonymous; reprinted from *CMW News*
8 Nalini Browning, Piercy, California, USA
9 Margaret Leuverink, Toronto, Canada
10 Letter to Rudite Emir, Los Altos, California, USA
11 Veronica Hausman, Fremont, California, USA
12 Kalidasan, Mumbai, India
13 Isabel Taylor, Washington, D.C., USA
14 Leela Nambiar, Chennai, India
15 Swami Swaroopananda
16 Anonymous
17 Srinivas and Lakshmi Sukumar, Saratoga, California, USA
18 Vimala Arjun; reprinted from *Tapovan Prasad*, May 1994
19 Veronica Hausman, Fremont, California, USA
20 Veronica Hausman, Fremont, California, USA
21 Veronica Hausman, Fremont, California, USA
22 Br. Atma Chaitanya; reprinted from *Chinmaya Sandeepany*
23 Asha Kamdar, Mumbai, India
24 Malti Prasad, Los Altos, California, USA

BLESSINGS AND TRANSFORMATIONS

1 Rudite Emir, Los Altos, California, USA
2 Swami Chidananda, reprinted from *CMW News*
3 Rudite Emir, Los Altos, California, USA
4 Anonymous
5 Anonymous
6 Rudite Emir, Los Altos, California, USA
7 Rudite Emir, Los Altos, California, USA
8 Mimi Robins, Brookline, Massachusetts, USA
9 Bhanumathi Rao, New Delhi, India
10 Anonymous
11 Anonymous
12 Swami Chidananda
13 Anonymous
14 Anonymous
15 Veronica Hausman, Fremont, California, USA

HIS ATTRIBUTES

1 Swami Swaroopananda; reprinted from *Chinmaya Sandesh*
2 Br. Someshwar
3 Gulu Advani, Los Altos, California, USA
4 Uncle Mani (Anant Narayan), Mumbai, India
5 Hamir Vissanji, Mumbai, India
6 K. C. Patnaik, Mumbai, India
7 Bill Browning, Piercy, California, USA
8 K. C. Patnaik, Mumbai, India
9 K. C. Patnaik, Mumbai, India
10 Jairam Jaisinghani, Mumbai, India

11 Br. Someshwar, as retold by Vijaya Chilton, Owings Mills, Maryland, USA
12 Swami Siddhananda
13 Swami Purushottamananda
14 Rudite Emir, Los Altos, California, USA
15 Sheela Sharma; reprinted from *Chinmaya Mission New Delhi News Bulletin,* November 1995
16 Swami Brahmananda, as retold by Prafulla, Bangalore, India
17 Ram Kirpalani, College Point, New York, USA
18 Praveen Kumar Tiwari, New Delhi, India

MIRACLES

1 Rudite Emir, Los Altos, California, USA
2 Krishna Varma, New Delhi, India
3 Leela Nambiar, Chennai, India
4 Jamna Batra, Mumbai, India
5 Anonymous
6 Anonymous
7 Anonymous
8 Krishna Varma, New Delhi, India
9 Rudite Emir, Los Altos, California, USA
10 Radhika Krishnakumar, Chennai, India
11 Asha Chakrabarty, Mumbai, India
12 Anonymous
13 Asha Kamdar, Mumbai, India
14 Mimi Robins, Brookline, Massachusetts, USA
15 Gulu Advani, Los Altos, California, USA
16 Anonymous
17 Nalini Browning, Piercy, California, USA
18 Anonymous
19 Kalidasan, Mumbai, India
20 Radhika Krishnakumar, Chennai, India
21 As quoted in *Journey of a Master* by Nancy Patchen
22 Rama and Dyumani Chander, Sidhabari, Himachal Pradesh, India

GREATNESS IN SMALL THINGS

1 Swami Sreedharananda; reprinted from *Chinmaya Sandeepany*
2 Swami Chidananda
3 Asha Chakrabarty, Mumbai, India
4 Rudite Emir, Los Altos, California, USA
5 Bharati Sukhatankar, Belgaum, India
6 Padmashree, Bangalore, India
7 Brni. Sadhana
8 Brni. Sadhana
9 Durga Singh, Kathmandu, Nepal
10 Indra Advani, Los Altos, CA, USA
11 Anonymous
12 Swami Dheerananda; reprinted from *CMW News,* July 1997
13 Nalini Browning, Piercy, California, USA

14 Arun and Asha Desai, Bellevue, Washington, USA
15 Anonymous
16 Swamini Samvidananda
17 Bill Browning, Piercy, California, USA
18 Rudite Emir, Los Altos, California, USA
19 Bharati Sukhatankar, Belgaum, India
20 Bharati Sukhatankar, Belgaum, India
21 Rajendra Prasad, Palo Alto, California, USA
22 As retold by Srichand Krishnani, Mumbai, India, who heard the account given by Gurudev at a *satsang*

GOD AND GOD'S WORSHIP
1 Gopal Sarma, Groton, Connecticut, USA
2 Anonymous
3 K. Hemalatha Ramachandra Reddy; reprinted from *Tapovan Prasad*, August 1994
4 Rudite Emir, Los Altos, California, USA
5 Veronica Hausman, Fremont, California, USA
6 Veronica Hausman, Fremont, California, USA
7 Br. Someshwar; reprinted from *CMW News*
8 Swamini Nishtananda
9 Bill Sheldon, San Rafael, California, USA; Luis Jauregui, Oakland, California, USA
10 Lee Shultz, Carnation, Washington, USA
11 Anonymous
12 Br. Someshwar; reprinted from *India Post*, February 9, 1996

EGO
1 Christine Grimmer, Sydney, Australia
2 Rudite Emir, Los Altos, California, USA
3 Rudite Emir, Los Altos, California, USA
4 Rudite Emir, Los Altos, California, USA
5 Anonymous
6 Rudite Emir, Los Altos, California, USA
7 Veronica Hausman, Fremont, California, USA
8 Brni. Robyn Thompson
9 Brni. Robyn Thompson
10 Veronica Hausman, Fremont, California, USA
11 Anonymous
12 Anonymous

SADHANA
1 Dr. Asha Chakrabarty, Mumbai, India
2 Rudite Emir, Los Altos, California, USA
3 Narain Bhatia, Mumbai, India; reprinted from *Chinmaya Sandeepany*
4 Brni. Robyn Thompson
5 Isabel Taylor, Washington, D.C., USA
6 Anonymous
7 Sheila Lal Keswani; reprinted from *Chinmaya Sandeepany*
8 Anonymous

9 Anonymous
10 Nalin Vissanji, Mumbai, India
11 Swami Shantananda; reprinted from *CMW News*
12 Letters to Rudite Emir, Los Altos, California, USA
13 Veronica Hausman, Fremont, California, USA
14 Brni. Sadhana
15 Prarthna Saran, New Delhi, India
16 Veronica Hausman, Fremont, California, USA
17 Rudite Emir, Los Altos, California, USA
18 Michael Mayzel, Toronto, Canada
19 Brni. Sadhana
20 Bharat B. Gupta; reprinted from *Tapovan Prasad*, May 1994
21 Anonymous
22 S. Peethambaram, Chennai, India; reprinted from *Swami Chinmayananda–As I Know Him*
23 S. Peethambaram, Chennai, India; reprinted from *Swami Chinmayananda–As I Know Him*

DISCIPLINE

1 Rudite Emir, Los Altos, California, USA
2 R. Padmanabhan; reprinted from *Tapovan Prasad*
3 Nalini Browning, Piercy, California, USA
4 R. Krishnamoorthy, Secunderabad, India
5 Uma Jeyarasasingam, Los Altos, California, USA
6 Sheela Chitnis; reprinted from *Swami Chinmayananda–As I Know Him*
7 Swami Purushottamananda
8 Swami Purushottamananda
9 Prafulla, Bangalore, India
10 K. C. Patnaik, Mumbai, India
11 Anonymous
12 Swami Purushottamananda
13 Swami Chidananda
14 Anonymous

MEDITATION

1 Letter to Rudite Emir, Los Altos, California, USA
2 Anonymous
3 Rudite Emir, Los Altos, California, USA
4 Swami Tejomayananda
5 Letter to Rudite Emir, Los Altos, California, USA
6 Anonymous
7 Rudite Emir, Los Altos, California, USA
8 Swamini Sharadapriyananda; reprinted from *Chinmaya Sandeepany*
9 Swamini Sharadapriyananda; reprinted from *Chinmaya Sandeepany*
10 Anonymous
11 Prabhakar S. Shirwadkar; reprinted from *Tapovan Prasad*, May 1989
12 Anjali Singh, New Delhi, India; reprinted from *Chinmaya Sandeepany*
13 Bharati Sukhatankar, Belgaum, India
14 Anonymous

TEACHERS AND TEACHING

1 Rudite Emir, Los Altos, California, USA
2 Anonymous
3 Anonymous
4 Neeru Mehta, Ahmedabad, India
5 Uma Jeyarasasingam, Los Altos, California, USA
6 Anonymous
7 G. B. Bhatia, Mumbai, India
8 Brni. Robyn Thompson
9 Michael Mayzel, Toronto, Canada
10 Letter to Rudite Emir, Los Altos, California, USA
11 Letter to Solange Berg, San Francisco, California, USA
12 Rudite Emir, Los Altos, California, USA
13 Bharati Sukhatankar, Belgaum, India
14 Letter to Rudite Emir, Los Altos, California, USA
15 Letter to Rudite Emir, Los Altos, California, USA
16 Letter to Rudite Emir, Los Altos, California, USA
17 Letter to Jorge Luis Jauregui, Oakland, California, USA
18 Swami Tejomayananda; reprinted from *Chinmaya Sandesh,* Mumbai, May 1994
19 Uncle Mani (Anant Narayan), Mumbai, India
20 Uncle Mani (Anant Narayan), Mumbai, India
21 Swami Swaroopananda; reprinted from *Chinmaya Sandesh*
22 Letter to Ashwin V. Parikh, Houston, Texas, USA
23 Letter, anonymous
24 Rudite Emir, Los Altos, California, USA
25 Swami Subodhananda
26 Letters to Jorge Luis Jauregui, Oakland, California, USA
27 Swami Purushottamananda
28 Swami Dheerananda
29 Swamini Samvidananda
30 Swami Jyothirmayananda
31 Anonymous
32 Anonymous
33 Anonymous

NATURE

1 Neeru Mehta, Ahmedabad, India
2 Swami Swaroopananda; reprinted from *Chinmaya Sandesh*
3 Bharati Sukhatankar, Belgaum, India
4 Padmashree, Bangalore, India
5 Padmashree, Bangalore, India
6 Padmashree, Bangalore, India
7 Anonymous
8 Brni. Sadhana
9 Jairam Jaisinghani, Mumbai, India
10 Rudite Emir, Los Altos, California, USA

11 Brni. Sadhana
12 Anil Sachdev, New Delhi, India
13 Swamini Nisthananda
14 Swami Shantananda
15 Brni. Sadhana
16 G. B. Bhatia, Mumbai, India
17 Swamini Nisthananda
18 Shubhra Tandon, Woodstock, New York, USA
19 Swamini Nishtananda
20 Rudite Emir, Los Altos, California, USA

BEYOND THE BODY

1 Letters to Solange Berg, San Francisco, California, USA
2 Swami Purushottamananda
3 Letter to Solange Berg, San Francisco, California, USA
4 Letter to Solange Berg, San Francisco, California, USA
5 Shubhra Tandon, Woodstock, New York, USA
6 Apparao Mukkamala, Flint, Michigan, USA
7 Nalini Browning, Piercy, California, USA
8 Rudite Emir, Los Altos, California, USA
9 Vilasini Balakrishnan, Silver Spring, Maryland, USA
10 Rudite Emir, Los Altos, California, USA
11 Vilasini Balakrishnan, Silver Spring, Maryland, USA
12 Apparao Mukkamala, Flint, Michigan, USA
13 Shakuntla Bindra, New Delhi, India
14 Rudite Emir, Los Altos, California, USA
15 Brahmaleen Swami Nityananda, as retold by Br. Someshwar
16 Sheela Kirpalani, College Point, New York, USA
17 Anonymous
18 Bharati Sukhatankar, Belgaum, India
19 Asha Kamdar, Mumbai, India
20 Anonymous
21 Rudite Emir, Los Altos, California, USA
22 Gail Larrick, Tucson, Arizona, USA
23 Rudite Emir, Los Altos, California, USA
24 Ghelubhai Patel, Mumbai, India
25 Swami Subodhananda
26 Swami Subodhananda
27 Christine Grimmer, Sydney, Australia
28 Indra Advani, Los Altos, California, USA
29 Uncle Mani (Anant Narayan), Mumbai, India
30 Letter to Rudite Emir, Los Altos, California, USA
31 Letter to Dinkar and Jayashri Naik, Sugar Land, Texas, USA
32 Kshama Metre, Sidhabari, India
33 Shubhra Tandon, Woodstock, New York, USA

34 Kshama Metre, Sidhabari, India
35 Asha Kamdar, Mumbai, India; Kshama Metre, Sidhabari, India
36 Kshama Metre, Sidhabari, India
37 Kshama Metre, Sidhabari, India

LAST GOOD-BYES

1 Michael Fantus, Washington, D.C., USA
2 Anjali Singh, New Delhi, India
3 Prafulla, Bangalore, India
4 Rudite Emir, Los Altos, California, USA
5 Rudite Emir, Los Altos, California, USA
6 Veronica Hausman, Fremont, California, USA
7 Brni. Sadhana
8 Krishanlal Chopra, Sidhabari, Himachal Pradesh, India
9 Swami Tejomayananda; reprinted from *Tapovan Prasad*, February 1998
10 Radhika Krishnakumar, Chennai, India
11 Shobha Joshi, Mumbai, India
12 Rudite Emir, Los Altos, California, USA
13 Anjali Singh, New Delhi, India
14 Sheel Dewan, Mumbai, India
15 Nalini Browning, Piercy, California, USA
16 Nalini Browning, Piercy, California, USA
17 Anjali Singh, New Delhi, India
18 Nalini Browning, Piercy, California, USA
19 Tina Bedi, New Delhi, India
20 Radhika Krishnakumar, Chennai, India
21 Uma Jeyarasasingam, Los Altos, California, USA
22 Anonymous
23 Shubhra Tandon, Woodstock, New York, USA; reprinted from *CMW News*
24 Brni. Sadhana
25 Sheel Dewan, Mumbai, India

WHO WAS HE?

1 Letter to Solange Berg, San Francisco, California, USA
2 Rudite Emir, Los Altos, California, USA
3 Rudite Emir, Los Altos, California, USA
4 Brni. Sadhana
5 Swami Swaroopananda and Brni. Sadhana
6 Bharati Sukhatankar, Belgaum, India
7 Dr. Suhasini; reprinted from *Chinmaya Jyothi*, Hyderabad, India
8 Nalini Browning, Piercy, California, USA
9 Reprinted from *Tapovan Prasad*